Another Summer in Kintyre

Also by Angus Martin

History

The Ring-Net Fishermen
Kintyre: The Hidden Past
Kintyre Country Life
Fishing and Whaling
Sixteen Walks in South Kintyre
The North Herring Fishing
Herring Fishermen of Kintyre and Ayrshire
Fish and Fisherfolk
Memories of the Inans, Largybaan and Craigaig, 1980-85
An Historical and Genealogical Tour of Kilkerran Graveyard
Kintyre Birds
The Place-Names of the Parish of Campbeltown *(with Duncan Colville)*
The Place-Names of the Parish of Southend *(with Duncan Colville)*
Kilkerran Graveyard Revisited
Kintyre Families
Kintyre Instructions: The 5th Duke of Argyll's Instructions
        to his Kintyre Chamberlain, 1785-1805 *(with Eric R. Cregeen)*
By Hill and Shore in South Kintyre
Kintyre Places and Place-Names
A Summer in Kintyre: Memories and Reflections
Place-Names of the Parish of Kilcalmonell
Place-Names of the Parish of Killean and Kilchenzie
Place-Names of the Parish of Saddell and Skipness

Poetry

The Larch Plantation
The Song of the Quern
The Silent Hollow
Rosemary Clooney Crossing the Minch
Laggan Days: In Memory of George Campbell Hay
Haunted Landscapes: Poems in memory of Benjie
Paper Archipelagos
Always Boats and Men *(with Mark I'Anson)*
One Time in a Tale of Herring *(with Will Maclean)*

Another Summer in Kintyre

Angus Martin

Published by:

The Grimsay Press
An imprint of Zeticula Ltd
Unit 13
196 Rose Street
Edinburgh, EH2 4T
Scotland

http://www.thegrimsaypress.co.uk

First published in 2015

Cover photograph: The bed of Lussa Reservoir exposed during drought, c. 1974. Photograph © George McSporran 2015

ISBN 978-1-84530-155-2

'For, as I draw closer and closer to the end, I travel in the circle, nearer and nearer to the beginning.'

Charles Dickens, *A Tale of Two Cities*.

Contents

4 April: A rock face at the First Water 3
5 April: Down to the shore 5
6 April: Blue-rayed limpets and bird pellets 6
    Alastair Thompson and the First Water 6
    The *Quesada*, 1966 11
8 April: A rock chair in Queen Esther's Bay 12
    Saint Kieran's Cave 14
    Excavation of Saint Kieran's Cave 16
    Christmas Eve in the Cave 18
    A wet Sunday in 1984 19
    Auchenhoan Head 20
    A cliff fall, 1889 22
    The Fiddler's Rock and Archie McAllister 22
    A cliff rescue in 1964 25
    The Bloody Bay 26
    Wreck of the *Accord*, 1993 27
    The loss of the *Lena*, 1898 28
    Otters 30
11 April: Seals, a gull and wilkers' caves 30
15 April: Largiebaan 33
24 April: Corphin 35
25 April: Cuckoos 37
    Wreck of the *Dotterel*, 1923 38
26 April: Four boys 41
27 April: Pirate and Cowboy 42
28 April: Watching an eider 43
    A shore walk in 1988 44
29 April: Storm erosion 45
30 April: Stockadale 47
    Arinanuan 51
    Death of John Porter, 1989 53
    Death of Donald MacArthur, 1902 53
    Willie MacGougan, shepherd 55
    Some thoughts on Gaelic 56
    Archibald Mitchell, shepherd 58
    Violence in Torrisdale Glen, 1821 60
    Missed by the bus 61
6 May: New Orleans 62

11 May: Overtaken	66
15 May: Ballimenach brae and memories of Tangy	67
The Corphin mermaid	68
16 May: Ru Stafnish	70
Orange-peel	71
20 May: Whales	72
21 May: Painted Ladies on Knock Scalbert	73
23 May: The Pirate's Grave	74
Jock Smith at Feochaig	78
Wreck of the *Charlemagne*, 1857	79
Two Donalds	84
A flock of sheep	85
The SS *Elisabeth*, 1935	85
An abortive camp at Feochaig, 1966	87
26 May: The Bastard	89
A mystery spring and Pursells	90
30 May: John Harvey, Gartnacopaig	91
Leslie Hunter's Granny	93
Largiebaan cliffs	95
3 June: Hillside aglow	96
6 June: Second Water	96
Sandy Helm	98
Abandoned in the night	99
Eddie Stone	101
Bush and bees	101
8 June: Balnabraid	103
11 June: Minen	106
15 June: The Old Road	110
Three cows	111
Willie Watson and turnip-thinning	112
16 June: High Glenadale	114
3 August 2013: High Glenadale	119
Duncan MacDonald	121
Cars off the road on the Learside	122
Bicycle accidents on the Learside	123
18 June: Polliwilline and 'Queen Esther'	128
19 June: Homeward	131
23 June: To Lussa Reservoir	132
George Campbell Hay and Annie MacDougall	133

East Skeroblin Cottage 134
An unexpected meeting 135
Bordadubh 136
Malcolm MacMillan 139
Betty McMillan 140
The hydro-electric scheme 144
Jimmy Allan 145
Blues in Collusca 148
McConnachies in Strathmollach 150
27 June: Thoughts on Ballimenach brae 152
Adders 154
27 June: Corphin 155
1 July: Creag nan Cuilean 158
Post Office and Captain's Well 160
Two pints of 'Belhaven' 161
Clegs and ticks 162
6 June 1984 164
6 July: Arinascavach 165
Bogie Roll and Rock 'n' Roll 167
Two drownings 168
Peter Morrison 170
Alastair McKinven 171
Sliabh 175
9 July: The Inneans 176
10 July: Inneans remembered and Ben Gullion 177
13 July: Largiebaan Caves 180
15 July: McCambridge's wholewheat bread 183
20 July: The dog Chomsky 186
22 July: The Stinky Hole 187
The Sheep Fanks and Bobby Martin 189
23 July: Home by the Learside 191
28 July: Five cyclists on Ben Gullion 194
31 July: Knockbay 195
5 August: Dreams 197
7 August: Feochaig to Glenahervie 198
Adders again 202
McEachrans and McKerrals, Glenahervie 204
Amelia McKay, Erradil 205
Two cliff fatalities 207

14 August: Butterflies and blaeberries · 207
19 August: Knock Scalbert and the Queen's Silver Jubilee · 209
    The Scottish Independence Referendum · 210
26 August: Killypole · 211
27 August: The Maidens' Planting and bramble-gathering · 214
    Keil Cave and Travellers · 215
    Small Tortoiseshells · 219
17 September: Auchenhoan · 220
20 September: Small Coppers · 221

Illustrations

1. Face rock at the First Water, 2014.   4
2. First Water, 2007.   7
3. Teddy Lafferty and Tommy Thompson at 'caravan', Second Water, c. 1953.   8
4. Jimmy MacDonald on rock chair at Queen Esther's Bay, 1984.   13
5. Norman Morrison during the Saint Kieran's Cave excavation, c. 1924.   17
6. Teddy Lafferty and Jimmy MacDonald on a rainy Sunday, First Water, 1984.   19
7. Auchenhoan Head from north, 1981.   21
8. Fiddler's Rock, 1981.   24
9. The trawler *Accord* aground in the Bloody Bay, 1993.   28
10. Five goats on Cnoc Moy, 2014.   34
11. Pirate Easter egg on Corphin brae, 2014.   42
12. Storm damage at Keil, 2014.   46
13. Duncan Macdougall at Stockadale, 2014.   51
14. Sarah and Angus Martin sheltering at New Orleans, 1988.   65
15. Ru Stafnish from the sea, 1998.   70
16. The Pirate's Grave, 1988.   76
17. SS *Elisabeth* aground at Feochaig, 1935.   86
18. John Harvey at Gartnacopaig, 1982.   91
19. Sarah Martin with bike at Second Water, 1994.   97
20. Second Water, looking north, 1989.   99
21. Martins and McSporrans in Auchenhoan hills, 1988.   105
22. Mid Minen, 2014.   107
23. Willie Watson's medal for turnip-singling in 1958.   112
24. Stone pillars at High Glenadale, 2014.   116
25. Jan and Iona Hynd at High Glenadale, 2013.   120
26. Derek McKinven and Alastair Thompson with bikes, Ballimenach brae, c. 1966.   124
27. Portrait of 'Queen Esther' by Charlotte Brodie Eastin, 2015.   130
28. Malcolm Docherty's assemblage at Polliwilline, 2014.   131

29. Nicola Coffield and John MacDonald at Lussa Reservoir, 2014. 135
30. Campbeltown Grammar School Bordadubh work force, 1974. 136
31-34. Work scenes at the hydro-electric scheme, Lussa, c. 1951 .
31. The power station at Gartgreillan showing the railway,
     and the temporary workers' accommodation and
     canteen. 146
32. A digger, used for excavating the foundations of the
     pipeline supports. 146
33. A 'puggy', being driven by Peter McKerral, Peninver, on
     its railway, moving a section of pipeline. 147
34. A traditional load-pulling 'machine'. The chain-traces
     of the horse, name unknown, are visible. 147
35. The bed of Lussa Reservoir exposed during drought, c. 1974 . 149
36. Lachlan Gillies with his great-grandmother Margaret
     McAllister, 2015. 152
37. Pennywort at Corphin, 2014. 156
38. Captain Hector Macneal of Ugadale, c. 1900. 160
39. Judy Martin, Margaret McKiernan and Davie
     Robertson at Arinascavach, 2014. 169
40. Alex McKinven with Drift, Dalbuie, 1955. 172
41. Sliabh before afforestation. 176
42. John Watson in Inneans Bay, 1982. 177
43. John McCallum at Largiebaan, 2014. 182
44. Chomsky and Judy at Fin Rock, 2014. 186
45. John Brodie with bike, Kildalloig, 2014. 188
46. Bobby Martin at the Sheep Fanks, 2014. 191
47. The author in the maw of a rock, Feochaig shore, 2014. 199
48. 'Wood Bay' looking north, c. 1982. 201
49. Teddy Lafferty with tent, Glenahervie Bay, c. 1982. 203
50. A Travellers' camp in Kintyre, c. 1935. 217

Introduction and Acknowledgements

This book is modelled on *A Summer in Kintyre*, in the introduction to which I allowed that I might write a follow-up if *A Summer in Kintyre* was well enough received. It was, by my standards, well enough received, but the book was hardly published when I started another. The title, *Another Summer in Kintyre*, has the merit of continuity and clarity – unless confused with the first – but I earlier considered and rejected a few possible titles (one of them was *Aggravated Haeomorrhoids*, a reference to the time I spent on the saddle of my bicycle in the summer of 2014!)

The main criticism directed at *A Summer in Kintyre* was that some of the place-names it contained were so obscure they didn't appear on any maps. I accept that point, and this time around, since I detest map-making, I have incorporated Ordnance Survey grid references into the index.

On 12 July 2015, given favourable weather, I hope to celebrate the 32nd anniversary of the death of Chris Wood, saxophonist and flautist, with a hike, and perhaps more, but I can't imagine at present what 'more' might be. Should any admirer of Chris Wood's music be interested in accompanying me on the hike, get in touch. And if any reader has ideas for a hike with an interesting motivation or destination, likewise get in touch.

For assistance with this book, sincere thanks, in alphabetical order, to: Jimmy Allan, Catherine Barbour, Iain Campbell, the staff of Campbeltown Public Library, Jackie Davenport at Argyll & Bute Council Archive, Christine Duncan, Teddy Lafferty, Jimmy MacDonald, Murdo MacDonald, Duncan Macdougall, Margaret McKiernan, Alex and Margaret Mackinnon, Alastair McKinven, George McSporran, Elizabeth McTaggart, Bobby Martin, Judy Martin, John Menzies, Peter Morrison, Les Oman, Davie Robertson, John Smith, Agnes and Allister Stewart, Alastair Thompson and William Watson.

Apologies to anyone I have inadvertently left out, and apologies too for any errors this book still contains. If you spot any, let me know.

Angus Martin, 26 March 2015.
13 Saddell Street, Campbeltown, Argyll PA28 6DN.
judymartin733@btinternet.com

Another Summer in Kintyre

4 April: A rock face at the First Water

The opening line in *A Summer in Kintyre*, this book's precursor, is: 'The conception of this book can be dated to 10 July 2013, 6.30 p.m., at Sròn Gharbh.' This one's conception can be dated to 4 April 2014, 7.15 p.m., at the Blin' Man. I was given that name for the rock face by a friend in Canada, Alastair Thompson. He believed he heard it from a maternal uncle, Gilbert Muir, who was shepherd in Auchenhoan when, in the 1960s, Alastair and friends frequented the First Water.

That rock face/face rock is to the immediate south of the First Water, which is a little bay on the Learside, the coast extending from Kildalloig to Polliwilline. The stream running into the bay is the 'Water' and it is 'First' because there is another stream further south known as the 'Second Water'. The southern one rises between Auchenhoan Hill and Arinarach Hill and makes its way through Balnabraid/Corphin Glen to the sea, gathering, as it goes, from little feeder streams coming off the flanks of the glen. In terms of volume, the Second Water is 'first', but the ordering of the names suggests that the streams were named from the Campbeltown end, 'First' being the first one reached.

The simplest route into the First Water is by a track which leads from the first gate past the little roadside coniferous plantation after the brae down from Auchenhoan farm. As one rounds the bend of that track, the rock profile will appear in view. I once had a name for it, but struggled to remember it. Two days later, on 6 April, I decided it resembled a Native American, which reminded me that I met the chief of a North American tribe at the Second Water in 1988. I was sitting having lunch in a mail-van when a car drew up and a tourist emerged and engaged me in conversation. He wrote his name on a newspaper I was reading, but I no longer remember it.

On 26 May, cycling on the Learside with George McSporran, he remembered the name of the rock profile as the 'Red Indian', and allowed that he'd heard it from me, so I'd forgotten a name I coined myself. The rugged nose resembles that of a stereotypical Plains Indian and there is also the suggestion of a feathered head-dress. The name Alastair had for it, the Blin' Man, also intrigued me, because a tidal rock at the north end of the bay is marked on Admiralty charts as 'Blindman's Rock'. Either the two rocks became confused or there was a near-identical name for each, one of them presumably derived from the other.

1. Face rock at the First Water, looking south-east, 2014. Photograph by the author.

Owing to its remoteness, that profile at the First Water is obscure, but I can think of two features in Kintyre which were well enough known to attract visitors, even if they don't now. Of course, ours is a time of rampant image-proliferation – through television, computers, mobile telephones, and other electronic media, along with the older paper forms: newspapers, magazines, books – and no one, I fancy, is going to travel miles to look at a rock which is supposed to resemble a human face. Indeed, very few folk nowadays, even if they happened to be near such a rock, would be likely to notice it – many of them would be preoccupied texting or talking into mobile 'phones. Nature, in all its marvellous variety, is, for many, merely the backdrop to an electronic otherworld entered through a device which fits the palm of a hand.

Looking north from the car-park at Machrihanish there was the Negro's Head, which in 1835 William Smith Jnr., in *Views of Campbelton*, described as '... a fancied resemblance ... to the features of a Negro'; but he himself didn't consider the effect 'particularly striking'. The profile is formed by the rock face of the grassy headland called the Dun – Gaelic *dùn*, a fort, or, as in this case, a rounded hillock – opposite the Old Clubhouse. Its later name was the Queen's Head, and it does distinctly resemble Queen Victoria in old age,[1] but since the image probably derived from coins minted in Victoria's later life, and out of circulation since decimalisation in 1971, that name, too, has slipped into obscurity.

In *Tarbert in Picture and Story* (1908, pp. 107-8), Dugald Mitchell published a photograph of 'The Man-Faced Rock', a feature on the west side of the road south from Tarbert, beyond the Carraig and just before the old steamer pier on the West Loch. Two women in the dress of the period are posed in front of the rock, with its well-proportioned forehead and nose.

That day, on my way back to the First Water with driftwood, I stopped for the first time on the grassy top of the 'Red Indian' and found it 'excellent for observation and also comfortable, with a good feel to it'. I e-mailed Jimmy MacDonald that evening to recommend it as a perch for bird photography, but he'd beaten me to it; he and Katrina Macfarlane had sat there the previous year.

5 April: Down to the shore

Between the First and the Second Water, I'd found a hefty branch of seasoned hardwood jammed in rocks. It took me four trips to saw, and I carried four logs at a time back to my bike concealed in whins above the First Water. I'd found the shore dangerously slippery underfoot the day before, and today the tide was almost in, so I decided to look for a way down the cliff to where the branch lay. 'Cliff' exaggerates the terrain, which drops from no great height from the fenced edge of a field. When the branch came in sight, I searched for a likely route, and found one. I was just about to start down, when a cock pheasant I hadn't seen erupted from the undergrowth below me, startling me with a demonic cackle. A minute later, I slipped on mud and went sliding down the slope on my backside. A jacket sleeve and the cuffs of my shirt and jersey were caked with mud, which I tried to wash off in a sea-pool.

6 April: Blue-rayed limpets and bird pellets

The following afternoon, on my way south to cut the last of the branch, I stopped at a mossy hump to photograph a sandstone terrace with attractive erosion patterns, and noticed something else, at my feet – a couple of tiny shells. They were blue-rayed limpets (*Patina pellucida*) and I wondered how they'd got there. For a start, I'd never seen these shells anywhere on the Learside and associated them with Atlantic beaches. The explanation was close by – a disintegrating bird pellet consisting almost entirely of the shells. That species of limpet is tiny, contains little meat, and, in any case, the shells had clearly been swallowed whole, with or without the animals attached.

Many bird species expel indigestible food parts as compressed pellets, and the form and content of the pellet help identify the species. Owl pellets characteristically contain bones, which the birds' digestive juices cannot dissolve. Birds of prey, however, can dissolve bones, so these are absent from their pellets. The pellets of crows generally contain a collection of tiny stones or some other form of grit for crushing seed in the gizzard, in addition to plant material, bones and insect chitin. Crows are, of course, voracious feeders and great opportunists, but my guess is that, from its looseness and singularity of content, I was looking at a gull pellet.

But, to the blue-rayed limpets themselves, from whatever bird's crop they were disgorged. Shells found on beaches are often dull-looking, but these were so fresh that, even from my standing position, the electric-blue lines were quite distinct. The shell I examined was yellowish-brown and quite translucent, but, had its occupant lived, the beauty would have faded. The young limpet lives on the fronds of the Laminaria seaweeds around the lowest tide mark, and the shell's flattish form enables the animal to keep a hold, even as the tangles are swirled about in storms. As the limpet grows, its shell darkens and begins to peak, and it migrates down the frond to the hold-fast – the base of the tangle, which is anchored to a rock – and excavates the shelter in which it will spend the rest of its life.

Alastair Thompson and the First Water

I first met Alastair Reid Thompson in 1964, my first year in Campbeltown Grammar School. I had never encountered him before and have no recollection of how our friendship formed. We belonged to a group which consisted also of Derek McKinven, Robert Davison and Murdo Macleod, but for my part these friendships scarcely existed outside school. Since Murdo lived in Southend, where his father was schoolmaster, I didn't see him after school, and since none of the others lived near me in town, and I had a separate set of friends in Crosshill Avenue, anyway, we tended not to associate after school. There was another reason: Alastair, Derek and Robert were at that time drawn to the Learside, whereas the Dalintober bit in me predisposed me to Kilchousland.

2. *The First Water bay, looking north, 2007. Photograph by the author.*

The wall overlooking Stewart Green was our meeting-place during school intervals. Much adolescent nonsense must have been spouted there, but I remember nothing of that. All I remember is that Alastair cut his initials, 'ART', into a cap-stone of the wall, and that we'd chuckle callously at an old dog with huge testicles which passed daily under the wall with his master. There was probably something wrong with the dog, and there was certainly something wrong with us, but nothing that maturity wouldn't cure.

I'd forgotten that all of us had carved our initials on the wall until I read a copy of a letter I sent to Alastair on 25 March 1969. (He kept all my correspondence and copied it to help me with this book: much of it, in particular the juvenilia, inevitably provided very uncomfortable reading.) 'Three years have passed since we carved (in summertime was it?) those fabled initials (don't ask me what a fabled initial is – it just sounds good!) into the lichened stone. Yes, I was idling alone in the sunshine where we used to stand (Rab, Murdo, Derek, you & I) scratching at the stone, and there it was – ART; searching further I uncovered the marred and worn and barely discernible AM. I failed to find any others, so it seems we alone survive there.'

As mentioned earlier, Alastair's uncle, Gilbert Muir, was shepherd in Auchenhoan when Alastair was growing up, and Gilbert's wife, Chrissie Helm, was reared there, so Alastair had a foothold in the place. The boys' absorbing project was the construction of a hut at the First Water. I was taken once to see it and remember a floor and a frame on the level grassy foreshore south of the burn. If you cross the stile at the foot of the track and look right, you are looking at the site. Twenty years after the project was abandoned, I could still trace the lines of the foundation. By then, of the three builders only Derek remained in town.

3. Teddy Lafferty (R) with Tommy Thompson, who is displaying a dead adder at the Second Water 'caravan', c. 1953. Photograph courtesy of Teddy Lafferty.

Alastair recalls that the hut was inspired by 'envy' of two converted vans at the Second Water. One, at the foot of Balnabraid Glen, was a Ford ambulance which had earlier been converted into transport for the Ru Stafnish radio station technicians, of whom Robert Davison's father was one. In January 1952, the vehicle skidded on ice on the hairpin bend down to the Second Water and plunged into the burn below. Charlie McMillan, himself a Ru Stafnish driver, acquired the van for the token sum of £5 and it was fitted with bunks, a card-table and a small stove for the use of the 'Coasters', as the Learside ramblers were known.[2] The leading Coaster at the time was Jamie 'Loafs' Morran, whom Alastair associates with that 'camp'.

The other one was a converted Co-op van, sited at the north end of the bay by an insurance agent in Campbeltown, Dan Morrans – near-identical surname, but a different family – for the use of himself and his brothers. Teddy Lafferty remembers that van arriving a year or so earlier, so it probably dates to 1950. It contained bunks, but had no stove, and cooking was done on a driftwood fire outside. Around that time, Dan owned a cine camera and was active as an amateur film-maker. Some films featured local characters in fictitious roles, but others were documentary, and footage shot at the Second Water survives, though I have yet to view it.

'At one time during that period,' Alastair recalls, 'there was a bunch of "Rocker" guys from Clydebank who would motor to Campbeltown to chase girls, etc. They made themselves at home at the camps. I'm not sure if there was any formal arrangement with the "owners" – likely not.'

Alastair recalled that the First Water hut was 'dimensioned around' finds of timber washed ashore, and was to be of simple design: bunks on one side, table and chairs/benches on the other, with a door and possibly a window facing the sea. It was a pity the hut was never finished, but, had it been, I suspect it would have been discovered and vandalised. He and his companions invested a good deal of time and effort in finding suitable wood on the Learside shore. It would be carried to the bay on their shoulders or, if too heavy, the weight would be shared, 'not always an easy task on that shore,' as Alastair observed. 'We were teenagers,' he added, 'and in our world being strong was worthy of admiration.'

One time they found three desirable hardwood pallets, but they were on the north side of Auchenhoan Head and too far from the First

Water to carry. No problem, though – they would lash them together, one on top of another, and raft them round the Head. Alastair was 'elected' to paddle the raft, and he left his jacket, shirt and shoes with Derek and Rab and proceeded to attempt a launch. Fortunately for him, the tide was ebbing and the plan was abandoned, but, by another stroke of good fortune, on their next visit to the coast they found that the sea had delivered all three pallets to the First Water.

One day, while the boys were working on the frame, a group of Grammar School 'brainiacs', accompanied by Ronald Togneri of the Art Department, appeared in the bay and were surprised to see the work-in-progress. 'We explained that the purpose was to have a place to study,' Alastair recalled, but no one, least of all Mr Togneri, would have given that commitment to academic excellence any credence.

The most dramatic event at the First Water, a bracken fire that raged out of control, happened by accident. Alastair recalls that the fire started 'innocently enough' with a patch of ground being cleared for some now forgotten purpose. The blaze quickly spread up the north slope of the bay, and Alastair remembers that a shirt newly purchased from N. L. McMillan's clothes shop was practically ruined during the emergency. It was his 'good' – that is, dress – shirt, and he shouldn't have been wearing it to the Coast. He used it in beating out the flames and soaked it repeatedly in the burn to improve its fire-fighting efficacy.

The incident was recalled in a letter I wrote to Alastair on 10 January 1982. Rab Davison and Derek McKinven had visited me on New Year's Day, but I was already in bed and 'had to bid them goodbye after a hasty greeting from the half-opened door'. They returned later in the week and were more hospitably received: 'We enjoyed a good yarn till one in the morning. They had gone together to the Learside and got talking about the ill-fated hut and some of your adventures on the coast – the raft incident &, perhaps less comfortable to recall, the firing of the hill. We all wished that you could have been there to share these and other memories.'

Alastair clearly remembers 'the day the *Quesada* went down'. He, Derek and Rab were at the hut site, but the day became increasingly stormy and they made their way back to Auchenhoan with their tools. 'It was so windy from the west, we had to duck down at various mounds to shelter and rest and were exhausted when we reached the farm.' Gilbert Muir put their bicycles in his van and ran the boys to town. 'After the news of the disaster and the storm', they returned to the First Water and spent time 'looking over the sea and realising that it still held its victims'. They decided against 'scouring the shore' that day.

The *Quesada*, 1966

Almost half a century on, the loss of the Campbeltown motor-yacht *Quesada*, south-east of Davaar Island, is embedded in the memories of those still living who survived the tragedy and those who are old enough to remember it. It remains an emotive and a controversial subject, which some future local historian may examine in depth.

My memory, for what it's worth, places me at the War Memorial in Campbeltown. The date is Monday, 23 May 1966. I'm on a message-bike, delivering parcels for George MacKay, butcher in Longrow, before I make my way to the Grammar School for the morning bell. Another message-boy, Robert Anderson, is cycling towards me and stops to tell me that the *Quesada* is gone and men have been lost.

The fatalities were: John McMillan, owner, Archibald Gillies, Kenneth Copping, Jack McCallum, John Paterson, James Wallace, Anthony Kennedy and Angus McGeachy. The survivors were: Archibald Stewart, John Barbour, David S. Johnson, Duncan McI. McKinven, John G. Docherty, Hugh Colville, James Colville, Archibald W. Ferguson, S. Lamont Conley and J. G. Durnan.

She left Campbeltown at around 7.45 a.m. on Sunday 22 May on a cruise, principally for members of staff of Paterson's Garage in town. The planned destination had been Northern Ireland, but a gale forecast for the Malin sea area prompted instead a trip to Lochranza, Rothesay and Tighnabruaich. The party had time ashore in each of these ports, and at about 10.30 p.m. the *Quesada* left Tighnabruaich to return to her home port. The passage to Skipness was 'smooth and uneventful', but afterwards the wind began to freshen and rose steadily to gale force 8 from the north-west.

About a quarter-of-a-mile north of Davaar Island, the port engine failed, and instead of gaining the safety of Campbeltown Loch, the vessel, her steering now restricted, 'proceeded on her starboard engine to the east and south of Davaar island'. Ten minutes later, the starboard engine also failed, 'and the vessel was down by the stern and drifting in the wind'. Just before 1 a.m., a distress flare was seen south of Davaar Island, and about fifteen minutes later Campbeltown life-boat was launched. But a Campbeltown fishing boat, the *Moira*, had already put to sea with a volunteer crew: Neil Speed, her skipper, Jim Meenan, skipper of the *Stella Maris*, Archibald Galbraith, Duncan McArthur, Sweeney Copping, Norman Thomson and Campbell Stewart.

These men had been aboard their boats preparatory to going out later in the morning, and an official report praised them in these terms: 'The skill, cool courage, intelligence and character shown by these men, which resulted in the saving of ten lives in a full gale, from a sinking vessel, with spindrift making vision impossible, and in confused seas, is deserving of the highest praise and commendation. Neil Speed's skilful handling of the *Moira* alongside the sinking *Quesada*, with James Meenan's direction of operations, are in the highest and best traditions of the sea.'

After the survivors had been landed at Campbeltown, the *Moira* returned to sea and continued the search until the afternoon, along with the life-boat and other Campbeltown fishing boats, the *Stella Maris*, *Mary McLean*, *Golden Hind*, *Little Flower*, *Boy Danny* and *Regina* Maris, but no further survivors were found.[3]

8 April: A rock chair in Queen Esther's Bay

When I arrived in Queen Esther's Bay, the enclosed inlet between the Bloody Bay and the First Water, with rucksack and saw, I was in a reflective mood, but it was 'one of those days when the past is more burden than inspiration', as I jotted in my journal. I'd been remembering, as I sat, family members and friends I'd shared the bay with over the past thirty-odd years. Normally the solitary state doesn't bother me, but that day it did.

I was lifted out of that mood for a while by the memory of a photograph I took there in the summer of 1984. The subject of the photograph had disappeared, as I had known for many years without troubling myself to find an explanation, but now an explanation interested me. The subject was a chair-shaped rock in the shingle beach on the north side of the bay. Jimmy MacDonald, for scale, is seated on the rock, which is the size and shape of a real armchair, but without arm rests – Nature cannot always be relied upon to deliver perfection!

4. *Jimmy MacDonald on the rock chair at Queen Esther's Bay, 1984. Photograph by the author.*

Four winters ago, at George McSporran's suggestion, Teddy Lafferty and I looked through our slides and selected forty or fifty which we took to George's house and added to his own selection. We viewed the lot in an evening of nostalgia. One of my choices was Jimmy in the stone chair, and, seeing the image again, after many years, I began to wonder what had happened to the chair. I later asked Teddy about it, since he'd spent more time than I in Queen Esther's Bay. Yes, he had sat on it and had meant to photograph it, but never got around to it. The Pirate's Grave, another missing stone on the Learside, was likewise on his list of subjects to be photographed and likewise wasn't and never would be.

Back in Queen Esther's Bay that day in April, I looked at where the chair had been and photographed the spot for comparison with the slide. Judy, my wife, examined the two images with me and agreed that, since the level of the shingle – gauged against a rock outcrop – had altered little in the intervening thirty years, the obvious explanation for the chair's disappearance was destruction, presumably in a storm.

(I wrote at length about Queen Esther's Bay in *A Summer in Kintyre*, pp. 183-84, and Esther herself is described in this book on p 128.)

Saint Kieran's Cave

From Queen Esther's Bay, I walked north to Auchenhoan Head to have a look in Saint Kieran's Cave. Towards the back of the cave lay a sheep corpse, from which someone – a disciple of the macabre, presumably – had removed the decomposing head and propped it on a rock. I noted that the interior was 'very wet' – it invariably is – and that water was running noisily off the cliff face. Indeed, a mass of vegetation – mostly greater woodrush – had been peeled off the cliff, presumably by a torrent, and was strewn on the grassy foreshore.

I also noted that the 'stone relics' were 'still in place'. These are intrinsic to the cave's distinction, and there are three: a boulder incised with an Early Christian marigold design, a socket-stone in which a cross had probably been mounted, and a hollowed rock which collects water drips from the cave ceiling. That rock-basin doubtless collected the water supply for generations of cave-dwellers – there is no spring or stream nearby – but I understand that its water was also formerly used for baptisms.

Many Kintyre caves were still occupied by destitutes and travellers throughout the nineteenth and even into the twentieth century, but

Saint Kieran's Cave was evidently not one of them. I assume that it became too wet for comfort. Thomas Pennant, in 1772, remarked of the 'round bason [*sic*], cut out of the rock', that it was 'full of fine water' and that sailors often landed at the cave to cook their food. An 'antient pair, upwards of seventy years', he added, 'once made this their habitation for a considerable time.'[4]

The stone carving is the cave's main attraction and is probably more than a thousand years old. It may well have sat on the floor of the cave for the duration of its symbolic life, but I must admit to concern for its security, though it is probably too heavy to manually remove. In the nineteenth century, there were traditions of the stone's being 'often taken away, by the cupidity of the credulous, or the maliciously mischievous, but by some inexplicable mystery or inherent virtue in the sainted character of the relic, it was invariably restored to its place, and found the following day'.[5] I wouldn't trust to supernatural intervention these days, so the question remains: is the carved stone safe in the cave? Should it be removed to a museum in which it will be just one among hundreds of artefacts to be glanced at by processions of visitors, or should it remain in its spiritual home, drawing a few hundred dedicated visitors each year?

In 1894, Lord Archibald Campbell, second son of the 8th Duke of Argyll, donated to the Kintyre Scientific Association's little museum in Kirk Street, Campbeltown, a rubbing on cloth of 'the pattern on the surface of the ancient stone in St. Kieran's cave'.[6] His wife, Janey Sevilla Callander, was a society beauty, of whom the American artist James McNeill Whistler painted several portraits. Anna Matilda McNeill, Whistler's mother, was descended from an Argyll family, and I wonder if the Campbells and Whistler, who were friends in London, discussed that shared Argyll connection?

There are several Saint Ciarans in history, but the cave is assumed to commemorate the sixth century Irish missionary, Ciaran of Clonmacnois, patron saint of Campbeltown (in its earlier Gaelic identity, *Ceann Loch Chille Chiarain*, 'Head of the Loch of Ciaran's Cell'). The local tradition that the cave was occupied as a religious retreat by Ciaran will never be proven, nor will it ever be disproven; but its credentials as a stellar site in the history of Christianity in Kintyre remain incontestable.

Saint Kieran's Cave should be a 'tourist attraction', but its inaccessibility counts against it. The Cave Painting on Davaar Island is no easier reached, but attracts thousands more visitors every year. Why should that be? One cave is an authentic archaeological/religious site, the other contains a nineteenth century gimmick; one cave has an atmosphere of sanctity, or at least of mystery, and the other has little atmosphere of any kind. That the crucifixion painting is much better known is attributable both to its promotion as a tourist attraction and to the island's having a greater visible presence; Saint Kieran's Cave is obscure, and long may it remain a destination of the few.

Excavation of Saint Kieran's Cave

The cave was excavated in 1924 and 1925 by volunteers from the Kintyre Antiquarian Society, supervised by Ludovic McLellan Mann (1869-1955), then an eminent but controversial prehistorian. In the Royal Commission on the Ancient and Historical Monuments of Scotland's Kintyre volume (1971), the excavation report was completely ignored. The only explanation I can suggest is that the excavation was considered to have been incompetent and the findings unreliable.

The report[7] was written by Norman Morrison, who, in the sheer range of his self-taught attainments, both scientific and literary, had few peers in what was an extraordinarily gifted group. He was joined on the excavation committee by Colonel Charles Mactaggart, a member of the family of Campbeltown lawyers, and retired from a distinguished career in the Indian Medical Service; 'Mrs Galloway', the widow of mining engineer and intellectual all-rounder, T. Lindsay Galloway, and a rare bird at the time in Kintyre, a female antiquarian and Fellow of the Society of Antiquaries of Scotland; Duncan Colville, a stalwart of the Antiquarian Society who would live to the age of ninety-seven and distinguish himself as the pre-eminent amateur archaeologist in Kintyre and an expert in a broad range of local studies; finally, Neil MacArthur, a prominent Campbeltown building contractor, who undertook to 'provide the labour and supply the necessary implements'.

Work began on 26 July 1924 and proceeded intermittently until June of the following year. Six trenches would ultimately be excavated. Morrison explained the procedure thus: 'After removing the surface rubbish, the method we then adopted was to cut the soil in layers of four inches, and every shovel of earth was riddled to ensure that no relic would escape our notice.' The first artefacts to appear, at a depth of twelve inches, were two 'dressed flints', and the excitement these finds generated was likened by Morrison to the experience of an angler 'who hooks and lands his first fish of the day'. The report is not without unintentional humour: 'An hour afterwards, Mr Mann suddenly jumped into the trench and brushed aside the man who was shovelling the earth. He then bent down and picked up a bone needle in a perfect state of preservation.'

5. *Norman Morrison inside Saint Kieran's Cave during its excavation, c. 1924. He is wearing a neck-tie in the centre of a party of Neil MacArthur's workmen, with shovels and riddle. From the Kintyre Antiquarian Society archive, Argyll & Bute Council archive, Lochgilphead.*

Against the back wall of the cave, the second trench yielded an adult human skeleton, the upper part of which, with the exception of the skull, had been crushed by a rock fall. The report's objectivity begins to wobble at this point, with Morrison's assertion that 'this individual must have been a notable person, probably a warrior or a saint'. On the smooth surface of a boulder embedded in the conglomerate rock, about five feet above the floor where the skeleton was uncovered, the party perceived 'incised sculpturing of a very early Christian period, consisting of a cross within an ellipse, a serpent-like figure in the attitude of striking, and other floriated designs'. Forty-one years later, in July 1965, the R.C.A.H.M.S. archaeologists who examined the cave noted only 'the mutilated remains of an incised carving'.

In the third trench, an object found at a depth of fourteen inches was described as 'a relic of the Viking period, trifling in itself, but full of meaning, a diamond-headed iron nail of a Norse ship'. Far from being 'trifling', had it belonged to a Norse ship it would constitute, even now, the only Norse artefact yet found in Kintyre! Significantly, it is not among the cave finds displayed in Campbeltown Museum.

I'll stop there. In the ninety years since the cave's excavation, archaeology has made tremendous multi-disciplined advances, utilising, for example, geology, chemistry, anthropology and even philosophy. It is all too easy to carp with hindsight, and being smart in print is safer than being smart in a pub or on the street. Next time I am in the cave, I'll think of Morrison and the rest of the volunteers, toiling enthusiastically, and when I step outside I'll imagine them on the grassy slope, sitting at lunch and looking out to sea.

Christmas Eve in the Cave

Norman Morrison was a policeman who was also a naturalist and whose specialist – and innovative – subject was adders. He was born on a croft in Lewis, but the last thirty years of his life were spent in Campbeltown, where he died in 1949. I often return, in books and articles, to Morrison and his exploits, for he had an original questing mind and was a gifted writer.

Some years after the excavation, he returned to Saint Kieran's Cave to spend a Christmas Eve there. As Christmas approached, he had become 'infected with a mysterious sentiment' which drew his thoughts 'in the direction of this magic cave'. Since, as he admitted, passing a night alone in an isolated tidal cave involves 'a test of nerve and courage', he enlisted a companion, whom he didn't name. They reached the cave in darkness, just before an incoming tide closed off the headland, and lit a fire with driftwood they'd gathered during a visit the day before. The account delivers descriptive and imaginative passages – he could 'picture with the greatest of ease the presence of the shades of saints, knights, and warriors' moving around him – before reaching its strange climax.

About a minute before the midnight hour a hush fell over Nature outside. The wind for the moment became silent, and even the waves toned down their wailing chant to a soft pleasant murmur, as if Nature were paying homage to the ushering in of another Christmas morn. As my watch registered the sacred hour of midnight the shrill note of an oyster-catcher was heard outside. Next moment it came shooting into the cave, flew right over the well and above our heads, then wheeled about, and with another pensive wail disappeared into the darkness of the outer world.

This creature in Gaelic is known as St. Bride's bird, and was considered by the early Celtic saints to be a sacred creature for services it had rendered to St. Bride. Naturally, we were startled at the sudden appearance and curious behaviour of this romantic bird. As might be expected, my mind at once flew back to the legend; but, of course, we now live in the age of cause and effect, so that we must say that the visit of this bird was a coincidence.[8]

A wet Sunday in 1984

6. L-R: Teddy Lafferty and Jimmy MacDonald in rain at the First Water, 24 June 1984. Photograph by the author.

On 24 June 1984, a Sunday, Jimmy MacDonald and I overtook groups of 'pilgrims' from St. Kieran's R.C. Church making their way around Auchenhoan Head towards the cave for a special mass. There were about twenty people, and the elderly among them in particular were having a hard time on the rocks, which were slippery in the rain. 'A most unpleasant day for such a venture,' I noted in my journal. It wasn't, of course, any better for Jimmy and me, and, to compound my misery, I had a headache all day, the legacy of a 'session' in the Ardshiel Hotel, which I unwisely prolonged at home by sipping malt whisky until four o' clock in the morning.

Iain Campbell, out for a drive, gave Jimmy and me a lift in his car and dropped us at the Sheep Fanks. Rain came on soon after, as I knew it would. I could see 'cloud battalions massing in the west', but didn't expect it to be quite so heavy or so continuous. Jimmy had seen Teddy Lafferty heading off with rucksack earlier that morning (probably while I was still in a drunken sleep) and we expected to meet him on the coast. We found his fire-place still smoking in Queen Esther's Bay, and, in the presumed absence of the man himself, were about to carry on when we heard a shout and the clatter of thrown stones. Teddy was huddled in a gully a little to the north of the bay, and we joined him for a while, before moving with him to the First Water, where we found a strip of dry shingle under a rock overhang. There were some dry sticks there and we got a fire lit and had tea and sandwiches. Soaking wet by that time, we set off in driving rain to return home by the Old Road. I have an abiding memory of the discomfort of that journey. I was wearing jeans, which were saturated, and with every step the cloth stuck to my legs. I later became a convert to corduroy trousers, and denim was banished from my wardrobe.

Auchenhoan Head

As the tide was coming in, I cut short my visit to the cave, since at high tide it is closed off. This, to coast walkers, has ever been a problem, the safest solution to which is to climb over the top of the headland and regain the shore at the opposite end. It was often, however, an option I preferred not to consider. When I have set out to walk a shore, I'd rather remain on that shore and avoid having to clamber up and then scramble down hundreds of feet.

7. Looking across the Lodan to Auchenhoan Head from the north, evening of 11 August 1981. Photograph by the author.

A solution to the problem appeared on 8 July 1980. My niece Barbara Docherty and I had set off for Queen Esther's Bay at 7.30 in the evening. When we reached Auchenhoan Head, the sea was up to the foot of the cliffs. Supposing that the tide was on the turn, I suggested we continue by the shore. Actually, the tide was still coming, and progress was slow and difficult. At one point we found the lower cliff impassable, so I suggested we ascend a bit to clear the impasse; but, having got some 20 feet up, I ran out of footholds and handholds and 'froze'. Barbara, too, hanging on below me, suffered a wave of apprehension. Even in my quaking state, however, the idea came to me that we might wade out of our dilemma, so we backed down to the foot of the cliff, removed our shoes and stockings, and continued up to our knees in water. Note in journal: 'All in all, quite exciting, as Barbara herself felt.' Note in book: for reasons of 'health and safety', the author no longer endorses the above expedient.

We were almost an hour getting round the Head, and when we finally reached Queen Esther's Bay, Barbara began gathering driftwood while I went to the First Water and filled the kettle. We had tea and ate a treacle sandwich each, after which, as the bay is rather enclosed, and was dark at that late stage of the evening, we moved to a little crag further north and sat there. The shadowed headland was before us, sunset clouds were spread across the northern sky and the sea was lapping the shore. As Barbara remarked, the beauty of the scene was inexpressible. We packed our rucksacks and set off along the shore to the First Water, where we cut up on to the road. Near Auchenhoan farmhouse, we heard a snuffling noise in roadside bracken, and, scaling a bank, found a hedgehog, which waddled quickly away up the field. We took the Old Road back, arriving home at fifteen minutes past midnight.

The derivation of the name 'Auchenhoan' is a contentious one,[9] but Gaelic writer Ronald Black suggests *Achadh a' Chuain*, 'Ocean Field', citing Arichuan (*Àirigh a' Chuain*, 'Ocean Shieling') in Kilmartin parish as a parallel. Another problematic name, of the neighbouring farm 'Ballinatunie' – 'Balintoan' in the 1751 Valuation Roll – he interprets persuasively as *Baile na Tòine*, 'Backside Farm', citing *Tòn Tìre* ('Land's Backside') in Mull and *Tòn ri Gaoith* ('Backside to the Wind') in Arran.[10]

A cliff fall, 1889

A young Campbeltown cabinet-maker, John Gilchrist, fell about 150 feet from Auchenhoan Head in March 1889. He and John McNair, a cooper, were walking on the shore below the headland when their progress was blocked by the tide. At some point near Saint Kieran's Cave, they began scaling the cliff 'to get on to the road', but Gilchrist lost his hold, fell to the shore and was knocked unconscious. His companion went for help, and at a 'shepherd's hut' – Auchenhoan, which would hardly have been a 'hut', but the steading which exists to this day – he found the shepherd, George Menzies. Together they carried Gilchrist to the 'hut', and, when he had regained consciousness, Menzies took him to town in a cart and found a doctor to attend to him.[11] Since nothing more was reported, presumably he survived.

The Fiddler's Rock and Archie McAllister

On my way back into the Bloody Bay to cut wood, I passed under the Fiddler's Rock, a miniature headland separated from Auchenhoan Head by a shingly creek. In *The Place-Names of the Parish of*

Campbeltown the name is explained thus: 'It is said that, viewed from above, the rock resembles a violin.'[12] This can only refer to the configuration of the narrow grassy summit, and seems to me rather too fanciful to be credible. Having said that, someone clearly looked at the rock and saw a fiddle shape there, perhaps because he believed that it should be there. If that is, indeed, the explanation, then the name should be 'The Fiddle Rock', though names do mutate over time; and 'Fiddler's Rock' is the form on an Argyll Estate map of 'Auchahoan' drawn in 1836. A likelier explanation may be that the rock commemorates an actual fiddler. Perhaps his musicianship was so execrable he was banished to the rock to continue his practice!

It is certainly associated now with a fiddler who is in no danger of expulsion from any musical gathering, Archie McAllister. His CD, issued in 2007, was titled *The Fiddler's Rock*. Archie's father, Duncan McAllister, was shepherd on Auchenhoan farm, but Archie was only six years old when the family left there in 1975, and his memories are understandably scant. He does, however, remember being with his father in a field overlooking the rock, which at the time was nameless to him: 'It was during the lambing and he was trying to get a ewe to adopt a lamb by putting a dead lamb's fleece on a lamb which had lost its mother, and I was amazed at what was going on with this process.' Archie was twenty-one years old when he finally heard the name 'Fiddler's Rock'. He was with his mother's brother, William McKillop, on a day trip to Ireland on the *Balmoral*, and while passing south along the Learside coast William pointed out the rock and named it. Later, when the time came to title the CD he had recorded, Archie thought *The Fiddler's Rock* most fitting, since he 'played the fiddle and was brought up so close to it'.

The album's most intriguing title belongs to a composition of Archie's, 'The Great Kilkenzie Strawberry Robbery'. I appeared with him and his accompanist, Sileas Sinclair, at a ceilidh in Glenbarr Abbey on 5 January. My contribution consisted of folk-tales and poems, and Archie, of course, provided the music. 'The Great Kilkenzie Strawberry Robbery' was one of the tunes he played that afternoon, and his introduction to it included a full account of the horticultural outrage and his role in it; but, to protect the guilty, I withhold particulars of the confession.

8. The Fiddler's Rock, 14 June 1981. Sheep have worn a path up the spine of the rock. Photograph by the author.

The Fiddler's Rock is very inviting, but I doubt if I have been on top of it more than half-a-dozen times, probably because I was already a cautious adult by the time I began frequenting the Learside. There was a day, however, when I climbed it twice, encouraged by a young companion, Jimmy MacDonald. The date was 20 August 1984. We arrived in mist at the Bloody Bay in the early afternoon, and saw that Teddy Lafferty was already there. Jimmy and I went up the rock, and from the top I took several photographs, including two of Teddy tending his fire on the shore. We had a cup of tea with him, after which I decided we'd carry on south to the Dummy's Port. Teddy accompanied us along the shore a bit, but we all ended up peering into a rock pool rich in marine life, and when Jimmy asked if we could stay, I agreed.

He and I had a refreshing bathe at the First Water, and, while we were in the sea, Allister and Agnes Stewart appeared with their Irish setter, Kerry. They stopped and spoke with Teddy, and I exchanged a few words with them on my way back to the fire. After more tea and food, at Jimmy's insistence we climbed back on to the Fiddler's Rock. From my journal: 'Jimmy, to my irritation, occupied himself in throwing stones and other things off the top. We watched a small blue boat drifting and being rowed offshore, two men in her. Another boat had arrived in the mist earlier and cut off her engine, and seven men in her – we saw them later – began fishing. She remained visible for two or three hours. We could hear the voices of the men in the mist over the engine noise.'

The south face of the Fiddler's Rock supports a stupendous growth of ivy, and the puddingstone rock, with its multitudinous ledges and holes, is well provided with nest sites for birds. Teddy used to gather kindling sticks, which had fallen or been dropped from a ravens' nest there, and now that he is unfit to get to the shore, he dreams of pastimes like wood-gathering – ordinary things illumined in memory.

A cliff rescue in 1964

The Fiddler's Rock was the scene of a dramatic cliff rescue in May 1964. Two Campbeltown teenagers, Edward Russell and Terence Evans, were walking on the shore when Edward 'decided to make his way along the cliff face'. He 'began to feel his feet slipping', and, reaching a ledge about 65 feet up, called to his companion: 'I'm trapped – I need help!' Terence ran to Auchenhoan farmhouse for assistance, found a shepherd, Archie Lang, and hastened with him to the spot. Meanwhile, Gilbert Muir, the head shepherd, back from the hill, was told of the emergency, and he too hurried to the shore. Having looked at Edward's position on the cliff, he and Archie agreed that they couldn't manage a rescue on their own, so, while Archie 'stayed behind and kept talking to Edward', Gilbert returned to the farmhouse and telephoned Campbeltown Police. Constable Sandy Carmichael was first to arrive and was followed by Sergeant Malcolm MacMartin and Constable Ian McCall. Southend Auxiliary Coastguard had been alerted and was on its way with rescue gear, and Gilbert's brothers, Andrew and William, were also heading to Auchenhoan. The police had brought a 200-foot-long rope, and, as darkness was closing in, the rescue operation began at once.

Constable Carmichael picked his way carefully down the steep slope with the end of the rope and passed it down to Mr Gilbert Muir. The other two officers and the Muir brothers took the strain at the top. With some difficulty the rope was dropped on to the ledge and Edward wound it round his waist and tied it securely. Slowly he was swung off the ledge and dangled dizzily over the sheer face of the cliff for some 10 yards until he was pulled in at another ledge by Mr Muir, who then untied him and led him up a path to safety.

Edward, of 140 Ralston Road, was cold and white with strain, but, apart from slight bruising to his ribs where the rope had taken the strain, he was otherwise unhurt. He was taken to Auchenhoan where Mrs Muir gave him a cup of tea and home-made scones. Then he was taken home in the police car.

He afterwards paid tribute to the swift and selfless efforts of the police and of Mr Muir and his brothers to save him from 'an impossible position'. He added: 'I won't be trying any cliff walking for a long time.'[13]

The Bloody Bay

As one rounds the base of the Fiddler's Rock, the Bloody Bay opens out in the south. It must have had a Gaelic name before 'Bloody Bay' was coined, or perhaps that's a translation of the original name. It is a classic Kintyre *innean* – an amphitheatre-shaped cove – but that Gaelic element, which survives in clusters along the coast north of the Mull, on Sanda, and between Brunerican and Pennyseorach in Southend, is entirely absent from the east coast of Kintyre, though many bays other than the Bloody Bay qualify topographically. The total absence of *innean* place-names on the east coast suggests that the generic was never carried beyond Southend.

Many Gaelic place-names on the Learside, however, were replaced by names in English or Scots. Apart from farms and major topographical features, the majority of names reflect the influence of the Lowland settlement of South Kintyre which began in the seventeenth century. From north to south: Sheep Fanks, New Orleans, Wee Man's or Mecky's Cove, Bottleneck Cove, Covie Kieran or Saint Kieran's Cave, Fiddler's Rock or Meer's Heid, Bloody Bay, Queen Esther's Bay, First Water, Johnston's Bay, Second Water, Dummy's Port, Grey Face, Pishin' Mare, Pirate's Grave, Johnston's Point, Viking's Grave, Giant's Chair, and the Castles, which takes us to Polliwilline.

The origin of 'Bloody Bay'? There are several choices. One tradition from Teddy Lafferty refers to seven brothers who fought among themselves until only one remained alive, and he also heard of a horseman who fell over the headland to his death; another ascribes the name to 'an attempted landing by Norsemen,'[14] which may connect with a tradition sent to me in 1999 by Duncan Gilchrist, in Timsbury, Bath. According to his father, the cave was used as a 'secret hide-away chapel during the times of Norse pillaging'. Some locals, including a 'princess' with a child, were at the cave for the child's baptism when they were surprised by raiders approaching from both directions along the shore. The 'princess' strapped the child to her back and climbed up the cliff to avoid capture, but the Vikings were waiting for her there, and, as she was pulling herself on to the top, they hacked off her hands and she fell to her death.[15] I'll add a fifth bloody tale. Saint Ciaran, being blind, had a beautiful pet deer which went around the countryside collecting alms for him. A brutal chief, *Eòghann* (Hugh) by name, one day blinded the deer for the fun of seeing it fall over the cliff on its way back to the cave with the saint's food. But divine retribution soon overtook the evil Hugh. While sleeping on top of Ben Gullion, wrapped in animal skins, his own hounds tore him to pieces.[16]

Wreck of the *Accord*, 1993

In August 1993, the Irish trawler *Accord* ran aground at ebb tide in the Bloody Bay. Her crew was rescued by Campbeltown life-boat and Coastguards, but her hull had been breached on impact and she filled with water in the flood tide and was declared a loss.[17] George McSporran, his son Sandy and I were in the bay the next year, on 16

January, when I noted: 'Masses of splendid wood lying around – tons and tons of it. Will take a few bits back, but there's no means of doing justice to the supply.' Thirty years on, her ugly remains – most visibly, the winch, fuel tanks and metal superstructure – still litter the bay, and chunks of her oak timbers continue to wash ashore, but they are contaminated with oil from the bilges and I pass them by.

9. *The trawler Accord aground in the Bloody Bay, 1993. The Fiddler's Rock is in front of Auchenhoan Head, with Davaar Island on the horizon. Photograph by Teddy Lafferty.*

The loss of the *Lena*, 1898

The Bloody Bay was where the body of Andrew McKinven, fisherman in Campbeltown, washed ashore in 1898. He had gone out in his line-fishing skiff *Lena* with Alexander Huie at 6 a.m. on Monday, 2 May. A calm morning gave way to a south-easterly gale, in which the *Lena* was caught and capsized.

When James Wareham and sons Joseph and Alexander rowed out of harbour that morning, McKinven and Huie were preparing to leave, and followed under sail to Auchenhoan Head. The Warehams were hauling the last of their lines when the *Lena* arrived, and, as they had caught no fish, they waited 'to see what luck McKinven and Huie would have'; but the signs were not good with them either. When the Warehams left the fishing ground, between 9 and 10 a.m., the *Lena* was the last boat remaining, and her crew was still at work, McKinven rowing and Huie pulling in the lines. Around 11 a.m., a wind rose in the east, and by the time the Warehams reached harbour a gale was blowing.

By evening, word had spread through the town that the *Lena* had not returned. About 3 o' clock the following morning, two of McKinven's nephews, James and Lawrence McKinven, set out to search the Learside. On Kildalloig shore they found the mast and an oar belonging to the *Lena*, and, further south, the *Lena* herself, afloat but full of water. Still further south, in the Bloody Bay, a body floating face-up among seaweed turned out to be their uncle, fully clothed and missing only his cap. They continued south in the hope of finding Huie, but his body was never recovered.

McKinven's corpse was taken to his house in Fisher Row and examined there by Dr James Brown. The funeral took place two days later from Lochend Free Church, where the dead man was an elder, and where, on the day before his drowning, he had 'assisted in the dispensation of the Sacrament'. There was a large turn-out of mourners, including many fishermen and church officers. He was sixty-seven years old and left a widow and grown-up family. Huie left a widow and four children.[18]

On 15 May, in the Argyll Arms Hotel, Campbeltown, I met up with two McKinven cousins, Margaret Bond and Marion Gray, who found each other through internet research, and we discussed Andrew's drowning and McKinven family history in general. Margaret and Marion met for the first time on 13 May 2013, and, as Margaret remarked, 'immediately hit it off'. Margaret, who lives in England, admits that until she began her genealogical researches she 'had never heard of Campbeltown'. She visited the town for the first time in May 2011, when I met her for a meal. This time she had Marion with her, and we were later joined by a local relative, Alex McKinven, who had been conducting one of his history tours in town and had heard that the women were looking for him. He guessed, correctly, that he'd find them in the Argyll Arms, since Margaret and I had met him there three years before. The cousins naturally had plenty to say to one another, and, after a few more drinks and a 'photo shoot' using Marion's phone, I left them to it.

Otters

On my way back into Queen Esther's Bay, I looked at an otters' feeding spot I'd noticed on 24 October of the previous year. Otters are quite frequently sighted on that coast. My ratio is probably around once in every dozen visits, without looking for them and without necessarily travelling more than a few miles. Scats and food remains can be found abundantly on certain rocks they land on to feed, and individually and randomly on the shore. The spot I was looking at wasn't a rock, but a grassy hollow in a rock. I had noticed, in October, a clearly defined track into the hollow, a patch of grass which had been flattened by a body, or bodies, lying or rolling on it, some droppings, and, which interested me most, the fresh remains of a velvet swimming crab. I looked carefully at these scattered pieces. All eight legs were there, and the nippers, pouch and shell, which was broken in half, presumably for extraction of the innards. I guess that the unfortunate crab was a mere snack to the otter which snatched it from the seabed. Six months on, there were no signs of otters' having recently visited the hollow.

On 25 May, while George McSporran and I were on the shore north of Johnston's Point looking for the Pirate's Grave (p 74), I noticed a tail momentarily lift from behind an ebbed reef directly below us. When I trained my binoculars on the rock, I saw an otter and then a cub with it. I watched them for several minutes, but George, whose eyesight is keener than mine, couldn't see them, even when I handed the binoculars to him. Certainly, his view from where he was sitting was rather circumscribed. Both otters were gone, I suspect, before we ventured stealthily down the shore towards the reef. We later saw a black-backed gull swoop on to the reef and lift what I reckoned might be the head of a fish the otters had caught and fed on. A second black-backed gull appeared almost immediately and pursued the first, which dropped its prize into a rock pool from which its pursuer retrieved it.

11 April: Seals, a gull and wilkers' caves

I was daily approaching closer to the Dummy's Port. Though wood was scarce on that stretch of shore, I decided not to go any further in my search because I could see nine seals hauled out on a reef north of the port and was reluctant to disturb them. I was hearing them, too, and would hear them again on subsequent days. I've often listened to seals, but on this day their calls were reminiscent of recordings I'd heard of humpback whales. I thought of Judy Collins's version of 'Farewell to Tarwathie', which I'd first heard in the early 1970s. I was lying in a bath listening to a tape, and was captivated by the fusion of the whale 'songs' and Collins's slowed-down and otherwise unaccompanied interpretation of the old Scottish whaling song. The obvious one-word description is 'haunting'.

I heard the Collins version on BBC Radio 3's 'Late Junction' on 6 February, which happened to be my sixty-second birthday. I'd already routinely e-mailed Les Oman, but sent him a postscript saying that the Collins song had been played, and adding: 'I hadn't heard it for years and it still sends shivers down my spine.' His reply the following day: 'I always loved that song and was slightly incredulous that it came to my attention via an American singer, especially as I found it quite soon after in a book of Scottish traditional songs.'

Judy Collins was introduced to whale songs in the summer of 1969 by Roger Payne, a marine biologist with the New York Zoological Society. He approached her backstage after a concert and handed her his recordings, saying: 'I want you to figure out something to do with these whales. They're wonderful, and I'm entrusting them to you.' It took Collins a couple of months to conceive a creative use for the tape, and 'Farewell to Tarwathie', which appeared on her album *Whales and Nightingales* (1970), was the beautiful offspring.[19]

4 p.m. Watching a herring gull paddling offshore among floating wrack. It spotted something underwater, leapt into the air and dived for it. Nothing doing. Seconds later, it ducked from a sitting position, then ducked again and came up with a small shore crab which it flew with to a nearby tidal rock and immediately began stabbing at. Three minutes later, it was still trying to extract sustenance from the inner shell, which, in a crab that size, is the only part that provides morsels of food. At 4.05 the gull was again cruising among the wrack channels. It's a patient business – a specialisation, almost.

Thirty-three years ago, I was shown a cave in a cliff on that shore, but subsequently failed to locate it and have never seen it again. On 27 June 1981, I encountered Derek, an old school friend, south of the

Second Water. I had expected to meet him, knowing that this was 'his' winkle shore. He was gathering when I saw him, and, because the stooping man didn't quite resemble him, I called tentatively. He stopped work and came up to me and said he would walk with me to the Dummy's. Some way along the shore, he asked if I knew there was a cave thereabouts. I told him I didn't, so he took me to it.

It is a charming little den. He had split, two years ago, some of the sandy flags which had been breaking off rock faces, and, laying down these sections, formed, on the greater part of the cave floor, a nicely-made stone surface. Actually, the recess scarcely qualifies for the description 'cave' ... There isn't much shelter from weather and it isn't at all deep. It is pretty much full of paraphernalia: plastic fish-boxes, two bottles of sugar – still edible, I would say – an old damp frying-pan, and the spinner part of a spin-drier, from which he had intended to make a reading lamp. He had also formed a small wind-break, using stones, to one side of the entrance. All of which illustrates that people are <u>still</u> making shelters out of natural shore features. He was coming to this shore – from the Second Waters as far south as Feochaig – two years ago to gather wilks, and was in the habit, in early morning, of cooking himself breakfast on an old stove (still there, he says) on the shore, using that very frying-pan.

My friend never, to my knowledge, slept in that rock-shelter, but other wilkers not so long before him did live in Learside caves, usually in summer when the long daylight enabled them to increase their effort. Based in a handily placed cave, they were on the spot to exploit both daily tides, and thus double their earnings. The Cats' Cove on Polliwilline shore (p 128) was one of those caves. Willie McLellan and fellow-wilkers from Campbeltown used that cave in the 1940s and would spend up to a week there, sleeping on beds of bracken.[20]

Cave-dwelling wilkers occasionally appear in the April population censuses. In the Campbeltown census of 1901, Isabella McMillan – 'Sweetie Bella' in A Summer in Kintyre (pp. 153-54) – was in a 'Cave on Balnatunie shore', a peculiar description for what, I am certain, was the Wee Man's Cove at New Orleans (p 66). She was noted as a forty-year-old 'Whelk Gatherer'. Her companion, thirty-six-year-old Thomas Dunsmuir, appears to have had a long association with that cave. In 1894, when 'residing at The Cove, New Orleans', he was convicted of 'day trespass on the farm of Auchinahoane'. His crime was the setting of four rabbit snares and he was fined £1 10s with £1 15s 6d expenses, or thirty days' imprisonment.[21] Considering his economic circumstances, the likelihood is that he opted for jail.

15 April: Largiebaan

Agnes Stewart e-mailed the night before to offer me a lift, and confirmed the arrangement by 'phone that morning. She and her husband, Allister, collected me at 1, and by 1.30 the three of us were on the track to Glenahanty. She was counting butterflies and logged eight peacocks. Had I been on my own, I'd have found most of them difficult to identify in flight, but that species, emerged from hibernation, was evidently the big reddish one I'd lately been glimpsing in rapid motion. The one which did oblige by alighting, in a little roadside quarry, was in immaculate condition. We parted at the bridge past Glenahanty and I continued up the Bruach Dearg.

I wrote my name and a message in the little Kintyre Way geocache notebook stored in a plastic box under the stile past Largiebaan steadings, noticing that there had been only one entry since my inaugural entry on 11 March. Cath and Mike from Dunfermline wrote on 27 March: 'Doing Kintyre Way – Sunny dry day – started at Southend – on way to Machrihanish. 6 days to go to complete at Tarbert.'

I'd hung my walking-stick on the gate at the stile and walked on for about ten minutes before realising I'd left it, so I returned. The 'cromag' was given to me as a fiftieth birthday present by Judy and my daughters in 2002. It was carved by Richard Semple, a retired farmer and a friend of Allister and Agnes. I'd noticed Allister's crook earlier and asked him who had made it, thinking it too might be one of Richard's, but Allister said he had made it himself, and showed me the handle, which was of blue plastic. It had come from a butcher's block in the Stewarts' shop, Allister having turned to that material when experiencing difficulty in finding horn.

I headed straight out to the cliffs by the Kintyre Way, then began heading up, following the cliff edge. During the climb, I disturbed a sparrow-hawk which darted from a ledge. There was a strong, gusting wind, and in my search for shelter I ended up well below the usual sitting places. Near where I settled, there was a little rock hollow, walled at its entrance. I thought it might be an improvised twinning-pen, since the space would just accommodate a ewe and a lamb.

10. Five goats on Cnoc Moy, 15 April 2014. Photograph by the author.

I decided to go for the late bus at Machrihanish, and, avoiding the descent of the Kintyre Way to Innean Mòr sheep-fank, kept well up on the flank of Cnoc Moy. The detour probably didn't save me any time, but I was rewarded with a sighting of two red grouse and a photograph of wild goats, which, by the mere chance of their configuration on the skyline, I consider my best ever picture of the shaggy beasts. As I rounded the hill, I lost the wind, which had dogged me all day, and was suddenly conscious of silence, through which the bleating of sheep on the opposite side of the glen reached me. I noted later that I 'felt a little wave of melancholy sweep across my mind ... I suppose these are the desolate voices of other evenings in the past, and speak for absent companions; or maybe sheep just sound sad and cause me to feel the same!' I had half-an-hour to wait at Machrihanish and sat on the bench beside the bus-shelter. Wavelets were rolling on to the beach in quick succession, illumined by the street lighting as they broke, and a full but hazy moon hung in the south.

24 April: Corphin

I arrived in the Dummy's Port at 2.10 p.m. by a descent from the road, a more sensible option than walking the shore from the Second Water, and back again, since I intended that day to extend my wood-gathering south towards Ru Stafnish. I was recovering from a cold, but had had enough of being confined indoors. During the ride I had been pondering the question of where I might safely leave the bike.

My previous bike had been stolen from the Paddling Pool the year before, and I was wary of a repetition. I'd left it behind a bush one evening I went for a stroll, and when I returned, in darkness, little more than an hour later, it was gone. It was an old machine and virtually worthless, and, since I'd chained one of the wheels to the frame, I suspect that morons had lifted it and thrown it somewhere out of sight, perhaps even into the loch. I soon afterwards had a replacement, thanks to Jenny MacFarlane, and the thirty-year-old white Peugeot 'Laser' has since given me exemplary service.

I identified the roadside quarry above Corphin ruins as a suitable hiding-place for the bike, and chained it behind a mound. Having scrutinised the quarry from the road and satisfied myself that the bike was concealed, I headed down to the shore.

From the main road, a track leads through a field to Corphin, which consists of two drystone 'long houses', humans in one end and cattle in the other. These were the ubiquitous dwellings of the farming community until replaced in the nineteenth century by more substantial steadings, but the Corphin houses never were replaced. Instead, a small sheep-fank was constructed beside them. The farm was tenanted by McIsaacs – a family long established in the southern Learside (p 94) – from 1757 until 1856, when John Spiers from Arran took the lease, along with that of Auchenhoan and Ballinatunie, and put a shepherd, James Cook, into Corphin. James and his wife were alone there, but in 1792 the farm had supported twenty persons.[22]

One of these Corphin McIsaacs, Donald, was a fisherman, and his stone hut still stands on the shore below Corphin ruins. He was deaf and dumb, hence the place-name 'Dummy's' or 'Dummy's Port'. His fishing activity was doubtless seasonal, and he probably stayed with his family up the hill during winters. His life on the coast must have been a fairly solitary one, but, then, his disability would hardly have been conducive to sociability in any circumstances. The two 'ports' – passageways cleared of rocks for the beaching and launching of boats – are still visible north of his hut. The hut's interior measures about nine by eight feet, so there would be room for bedding, a fire-place, perhaps a table and chair, and not much else. That structure is drystone, but on the north end, next to the doorway, a small extension was added, perhaps as a store, and it was constructed with lime mortar.

When Corphin was turned over to sheep, the McIsaacs moved south to Dunglas. Argyll Estate records show that John McIsaac, 'tenant in Corphin' and Donald's nephew, got the lease of 'Dunglass and pendicle of Inisroel' in 1857 for the standard nineteen years, at an annual rent of £220, and that when the lease expired he was given notice to quit. Old Donald died at Dunglas in November 1871. He went out one morning to herd cattle, and when the cattle came home in the evening without him, a search party found him 'lying at the side of a dyke quite dead'.[23]

Among those identified as sympathising with Argyll's Rebellion in 1685 was Donald McCavish in 'Coraphen'.[24] He appears to have escaped punishment, but two prominent Kintyre rebels were executed, Colin Campbell of Skipness and Major John Campbell in Cleongart, whose arms were cut off before he was hanged in Inveraray. Among the rebels who were banished, Samuel Huy, having refused to acknowledge the authority of King Charles II, first had his ears cut off. The standard of that Protestant rebellion against the imposition of Episcopacy was raised at Campbeltown Cross on 20 May, 1685, by the 9th Earl of Argyll, Archibald Campbell, but within a month the rising had collapsed, and Argyll was captured and executed in Edinburgh.[25]

I copied many years ago from the Southend Parish register of deaths a pathetic entry of 1859. A ninety-year-old woman, Mirren MacCallum or MacLean, was found dead on 'the farm of Corvine' from 'Exhaustion brought on by fatigue and exposure to cold'. She was reckoned to have died between 21 March and 1 April and her parents were unknown.

One of the earliest entries in the Campbeltown register of poor was a seventy-three-year-old seamstress, Janet McEachran, born at 'Corraphin'. She was the widow of Thomas Murphy and had 'no friends able to assist' her in her old age. She was admitted to the poorhouse in February 1847 and died there.[26]

25 April: Cuckoos

At 4.20 p.m., between Corphin ruins and the shore, I heard my first cuckoo of 2014. Agnes Stewart, whom I met on the road, also heard the call that day. As many readers will know, the cuckoo is a bird of superstition. I have written so often about these superstitions, I am almost embarrassed to find myself having to repeat them; but this time I'll deliver the ultimate summary. If you don't hear the bird this year, then you won't hear it next year either, because you'll be dead; and you'd better hear it with food in your stomach.

I shan't pretend indifference to the cuckoo business, but since adopting the superstition I have never failed to hear the call, so the question of how I would react if I didn't remains academic. In 2014, however, George McSporran almost found himself in that dilemma. By 23 May, a month after he should have heard the bird, he was still waiting. We were pushing our bikes up Ballimenach brae that afternoon when an approaching Forestry Commission van slowed down and stopped, and the driver lowered his window. He was an acquaintance from Tarbert, Brian Baird, and his appearance was fortuitous, because our conversation was interrupted by the long-awaited call. The bird was perched close by in a roadside spruce plantation, and, as I noted on the spot, provided an 'emphatic guarantee of another year in the world'. This observation was, of course, for the benefit of George, who later confessed that he was 'really starting to get worried'.

Having, unusually, spent most of the spring cycling on the Learside, I found myself for the first time a witness to 'cuckoo fever'. I encountered several people – local and familiar to me – whose reason for being there was to hear the bird; and the anxious query, 'Hae ye heard the cuckoo?', was one with which I became familiar. But the one stranger, a Gaelic speaker, was the most interesting of all. On 29 April, I met Agnes Stewart at Kildalloig, and, while we were talking, a car stopped. Agnes asked the driver if he had heard the cuckoo, and he replied that he had. She then asked him to repeat, for my benefit, a Gaelic saying she'd obviously heard him quote before. He gave me the phrase and repeated it. Agnes then asked me to translate it, and I offered: 'I am very gloomy if I don't hear the cuckoo.' The man said that was all right and asked if I had a little (*beagan*) Gaelic. I felt rather pleased with myself, but in truth I had recognised two key words, *cuthag* ('cuckoo') and *muladach* ('sad'), which latter was hanging on in the Campbeltown dialect thirty years ago, and may still be. And, of course, the transparent context of the test helped too! Agnes informed me later that she had met the man the day before and advised him that if he wanted to be sure of hearing a cuckoo, he should continue up Ballimenach brae to a certain point where she had heard three birds calling separately that very day.

There is great interest every year in the earliest date the cuckoo is heard, but for the first time I found myself wondering what the latest date might be. The superstitious lose interest in the bird once the vital call has been heard, but had anyone been noting dates for the last call? I asked a few friends to listen and report to me, and one of them, Agnes, stated her belief that calls invariably cease before the Summer Solstice. She was evidently correct – the last report I had was from her on 18 June – but I invite readers to listen out in future summers.

As I sat under Ru Stafnish, where I cut the day's load of wood, I noticed a little spruce in the oddest location I'd ever seen a conifer – growing out of a split in a rock just above high-water mark. Its tip had been nipped off, probably by a foraging deer, but it looked healthy enough even though it's sure to be awash in gales.

I also noticed what at first appeared to be an oddly eroded rock with a hole in it, but which, when examined through binoculars, became a big lump of iron. Note in journal: 'I presume *Dotterel* and there's a good story there.'

Wreck of the *Dotterel*, 1923

The little cargo steamer *Dotterel* of Port Glasgow grounded at Ru Stafnish on 17 February 1923. She was loaded with machinery, pipes and other materials for Lord Leverhulme's ill-fated improvement schemes on Lewis and Harris, but, on her passage north, blizzard conditions at the Mull alarmed her master. He decided to turn back and shelter in Campbeltown harbour, but instead ran the *Dotterel* ashore in the same blizzard. After a 'trying night', he and his crew of seven managed to get ashore and reach Campbeltown, where they were cared for by the Shipwrecked Mariners' Society. On the following day, they sailed to Glasgow in the S.S. *Kinloch*. Their ship was reported to be 'fast on the rocks' and 'badly holed', but arrangements had been made to salvage the cargo and ship it to

Campbeltown. The salvaging of the *Dotterel* herself was predicted, given 'favourable weather',[27] but the opportunity never came.

Was the cargo itself salvaged? Some of it may have been, but there is ample evidence that much – perhaps the least valuable of the materials – was left. From the Ru to Johnston's Point, sea-worn bricks and bits of bricks, along with broken drainage-tiles, still litter the shore.

The ship's fate would probably have been consigned to oblivion had it not been for a court case, in May of the following year, in which two Campbeltown men, Campbell Roddick, plumber, and Andrew Scally, riveter, were charged with theft from the wreck.

The first witness was John Plancy, described as a 'metal merchant' of 32 St. Leonard's Street, Edinburgh. His religion did not escape the notice of the court or of the *Campbeltown Courier*; he was 'a Jew born in Hungary' and took the oath 'in Jewish fashion'. He testified that he had bought the *Dotterel* from the Receiver of Wreck and had since engaged a succession of salvage squads, but with 'very disappointing results'.

At the time of the theft, Duncan Newlands – later a distinguished coxswain of the Campbeltown life-boat – was at work on the wreck, being paid according to results: 'so much per ton landed on Campbeltown Quay.' Plancy had given Newlands a letter authorising him to undertake the work, but 'he could not tell the exact date, as he was unable to read or write'. Newlands, however, had the letter, which had been written for Plancy by 'the shipping clerk at the quay'. The scrap was to be sent to John Henderson, metal merchant in Glasgow.

Early in April, Plancy had received a telegram informing him of a theft at the wreck. He travelled to Campbeltown and in the police station was shown iron plates and barrels filled with brass piping, all of which he valued at £14 or £15 and was satisfied had come from the *Dotterel*. When cross-examined by Archibald Stewart, solicitor, he disclosed that he had paid £24 for the wreck, but had already spent over £300 and 'got nothing back'. He denied knowing the two accused, let alone authorising them to remove any part of the wreck.

The next witness was Duncan Newlands, described as a seaman in Bolgam Street. He confirmed that he had been engaged by Plancy and produced the letter of authorisation dated 30 November. On 1 April, Newlands went to the wreck in his motor boat, accompanied by his brother George (p 162), and found that a recent gale had shifted and split the hull. The engine-room had been exposed, and, seeing the brass piping, the two men went to work, using a hammer and a hatchet, their only tools. They loaded about two tons of metal that day and landed it at Campbeltown. A breeze of wind the following day kept them in harbour, but they reached the wreck the day after that and discovered that the brass pipes and iron plates they had left for later removal were missing, along with their tools.

James McCaig, 'licensed broker' in Union Street, Campbeltown, testified that one of the accused, Roddick, had told him that 'they had got liberty from the Jew to take stuff from the wreck'. McCaig advised Roddick to 'work away if you have got liberty', and advanced £2 in anticipation of receiving some metal. On 2 April, Roddick and Scally together approached McCaig and said they had 'salved some brass rods, which were lying near the Learside road'. McCaig sent out his lorry next day to uplift the metal, which was brought to his store. The pipes were broken up and put in barrels and the lot sent to Glasgow. McCaig paid for six hundredweights and gave Roddick and Scally £6, having deducted 10s for use of the lorry. 'The whole thing was done quite openly,' McCaig said. 'The accused did not ask him to send down the lorry in the dark. The lorry went down in the forenoon. Witness had no reason to suspect the men's story.'

The lorry-driver, George Dengate, recalled that Roddick and Scally accompanied him down the Learside to collect the scrap, 'which was lying by some old ruins about 200 yards from the main road'. Police Superintendent Paterson and Constable Hutchison had gone there with Dengate, and the constable described the location as 'about a mile from the wreck, at the side of a path leading from the wreck to the public road. No house was visible from the spot. The road was a lonely one'. From these descriptions, the 'old ruins' were clearly Corphin.

Andrew Scally gave this account to the court:

> ... he knew Plancy by seeing him coming about the town for a while. He was known as the Jew. Some time before the New Year he saw Plancy behind the Labour Exchange. He was talking to a group of men about the wreck being a bad speculation, and shouting out what he would do to the men he had employed on the job. He seemed to have a grievance against these men. Witness and Roddick being skilled tradesmen thought they

might be of some use at ship-breaking, and meeting Plancy at the Dalintober urinal later they asked him for a job. Plancy replied that he would rather he had never seen the d––––d wreck. He was finished with it and would employ no more men. They could take the whole d––––d job. He would have no more to do with it ... About three weeks after that they went to the wreck and had a look at it, but did not do anything. In the beginning of April they again went down, and seeing some tools lying on the shore, and the weather and tide being favourable, they had a day's work at it. They thought the Jew was finished with it, and that it was public property. They did not know that Newlands had been engaged to continue the work for the Jew. There was nobody in authority about the wreck. Some fishermen were in the vicinity picking up wood.

Roddick and Scally were found guilty. The Sheriff supposed the case to be the first of its kind in Campbeltown Court 'within living memory', and decided that 'under the particular circumstances ... a very modified penalty would be sufficient'. They were fined merely £1 each, which they paid there and then.[28]

26 April: Four boys

On my way to the Learside, I passed Agnes Stewart returning home along Kilkerran Road, and she shouted to me, 'You're late the day!' I was, but on account of the lengthening days I had ample time to accomplish what I had set out to do, which was to gather more driftwood. Near the top of Ballimenach Brae, I had another human encounter, this one devoid of the least appreciation of the life I enjoy.

I had already reached a relatively level stretch of the road and was back on my bike after a long push. I noticed, in a lay-by ahead of me, a car whose driver I had earlier signalled to overtake me on a bend, receiving, in acknowledgement, a courteous flash of his rear lights. There were three boys standing at the car, and when I stopped to exchange pleasantries, I noticed a fourth lying behind the vehicle smoking a cigarette. I was conscious of being the source of mild amusement, but the boys, having seen me cycling that road on previous days, were none the less curious as to my motivation.

A couple of them expressed unwarranted admiration of my cycling prowess, the smoker admitting that he was reluctant to walk the length of his back garden. I explained that I would be gathering wood on the shores, but the concept of the open fire elicited puzzlement. One of them asked me where I lived, and, when I replied 'Saddell Street', queried why I didn't cut wood there or, indicating the coniferous forest on either side of the road, here! I wasn't about to explain the superior quality of seasoned driftwood, and merely remarked that shore wood was 'better'. My parting remark was to compliment them on having heard the cuckoo – one was calling nearby all the while – and thus being assured of another year of life. This revelation 'killed them'.

27 April: Pirate and Cowboy

11. Painted Easter egg on Corphin brae, 27 April 2014. Photograph by the author.

While pushing the bike up Corphin Brae, I was noticing overhanging briers and decided I'd cut them back, so I walked downhill a bit with secateurs to start on those I'd already passed. While snipping away, I noticed something odd stuck on the fence. It was a boiled egg with a pirate's face painted on the shell, presumably placed there a week before on Easter Sunday. The discovery prompted the following entry in my notebook: 'If you do something different, you might learn something different.' I can't say I learned much from the find other than that someone had gone to the trouble of decorating a real egg, and presumably some child had rolled it on the brae, both of which practices are unusual now, compared with – yes, it's that phrase my daughters grew to fear! – 'when I was a boy'. Oh, and the egg itself hadn't been eaten, which wouldn't have happened 'when I was ...'

While sawing a log, a memory rose from the depths of my brain, probably surfacing for the first time 'since I was ...' It concerned a local 'worthy' who, rather than expend energy on sawing wood, would stick an end of a branch into the fire and sit pushing it into the flames until it burned away. He also indulged a fantasy that he was a cowboy living in a 'Western'. He'd answer a knock on the door by cycling down the hallway with his 'six-shooters' at his waist, and when you'd see him cycling in the street, if you shouted 'Go for your guns!' he'd instantly take his hands off the handlebars for a quick draw and fall off his bike. Or so the stories went 'when I was ...'

28 April: Watching an eider

On my way down to the Dummy's Port, I noticed two herring gulls flapping over something white offshore. That 'something' became, when I looked at it through binoculars, a male eider duck, with a smaller something, which I couldn't identify, in its beak. The gulls were clearly intent on dispossessing the drake of its catch, but after a few feeble sallies in its direction, they flew off.

I recalled having seen a similar incident before, and when I returned home I checked my journals. The date was 20 May 1984 and Jimmy MacDonald was with me. On our way home from the Dummy's in the evening, we watched, from the road above Johnston's Bay, a male eider diving repeatedly: 'Could see it moving whitely underwater – feeding on the bottom for, say, ten to twelve seconds at a time – but the remarkable part of it was that a gull was in continual attendance, optimistic of gain. A few times, the gull made efforts to dispossess the duck, but there was no more to it than that.'

Almost thirty years on, and alone, I decided to sit and observe the drake, and eat while he ate. I enjoyed watching him diving and then swimming underwater, beak tilted to the seabed and eyes searching for prey. The tide was ebbing and the water was shallow, and I could follow his white plumage as he foraged over a patch of sandy seabed, leaving a trail of big bubbles. Within the space of five minutes, I saw him catch three small fish, and judged him to be 'doing very well'. He gave each fish a shake in his beak before swallowing it. At 4.35, he sped out through a channel to the open sea, and five minutes later the tide had drained out through the channel, leaving the pool isolated.

One tree trunk I discovered jammed in a rock outcrop beyond the Ru still had rows of bracket fungi (*Coriolus versicolor*) attached to it, a survival I'd never seen before on driftwood. I felt a few of them and found them 'crispy' and presumably as dead as the tree itself. I could see Johnston's Point ahead, but had by then encountered a jumble of overgrown rocks and decided that the next stage of the driftwood survey could wait.

A shore walk in 1988

I thought back to a day in 1988 when Judy and I walked that coast with our first daughter, Sarah, who was just eight months old. We'd gone to Southend by bus on 30 April and spent the night with Donnie McLean in his caravan at Macharioch. Wind and rain assailed the van all night, but morning brought improvement and we decided, after a leisurely breakfast, to return home by the coast. I wouldn't care to attempt that shore now with a baby on my back, and since Sarah herself was now carrying a baby – inside her – the risk was magnified in my imagination.

I noted in my journal (1 May) that 'we found the going hard' and that 'I particularly felt the strain, burdened with Sarah on my back'. At the Second Water, we quit the shore, transferred Sarah from my back to Judy's, and completed the hike by road. The day after that walk, I felt stabbing pains in my chest and was so alarmed that I made an appointment with my doctor. By the time he examined me, I had already convinced myself that I had suffered a heart attack, but, to my relief, he identified the pain as muscular and blamed the baby-carrier. My sister Carol in Louisiana had passed it on to us, but its design – in particular, the crossed straps – was unsuitable for prolonged use over rough terrain, and it was replaced by a more suitable carrier which Donnie McLean no longer needed.

George McSporran experienced a similar health scare. When his son, Sandy, was about six years old, George took him to the Lake, south of Ballygroggan, to introduce him to fishing. There are plenty of rocks at the Lake – the name is corrupted from Gaelic *leac*, a flat rock – and with the strains of carrying Sandy down to the shore and of lying peering into the rock pools where lobsters and crabs could be lured by bait and snared, a day or two later he suffered chest pains which, like mine, were muscular in origin, but suggestive of imminent heart failure!

29 April: Storm erosion

I was back at the Ru and spent some time photographing evidence of the past winter's extreme storm damage, in particular mats of turf which had been stripped off rocks. Who knows how long the turf had taken to cover the bare rocks, creeping from the edges and establishing little habitats for flowers and insects? Now many of the rocks were bare again. But the damage along that coast was slight compared with what I'd seen at Southend, which was hardest hit.

Judy and I walked Brunerican Bay for driftwood on 20 January, a couple of weeks after the worst of the gales, and the damage was alarming. The whole beach had been thoroughly scoured and parts of it were unrecognisable: terraces of red sandstone, grass-green the year before, were now naked. The day, however, was not without its lighter side. During the bus journey to Southend, the driver presented one of the passengers with a bulging envelope, which, when opened, was found to contain false teeth. The recipient had lost them on a previous bus journey, and his reunion with the missing 'wallies' occasioned prolonged hilarity.

That day of destruction at Southend, 3 January, was the consequence of a tidal surge combined with an onshore gale, and I received news of it almost immediately by e-mail from Catherine Barbour, who farms Keil with her husband Cameron. At high tide that day, around 12.15 p.m., she and Cameron stood in the field in front of their farmhouse, watching in awe as huge waves crashed over the road and began knocking down their roadside wall. As the tide began to recede, they saw that part of the main road had also been destroyed. By 3 p.m., the field, which they know as the 'Cemetery Field', was awash with sea-water and strewn with seaweed, wall rubble, and countless dead worms, which provided a flock of oyster-catchers with a 'free buffet'.

12. *Storm damage at Keil, showing broken walls in Cemetery Field, 3 January 2014. Photograph, taken in low light and drifting spray, by Catherine Barbour.*

Late in the following day, Catherine reported that all was 'calm and quiet after yesterday's excitement'. A Council squad had appeared at 8 a.m. with diggers, a JCB 'Telehandler', two lorries, and shovels, and had levelled the 'mountains of sand' which had been thrown on to the road. The workers discovered that part of the road below Columba's Footprints had also been washed away, so the stretch of road between the car-park at Keil Cave and Keil Farm road-end was closed. While she and Cameron were stooping to the task of clearing stones from their field, sightseers thronged the scene, taking photographs and exclaiming in wonderment at the devastation. She later reflected that she might have 'missed a trick' that day: 'I should have been down at the Lodge gates with a big bag of pancakes and a pot of coffee, and I think I could have made a fortune, such were the crowds that appeared from dawn till dusk.'

Coastal erosion is hardly a recent problem. I have been noting its effects over the years. The causeway to Smerby Castle, for example, is gradually disappearing, and, at the Wee Holm, Polliwilline, a boulder which was once bedded in earth and grass on the foreshore is now a feature of the beach. Our first caravan was moored close to it, and Father (now Monsignor) Donald MacKinnon, on visits to Polliwilline in the 1980s, liked to sit on it and contemplatively smoke a cigarette.

30 April: Stockadale

In September 2013, Judy and I set off up Barr Glen to visit Stockadale, but failed to reach it.[29] Almost eight months later, she saw me off at the bus terminus in Campbeltown with a cheery 'Have a good time at Stockadale'. In 2013, she and I had taken that same 11.30 bus to Glenbarr, but had walked to the head of the glen and basically run out of time and energy. This day I was met off the bus by Duncan Macdougall in his car, and he drove up the glen to Arnicle.

I first met Duncan many years ago at Kintyre Antiquarian and Natural History Society winter lectures. He then had the shop in Tayinloan, but since his retirement he has lived in his native Glenbarr. When I told him about the aborted attempt to visit Stockadale, he offered to take me there, and we agreed to go in the spring before the bracken upsurge would impede route-finding.

The next farm up from Arnicle, on the north side of the glen, is Garvalt, a ruin now. I looked at Garvalt and its history in *A Summer in Kintyre* (pp. 235-36), but forgot about a nearby roadside well. Adam MacPhail, who farmed Skernish, told me of it in 1977. It was overhung by a tree, on a branch of which 'St Mary's Well' had been written; but he knew it as the 'Wishing Well', and he'd make a wish whenever he stopped to drink there. He remembered its water as the coldest he ever drank, and there was a cup at it for the convenience of travellers. He knew the well from times he was up at Garvalt cutting peats, but after he stopped the peats he never saw the well again. Duncan Macdougall also remembered drinking from the well, which was two or three hundred yards beyond Arnicle gate. On 9 August, he cycled up the glen to look for it, but found no trace. He believes that when trees were planted on Garvalt land, the Foresty Commission, in widening the track, obliterated the well.

Judy and I in 2013 had continued beyond Garvalt until the track ran out and we found ourselves in coniferous forest with no obvious route down to Stockadale. This time, however, Duncan cut off a track just past Garvalt and headed down towards Barr Water. We soon came to a ruined settlement, which, from its proximity to the shepherd's house, must have been the earlier Garvalt. Duncan led the way through deciduous woodland until Arinanuan came in sight and we knew our destination was near. When the belt of trees ended, we were on open ground and headed uphill until the ruins appeared in a space the forest-planters had left clear.

The name 'Stockadale' is from Old Norse – *stokka dalr*, 'valley of stumps, logs' – and is probably over a thousand years old. Like many other -*dalr* names in Kintyre, the location of the valley itself is lost, and the name survived attached to an adjacent feature, in this case a settlement. Interestingly, there are two other Norse place-names further down the glen, Amod and Arnicle, and they are also old settlements, though by strictest definition they are not settlement-names, since they lack a habitative element (*stadr*, *bolstadr*, *bol* or *saetr*). Amod represents *A-mot*, 'confluence' or 'river-meeting', and Arnicle is *Arna gil*, 'Eagle ravine'.

Descriptive place-names may depreciate over time, and afforestation certainly accelerates that process. Question: when is a Brown Hill (*Cnoc Donn*) not a 'brown hill'? Answer: when it's covered in conifers. Stockadale's relevance as a place-name would have vanished after the tree-stumps – presumably left from woodland clearance – rotted into the ground, and the name itself became obscure to Gaelic speakers. Discussing 'Glenstockadale', near Leswalt, John MacQueen, in *Place-Names in the Rhinns of Galloway and Luce Valley*, makes a similar point: 'When Norse ceased to be spoken in the area, the Gaelic word *gleann*, also meaning "valley", was prefixed, giving the modern tautological "valley of the valley of stumps."'[30]

Amod can still be 'read' in the landscape, because the merging streams remain, but Arnicle may only be imagined. Compose a typical steep-sided ravine, clothe its banks with heather and little birches and hazels and stud it with glistening grey rocks; drop an eagle, or, better still, two eagles into that space, roaring with peat-dark waters; on a high ledge construct a big, twiggy nest to which these, and perhaps successive generations of eagles, return year after year, and you witness the emergence of the name, like a chick from its egg. Well, maybe ...

Quite apart from being a Norse place-name which happens to have survived into the twenty-first century, Stockadale is also an example of a settlement – one of many in Kintyre – whose economic status has diminished to nothing. I looked at its historical record in *Kintyre Places and Place-Names* (pp. 106-7), but there is one interesting reference missing from that account. In K.A. Steer and J.W.M. Bannerman's *Late Medieval Monumental Sculpture in the West Highlands* (p 160), the entry on the MacEachern cross, now at the Old Quay Head, Campbeltown, examines the genealogy of that significant Kintyre family (spelling now standardised as 'McEachran') and notes that, in a rental of 1506, 'Stokadill' was leased to '*rectori Makachern*' (parson MacEachern) and that Colin MacEachern was guarantor for the payment of the Stockadill rent, '... the only recorded instance in which we find Colin MacEachern, who was chief of the MacEacherns of Killellan and maer of South Kintyre, standing surety for a rent in North Kintyre, although he frequently did so in South Kintyre'.

In 1686, Angus MacMillan in 'Stuickeideill' alleged before a Justices of the Peace Court that he had five goats stolen by Duncan MacMillan in Duchorrain – 'Deucheran', to the north-east of Barr Glen, once a farm and now a wind farm – but Duncan was 'assoilzied' (acquitted). Angus claimed to have found two of his missing goats in Duncan's possession, but Duncan, when 'put to the defender's oath', argued that the goats were his own and that he had had them for twelve months.[31]

In 1775, John MacLean in 'Stockadill' was up before the same court, as one of twenty-nine men from Muasdale and Barr Glen – a mixture of farmers, cottars and tradesmen – accused by Colonel Charles Campbell of Barbreck of taking wood from his lands without permission. A few admitted to taking a little brushwood or enough hazel to make a creel, but only one admitted to cutting any substantial quantity.[32] Timber at that time was a scarce commodity in Kintyre, and expensive to import, so land-owners regarded woodland plantations as a long-term investment requiring protection from the depredations of foraging livestock and needy humans.[33]

In 1811, James Telfer, 'writer', or lawyer, in Campbeltown, went to the Justices of the Peace Court to claim money owed to him for legal charges. One of the five debtors was John MacMillan, 'late in Colasca now in Stockdale', who owed £1 8s 9d.[34]

A couple of years back, I was asking myself: where is this Stockadale which was once so well known? It is not named on any Ordnance Survey map, but appears on the Langlands map of 1801 and was still occupied when the 1851 census was taken. It appeared to be virtually forgotten, though I was heartened when a Glenbarr angler, Frank McNaughton, told me in 2013 that he knew nearby Loch Mòr and Loch Beag as 'the Stockadales'.

Frank's friend, Duncan Macdougall, is also an angler, and while we were sitting at Stockadale, he told me a little story about the aluminium walking-pole he was using that day. On a day in 2011, while he was wading in Loch an Fhraoich ('The Heather Loch') in the hills above Tayinloan, the pole slipped off his belt and into the water and he couldn't find it. He had a rough idea of where he had lost it, and in 2013, when he was back at the loch and its water was very clear, he searched for it and saw it at a depth of about three feet. He hooked it out with his fishing-rod, and after two years' immersion it was in perfect working order.

We had sat to eat a late lunch after exploring the ruins. On our way there, I was suddenly overcome by an apprehension which stopped me in my tracks. Had I packed, or even filled, a flask of tea for the outing? I threw off my rucksack and rummaged inside it – sure enough, the flask was missing. I confess to having blamed Judy for the oversight, because while I was packing for the walk, with an eye on the clock, I was distracted by a rant she was delivering against Calmac, which had cancelled the first sailing of the Ardrossan-Campbeltown ferry, on which she had intended returning home the following evening with our daughter Amelia. She had gone to the New Quay that morning to buy tickets and found the Calmac office closed. While she was standing there in puzzlement, a car drew up and the driver informed her that a Kintyre councillor, John Semple, had advised on Facebook that the service had been postponed for a week owing to the *Isle of Arran*'s being required elsewhere. When she arrived home, she checked the Calmac website and found no information there. She then telephoned the company and spoke to a young man who was unaware of the cancellation. It was to be a day of transport difficulties for me, too, as I shall later relate.

Duncan had a small flask of coffee with him, and, after drinking a cup from it, he handed it to me, saying he'd had enough and I was to drink the rest. I was grateful for his consideration, because the ritual of tea- or coffee-drinking is integral to my enjoyment of the outdoors.

Several days after my visit to Stockadale, Agnes Stewart told me of a similar disappointment she experienced there about forty years earlier. She and Allister had a caravan at Bellochantuy, whence, with their daughter Agnes, they set off up Barr Glen during a spring holiday. Agnes: 'I had filled a flask of coffee for us, but had forgotten to take cups, so we had no coffee, and it was only when we had finished our lunch that we discovered that the door of Arinanuan was unlocked, and that inside was an array of crockery and cutlery, no doubt for the use of shepherds.'

13. *Duncan Macdougall at Stockadale, 20 April 2014. Photograph by the author.*

Arinanuan

From Stockadale, Duncan and I were looking across Barr Water to Arinanuan – *Àirigh nan Uan*, 'The Lambs' Shieling', in Gaelic – with its red-painted corrugated-iron roofs. As Duncan remarked, 'You wouldn't feel too isolated, because you've got the house across the burn.' Arinanuan, too, is unoccupied, but when Duncan's mother, Catherine Park, was in Glenbarr School in the 1920s, there was a McPherson family in Arinanuan. She remembered that when the river was in spate and the McPherson children couldn't cross the fords on their way to school, they had no choice but to return home. I dare say they might not have been too upset at missing a day's education! But fords are risky in spate, hence bridges.

On 24 May 1907, the head teacher at Glenbarr School recorded that seven out of the twenty children on the roll were absent 'on account of the heavy rain and the long distances they have to come to school'. One of the children lived five miles from the school, two between three and four miles with 'a stream to cross', two between two and three miles with 'a stream to cross', and one had already caught a cold. All of them, the school log entry concluded, 'cross a wet hill to reach the school'.[35]

In May 1879, a little girl, Janet Robertson, fell into Barr Water while playing below Blary, where her father Robert was shepherd. Her brother and another boy were with her but didn't see her tumble from the bank. The river was in flood and she was swept downstream. Her body was recovered from a pool below Auchadaduie steading.[36]

For the McPherson children, attending Glenbarr School involved a walk of four miles each way. They brought their dinner with them to school, and it was plain fare indeed – a girdle scone, which, before eating, they would moisten with water under a tap.

A little documentary glimpse of their father, William McPherson, was afforded in August 1923, when he competed in the first ever Kintyre Sheep Dog Trials. The event was held in brilliant sunshine at Gortan farm, on the edge of Campbeltown, and attracted a 'great concourse of spectators'. The steamer *Kinloch* made a special evening run for the benefit of visitors from Carradale and Arran, and doubtless the judge, John Henderson, Banlicken, also returned home to Arran by that steamer. The winning shepherd, Archibald McDiarmid, Auchenhoan, with his dog Jess, received £3 in prize money along with a silver cup presented by Mrs Macneal of Lossit. William McPherson's dog, Fly, 'made a great start, but was altogether too keen, and deficient in command and style'. With twenty points and a time of twelve minutes, William didn't make the first three, but received a special prize for being placed second in the 'best outrun', and returned to Arinanuan with ten shillings.[37]

Death of John Porter, 1989

My first visit to Barr Glen, in 1989, was entirely unplanned. On 9 September, a Saturday, Judy and I were preparing to set off on a hike, when, just before 10 a.m., she heard a maroon. I was a member of Campbeltown Auxiliary Coastguard at the time and telephoned the office to find out what was happening. Fifty-nine-year-old John Porter, who had a heart condition, had gone missing during a walk on Friday. He and his wife were from Hove in Sussex and were touring in a caravanette, which he'd parked at Arnicle. When he failed to return, his wife alerted the farmer, who searched as far as Arinanuan.

There was now a full-scale rescue operation in progress. By the time we arrived at Arnicle, a Royal Navy Sea King helicopter crew and a police team were searching, and support was assembling: Campbeltown and Southend Coastguards, mountain rescue teams from Dumbarton and Oban, and teams from the RAF and US Navy at Machrihanish, about forty men in all. Campbeltown Coastguard was instructed to search north from Arnicle as far as the Dubhloch, but we were recalled at 11.30 when police found John Porter dead in woodland near Garvalt.

I was home by 12.40, and with Judy, Sarah and Amelia caught the 1 o' clock bus to Drumlemble and walked out to Killypole. The day was still and sunny, and, while Judy fed Amelia at the steading, I played with Sarah at the lochside, someone else's tragedy already receding in memory.

Death of Donald MacArthur, 1902

In the morning of 7 February 1902, a group of men crossed the hills from Carradale Glen to Rosehill for the annual Largieside Agricultural Society ploughing match. The winning ploughman was David Smith, who took fifteen shillings and a silver medal home to Bellochantuy;[38] but, unknown to anyone there, the event would be overshadowed by tragedy.

At about five o' clock in the evening, Donald MacArthur, farmer in Auchenrioch, John Reid, ploughman in Brackley, and John Macdonald, farm servant in Auchenbreck, left the field and started back for Carradale Glen. At that time of year, they were, of course, heading into darkness. They called at Arinanuan and remained there until after eight o' clock. Thus far, they had travelled on a decent road, by the standards of the time, but it ended there, and beyond lay mere tracks through the hills.

When they resumed their journey, the shepherd at Arinanuan, John MacGougan, gave them a lantern and accompanied them a short distance, 'putting them on the hill path'. They soon lost the path, but carried on, in the wrong direction, as it transpired. Donald MacArthur succumbed to exhaustion, so his companions carried him. Heavy snow began falling and the lantern candles burned out. By then, Reid and Macdonald were themselves exhausted, so they laid MacArthur in a sheltered spot, covered him with their coats and waited there, doing what they could for him.

At about seven in the morning, both men set off, in opposite directions, to seek help. Reid arrived at Deuchran and Macdonald at Narachan. The Narachan shepherd, John MacCallum, hastened with 'hot tea' to Deuchran Hill, where MacArthur had been left, but he was unconscious by then, and, being unable to revive him, MacCallum left to find help to move him. He hadn't gone far when he met John Reid with the Deuchran shepherd (probably Neil MacLean, a Mull man). MacArthur was now dead, and they carried his corpse home to Auchenrioch.[39] Donald MacArthur was fifty years old. His father, Archibald, would die in 1916, a month short of his hundredth birthday, and by then the oldest person in Kintyre. His story is told in *Kintyre Places and Place-Names*.

MacArthur's death was the third from exposure in Kintyre within a fortnight. The first was Bridget McCall, wife of Alexander Townsley, 'travelling tinker', who was found on 24 January on Dhurrie farm, a living infant strapped to her back. She was presumed to have rested and then fallen asleep while returning to the family camp at Aros Moss.[40]

On 2 February, seven-year-old Hugh Cook was found on High Knockrioch farm by Donald Darroch, ploughman, and Mary McArthur, farm servant, who were on their way to town. Mary recognised the boy, who was a neighbour of her family in Saddell Street. He had followed a funeral to Kilkerran – where he himself would be buried three days later – and had then tried to reach the Black Loch, attracted by the ice-skating going on there. When he failed to return home, a search party with lanterns 'scoured the hill in the neighbourhood of Knockbay and towards Crosshill',[41] but he was already beyond them.

Willie MacGougan, shepherd

Willie MacGougan, whom I tape-recorded once at Largie, was in Arinanuan as a five-year-old when Donald MacArthur and his two companions called there in February, 1902. John MacGougan, who directed them on to the track to Carradale Glen, was his father. Willie was born in a thatched house with an earthen floor at Bàrr Uachdaraich (Upper Barr) in Barr Glen, on 6 December 1896. John MacGougan had married Mary Littleson at another Barr Glen farm, Killegruer, which is still occupied by a Littleson family – the only one left in Kintyre, in fact.

The name 'Littleson' looks English, and if a myth had been concocted to explain it – English sailor is shipwrecked at Westport, marries local girl and turns himself into a farmer – most folk would accept it; but it's yet another Gaelic name disguised. This one, like Pursell from McSporran (p 90), has, at least, the merit of logicality. It represents *MacFigeinn*, for *MacBhigein*, the root of which is *beag*, 'little', therefore 'Son of Little'. It appears to be not just a peculiarly Kintyre surname, but peculiarly Largieside, and originated, I suppose, as a nick-name.

I've mentioned that I visited Willie MacGougan once – the date was 3 March 1977 – and I have to add that I would have returned to him, because he was just the type of intelligent tradition-bearer I was keen to record. His housekeeper, however, ruled out further interviews. The rebuff hurt and puzzled me, because she had contributed quite cheerfully to the tape-recording session and I detected no ill-feeling during the visit. Whatever the explanation, the bulk of Willie's lore went to the grave with him two years later.

His information and stories helped me with two books, *Kintyre Country Life* (1987) and *Kintyre Places and Place-Names* (2013), and the only record of Càrn na Lòinidheach ('The Rheumatic Stone') in Rhonadale Glen and Cnocan Dùn Mòr ('Hillock of the Big Fort') at Rhunahaorine – each with a story attached to it – came from Willie MacGougan.[42] These were incidental references, and I have no doubt that had I sat with him, a map in front of us, the yield of place-names would have been sizeable.

I would certainly have returned to him in 1978, had I been able to, because that year was devoted to collecting Gaelic vocabulary in Kintyre, and I had been told that Willie was a Gaelic speaker.

By then, the number of surviving native speakers had dwindled to insignificance and the language was approaching extinction.

Some thoughts on Gaelic

The disappearance of Gaelic from Kintyre – lost in the span of a generation – has interested me for most of my life. The interest is personal as well as historical, because the language should have been my birth right and I still feel that English is essentially foreign to me. I covered the subject in *Kintyre: The Hidden Past*, but since then my understanding has deepened.

Donald McLean, who grew up in Campbeltown, wrote a series of articles, 'Campbeltown Fifty Years Ago', for the *Argyllshire Herald* in 1912 and 1913. His name suggests he might have had Gaelic, but he hadn't, and, in fact, he questioned the value of the language. His father was an accountant who, once a year, would be collected in a gig by Keith Macalister, laird of Glenbarr, and brought to Glenbarr Abbey to assist with rent collection and book-keeping. Donald would accompany his father as far as 'Portavooren' (Port a' Bhorrain), where he was dropped off to lodge with a McCorkindale family.

McLean described the farmer, Donald McCorkindale, as 'a big man, with a small wife and a large family; a baker's dozen, if my memory serves me right, twelve sons and one daughter'. Since his account must approximate to 1861, I checked the census for that year and found Port a' Bhorrain entered by its alternative name, 'Dalkeith'. The head of the house was Malcolm McCorkindale, a widower (aged 77); there was his son Donald (40), Donald's wife Janet (43), and seven children, the oldest nineteen and the youngest five. (There were actually two daughters among them.) Donald belonged to Auchadaduie in Barr Glen, and Janet, whose own name was MacNiven, to Muasdale, and they married in 1837.

McLean's account of life on the farm is engaging, and he could certainly write, but I'll concentrate on his frustrations with the language barrier which confronted him at Port a' Bhorrain. He and his bedfellows, the youngest McCorkindale boys, enjoyed pillow fights at night, but their lack of English and his lack of Gaelic precluded conversation. One afternoon, he and two of the boys went out and shot a bag of rabbits, but '... alas, owing to the language difficulty, our talk was limited. I thought to myself what a pity it was that these fine young fellows should be unable to talk the language of the commercial and business world which would have equipped them better for a fight for a better position there'. His conclusion was that Gaelic was 'well worth preserving as an addenda [*sic*] to a good English education and to keep alight the free and independent spirit of the Gael ...'[43] Unfortunately, as time would quickly prove, the addendum would be deleted in the state education system.

During the writing of this book, Hugh MacFarlane came into my thoughts (p 157). When I first visited him in Tarbert in 1974, he was nearly ninety, and, I soon discovered, had a rich Gaelic vocabulary; but he would not have claimed to be a Gaelic speaker. I wondered if he had been fluent in his youth and gradually lost his fluency as Gaelic died out in the community. The 1891 census noted that his parents spoke both Gaelic and English, but that all their children, including Hugh, aged seven, spoke only English. I was sceptical. How was fluency in Gaelic – or in English, for that matter – assessed, especially in children? There would certainly have been no time to conduct tests, even had the census enumerator been competent to do so. I presume that the say-so of the head of the household settled the question; and I shall add that there were native families unwilling to be associated with a language increasingly perceived to be redundant.

In 1891, according to census returns, fifty-nine persons in Kintyre spoke only Gaelic, and thirteen of them were in the part of Tarbert village which lies in Kintyre. These and other related statistics are reproduced in *Kintyre: The Hidden Past* (p 34). At the time I was writing that book, I had doubts about the accuracy of census statistics (let's make that any statistics!) and I now have even more doubts. I checked that census for the individuals in Tarbert identified as monoglot Gaelic speakers, and some strange anomalies emerged. One of the thirteen, Dugald MacFarlane, a seventy-six-year-old retired fisherman, was living with a son and daughter, who, according to the enumerator, had no Gaelic. How did they communicate? Mary MacFarlane, a seventy-six-year-old widow, was living with her thirty-two-year-old unmarried son, John, and both were down as Gaelic only. Could a fisherman of John's age in Tarbert in 1891 really have had no English?

In that same census, the infant sisters Lizzie, Isabella and Margaret Taylor in High Crubasdale, Muasdale, were marked as monoglot Gaelic speakers, since they hadn't yet started school, a correct, if irregular, census observation; but were they included among the fifty-nine?

(Incidentally, that search of censuses gave me a name I had earlier looked for and missed. In *Kintyre Places and Place-Names*, I discussed *Creag Eonaidh/Creag MhicCuilgein*, Gaelic names for a rock to which a fishing tradition was attached. I stated that I could find no trace of a John MacQuilkan after whom the rock could have been named, but there was such a man in Tarbert in 1891, a widower and retired fisherman in Bain's Cottage, and at seventy-two he was old enough to have inspired the place-names.)

Archibald Mitchell, shepherd

The last occupants of Stockadale appear to have been Archibald 'Baldy' Mitchell, his first wife Kate Conley, daughters Isabella and Flora and sons Archibald and Duncan, who were there in 1851. In 1861, Archibald, Kate, and their son Archibald, with his wife and two sons, were in Knock Kilmichael over on the Carradale side, and Stockadale was deserted. But by 1869 Archibald was back in Barr Glen, at Garvalt, where Kate died on 24 March. They had seven children together, to which Archibald would add three more with his second wife, Margaret MacCallum. He was sixty-eight years old and she was thirty when they married in 1870, two days short of the first anniversary of Kate's death; but though old enough to be Margaret's grandfather, he was clearly not deficient in sexual vigour.

On Old New Year's Day (12 January) 1874, Archibald received a purse of sovereigns 'as a token of regard for him, and to help to assist him in his old age'. The presentation was made by Robert Fraser, crackpot innkeeper at Drumore, Bellochantuy, not far from Killocraw, where Archibald was now shepherd. The newspaper reports don't mention from whom the money came, but presumably a subscription was raised among the friends who gathered in the inn and later 'voted themselves into a dancing party ... and tripped it to and fro' until early morning'. Described as the oldest shepherd in Kintyre, Archibald's age was misleadingly given as 'four score years and ten'.[44]

On his death certificate, a year later, his age was given as seventy-five, which, give or take a few years, would have been closer to the truth, though no birth record exists. In censuses, he gave his birthplace as Carradale, and in his marriage certificates his parents were named as Archibald Mitchell and Mary Thomson. He therefore appears to belong to one of the Mitchell families – perhaps, if it could be proven, *the* Mitchell family – in the Carradale district from the eighteenth century, and in Skipness from the seventeenth: one of the 1685 rebels (p 36) was Malcolm Mitchell in 'Corphean' (Coalfin).[45]

First, however, to his death in February 1875. He had moved again by then, and was shepherd at Lochsanish, a Laggan farm of which scarcely a trace remains. He had been in Campbeltown on the 4th, and at about 11 p.m. set off home, accompanied by a brother-in-law named MacLaren, who left him at the Poorhouse on Witchburn Road, 'thinking that [he] would manage to reach Lochsanish all right'. But the old shepherd never arrived home, and a search party failed to find him on the following day, a Friday. On Saturday came a report that some labourers who had worked through Thursday night, loading a ship with draff at the Old Quay, had heard 'stifled cries' from the end of the New Quay. Sure enough, when the quay was searched, Mitchell, 'although stiff in death ... was still clinging to one of the skeds [piles]'.

The reason for his return to town was the subject of speculation,[46] but the possibility that he was intoxicated that night remained unsaid. That he dipped into the purse of sovereigns – greater wealth, I dare say, than he had ever known before – to fund a spree in town may explain the fatal misadventure.

There is a curious sequel to all that. When Doug Cooper, a Canadian great-great-grandson of Archibald Mitchell, visited Kintyre for the first time in 1996, he was told that after his grandfather's brother Archibald Mitchell died in 1965, a gold sovereign was found among his possessions when his house, Baraskomill Cottage, was cleared.

The origins of several Kintyre surnames continue to intrigue me, and Mitchell is one of them. The Lowland origin of the Mitchell farming and whisky families in South Kintyre is not in doubt, but there were Gaelic-speaking Mitchell families in North Kintyre, the Carradale district in particular, and Archibald Mitchell, who drowned in 1875, belonged to one of these Gaelic families. I have already speculated in print on how these Mitchells might have got their name and their Gaelic. They might, like the Largieside Armour, Colville, Greenlees and Watson families, have crossed the border from the Lowland Plantation stronghold of South Kintyre into the Gaelic North and 'gone native'. Or 'Mitchell' may be an Anglicised Gaelic surname, but which one? The obvious candidate is *MacGhilleMhìcheil*, which certainly mutated into 'Mitchell' in Mid-Argyll; but, against that, all the evidence points to 'Carmichael' as its final form in Kintyre.[47]

I have a personal, albeit tangential, interest in the Mitchell conundrum, through Isabella Martin, who married a Duncan Mitchell. Their parents – Duncan Mitchell, crofter, and Mary MacConnachie, and Duncan Martin, shoemaker, and Mary MacCallum – were living in Torrisdale Glen when Duncan and Isabella married, and Duncan and Isabella themselves lived there until they moved to Dalintober. My friend Agnes Stewart (née Mitchell) is a great-great-great-granddaughter of theirs. Isabella's brother, John Martin, my great-great-grandfather, also took the road south to Dalintober, and married Elizabeth MacFadyen, who was born in South Knapdale, daughter of John MacFadyen, shepherd, and Margaret MacAlpine. But enough of genealogy!

Violence in Torrisdale Glen, 1821

The dark spirit of Thor must have descended on Torrisdale Glen in January 1821, at Old New Year, a time of uninhibited excess in a society which sanctioned few holidays. At about 11 a.m. on the 12th, twenty-seven-year-old Duncan Ferguson left his house at Torrisdale in the company of a neighbour, Alexander MacDonald, to watch a shinty match in Carradale Bay. In the avenue of Carradale House, about half-a-mile from the Bay, they encountered Archibald MacKay, farmer at Kirnashie and a son of John MacKay, tacksman of Carradale Estate. He had been sheltering from a shower of rain and emerged from behind a dyke holding an umbrella.

On seeing Ferguson, MacKay insulted him in Gaelic: 'Are you there, Big Prick?' An angry dispute ensued, with 'a good deal of cursing and swearing on both sides', and then the two came to blows. A crowd gathered, watching the brawl, until the police constable at Carradale, David Henderson, grabbed Ferguson and dragged him away. But MacKay was in no mood to desist and came at Ferguson brandishing his shinty-stick. Ferguson broke clear of the constable and again struck out at his adversary, but some men in the crowd immediately separated them, and Ferguson, fearing arrest, ran home.

Ferguson admitted to being 'a little the worse of drink' that morning, but 'not by any means intoxicated', and stated that he 'drank only one dram throughout the rest of the day'. He remained at home all that day, and at about 7 p.m. was seated at dinner with Duncan MacDougall, fisherman in Tonaduppin, when Archibald MacKay and his brother Donald appeared at the door, armed with sticks and shouting in Gaelic: 'Are you in Ferguson, you bugger? Turn out here!' Ferguson, by his own admission, was so 'terrified' that he fled through the house. The MacKays entered in pursuit, and, when they cornered Ferguson, Donald MacKay directed a violent blow at his head, but Ferguson raised an arm to protect himself and was struck on his right elbow, which was left badly bruised and swollen.

Ferguson managed to escape from the house and ran to a nearby wood, pursued by the MacKays. He reached the house of Alexander MacAlister, and, crying 'Murder!' at the window, begged him to come out. While he and MacAlister were in excited conversation, Ferguson's wife, with a child in her arms and another at her feet, appeared, crying uncontrollably, having imagined her husband 'murdered in the wood'.

Others were terrorised during the MacKays' rampage that evening. One of the innocent victims was Isabella Martin. She and her husband, Duncan Mitchell, shared the house with Ferguson and his family, and Isabella – then twenty-four years old – was struck by Donald MacKay. She was three months pregnant at the time, and four days later miscarried. She was still 'very unwell' when interviewed on 24 January, during the preparation of criminal charges against John, Archibald and Donald MacKay, and ascribed her miscarriage to 'the fright she took at the McKays' violence'.[48]

Missed by the bus

After all these diversions, I'm back in 30 April 2014. On the way to Stockadale I saw my first slow worm of the year and on the way back my first adder, a small dark-skinned creature, both disturbed unseen by Duncan Macdougall, who was ahead of me. We were back in Glenbarr at just after 4 p.m. and Duncan suggested I go to his house for a cup of tea, to pass the time until the school bus would come back through the village at 4.40. I got my tea, but not my bus.

I left Duncan's house in good time and waited at the bus stop. After ten minutes, I asked Peter Sinclair if he had seen the bus go through early. He was outside his shop, Glenbarr Stores, with a van load of plants for Islay, and we ended up talking about local history and in particular his great-grandfather, Hector Thomson, who was in Glenbarr shop before him, and also ran Glenbarr Temperance Inn, when such facilities were necessary for travellers and profitable for proprietors.

While I was talking with Peter, Duncan appeared to report that he had seen the school bus drive by on the main road while he was standing at his kitchen window, which confirmed my suspicion that the driver had somehow missed out the village on his way back to town. With that uncertainty resolved, the discussion of family history resumed outside the shop. Peter mentioned a visit he made to Ian MacDonald, the authority on Largieside history and genealogy, not long before his death at the age of ninety-three the previous year. Ian was in bed at his home in Lochgilphead, but when Peter mentioned Hector Thomson, Ian swung his legs out from under the covers, reached into a 'kist', removed a file from a pile of other files, flicked through it, and unerringly pulled out a paper containing the Thomson genealogy.

I said goodbye to Duncan and Peter, promising I would report the bus failure next day, in case any villager should suffer the same inconvenience in future, and made my way to the main road to wait for the next south-bound bus. I was joined in the bus shelter by a man and woman who were going to Clachan. When their north-bound bus stopped for them, I saw Judy on board – she was going to Glasgow to buy a baby sling – and we exchanged a wave. I filled my pipe and smoked until my own bus appeared, but I didn't get around to reporting the bus failure – I suppose this is the report – nor did I see Peter Sinclair again: three months later, he was dead.

6 May: New Orleans

I was heading for Ru Stafnish, but had been late starting, and there were showers of rain about, so I decided to shorten the outing and walk the shore from New Orleans to Auchenhoan Head. New Orleans is a curious name to have been attached to a Kintyre croft. Bob Wylie, fisherman there, told Duncan McLachlan that a returned emigrant had put the name on it, an explanation not without local precedents. The name on the earliest Ordnance Survey map, surveyed in 1866, is 'Carolina', yet 'New Orleans' was the name in a trespass case which went to court in 1858.[49] It is an interesting little onamastic puzzle, but not one which is likely to be solved unless the answer appears in a hitherto undiscovered document.

Why no picture postcard manufacturer ever capitalised on the correspondence with the city of New Orleans is incomprehensible to me. My sister, Carol Warren, has lived in Louisiana for most of her life, and whenever she returns to Kintyre on holiday I imagine that there is such a postcard – offering 'Greetings from New Orleans' and depicting a lonely cottage and a stony shore – which she could send to her family in America.

A couple of weeks before Christmas, while in the Kintyre Photography shop in Campbeltown, buying a selection of Stuart Andrew's magnificent cards of local snow scenes, I tested my idea on the photographer himself. He was decidedly unenthusiastic, pointing out that the market for picture postcards has declined so much that printing a batch of cards simply wouldn't be economic; and he also thought that a subject as obscure as New Orleans wouldn't appeal to tourists, who want familiar scenes.

New Orleans Glen, however, was once a popular picnic spot. In a tourist booklet, *Campbeltown, Southend and Machrihanish: The Official Guide*, published around 1907, it is described (p 22) as 'one of the prettiest glens in Kintyre, and ... an ideal spot for picnic parties. The glen is beautifully wooded, and a trickling rivulet courses down through banks rich with summer flowers. No visitor should leave Campbeltown without having visited this delightful dell'. An accompanying photograph depicts the entrance to the glen and a simple cottage, to which Bob Wylie added an upper storey. It has since been further extended and is now a holiday home let by Kildalloig Estate.

William McTaggart met his first wife, Mary Brolochan Holmes, at New Orleans in the summer of 1860, when he was staying in a cottage there, studying dawns for his painting *The Wreck of the Hesperus*. She was in the only other cottage nearby, which suggests that one had rented New Orleans Cottage and the other the 'Fisherman's Cottage', as it is now called. They were cousins, related through William's mother, Barbara Brolachan, and Mary's paternal grandmother, Mary Brolochan, and married in 1863.[50]

Norman Morrison enthused about the view from New Orleans in an essay 'Winter': 'While standing on the wooden bridge at the lower end of New Orleans Glen, the vista before me was of an enthralling and spellbinding attractiveness. To the south-east, the near horizon was bounded by the rugged and formidable headland of Auchanhoan, one of the most romantic and imposing headlands in Argyllshire.'[51]

I sat in the little cave to the south of the Wee Man's Cove, which is the first cave past New Orleans Cottage. Like its larger neighbour, it has clearly been occupied by humans: the interior has been levelled right to the back and at the entrance there is the foundation of a wall which probably served as a windbreak. Also at the entrance, there is a stand of nettles, which in such a location indicates past human presence. The mouth of the cave is overhung with a mat of ivy.

Iain Hood, Peninver, found part of a Bronze Age sword-blade right at the back of the cave when he swept it with a metal-detector in 1980. The artefact, which may have lain there undisturbed for around three thousand years, is now on display in Campbeltown Museum. I had wondered what could have happened to the rest of the sword. Roddy Regan, an archaeologist at Kilmartin Museum, explained that valued objects were often deliberately broken before ritual deposition in 'special places', such as caves or rock-shelters. Iain Hood, who died of cancer in 2014, was a dedicated ornithologist since boyhood and knew the remoter parts of Kintyre intimately.

I saw the little cave occupied in 1988. The date was 31 July and I was with Judy and daughter Sarah, not yet a year old. We left our bikes at the Sheep Fanks and, as the tide was high, climbed over Auchenhoan Head. In Queen Esther's Bay we met Teddy Lafferty and shared a pot of tea with him. There were two other parties on the shore – Duncan McInnes and family and Garry Muir and a friend – both of which had been thwarted by the tide in their attempt to reach Saint Kieran's Cave. The main topic of discussion among us was a gruesome case of matricide in Campbeltown the previous day. Teddy set off to take the Old Road home and we returned by the shore.

At the 'Ivy Cave', as I call it, we encountered one Tony Smith, his partner and their fifteen-month-old daughter. They had earlier been camped at the Doirlinn, but had moved from there and pitched their little tent inside the cave. We chatted for a while and I photographed them with a small fire in the foreground and tent and cave in the background. (I would have published that photograph here, but despite repeated searches, I couldn't find the slide.) They would doubtless be described nowadays as 'New Age Travellers', except they didn't appear to have any transport. Note in journal: 'We liked them.' Note in book: We never saw them again.

14. Sheltering from a thunderstorm in the 'Ivy Cave', New Orleans, Sarah and Angus Martin, 10 July 1988. Photograph by Judy Martin.

Three weeks earlier, on 10 July, we ourselves had sheltered in the cave. As before, we had cycled to the Fanks and left our bikes there. We stopped for a while beyond the Wee Man's Cove and ate lunch while Sarah amused herself on the beach. On our way back from Saint Kieran's Cave, we heard distant peals of thunder in the west. Heavy drops of rain began falling as we approached the Wee Man's Cove, and we hurried there for shelter. Inside the mouth of the cave, Judy noticed a pile of bird droppings and, looking up, saw a swallows' nest with chicks in it. We decided to leave the birds in peace and hastened back, in pouring rain, to the Ivy Cave, but the shower, which was heavy enough to obscure Davaar Island, lasted only ten minutes. To amuse myself in the cave, I wrote in pencil on a smooth chalk pebble, which Sarah had lifted from the shore, a message and the date, and put the pebble inside a shortbread wrapper and laid it on a rock ledge. (It was later discovered by Gordon and Helen Duncan, Campbeltown.) We were caught in another shower at the Fisherman's Cottage and sheltered against a shed. When the shower passed, we were rewarded with the sight of a rainbow, so close, it seemed, that we could almost touch it.

The following year (on 30 July 1989) we were given an explanation of the name 'Wee Man's Cove', the bigger of the caves, when we walked round Auchenhoan Head and into Queen Esther's Bay. We found Teddy Lafferty there, sitting half-asleep on a plastic crate. He told us that had he not decided to stay for ten minutes more, to watch a yacht sail by, we'd have missed him. We revived his fire, cooked our meal, and, while we were eating it, Teddy left; but not before he had mentioned an earlier encounter, which I recorded: 'Teddy met a family on the shore. Jock Smith's maternal aunt, a Johnston, was there, and she remembered the old Coasting days. He talked at length with her. She recalled the "Wee Man" of the cave. His name was Fred and he sold needles and thread in town. Her parents took him into their home at the head of the Longrow – a tenement since demolished to build the block of flats opposite Neil McLean's shop – then he got a house of his own in town. He kept all his money, just pennies and ha'pennies, in a jam-jar.'

A description in 1851 of a cave north of Auchenhoan Head can only refer to the Wee Man's. It appeared in 'Rambles in Kintyre', an anonymous article describing a walk along Kilkerran, past 'newly built Davaar House' and around the Head to Saint Kieran's Cave: 'We passed a cave of no great dimensions, at the mouth of which we had often formerly seen tinkers sitting on the grass or with tobacco pipes in their mouths, while rolling o'er their heads, from the entrance of the cave, clouds of smoke indicated that cooking operations were carried on in the inside.'[52]

11 May: Overtaken

While cycling along Kilkerran Road, on my way to Ru Stafnish, another cyclist passed me with ease. I wasn't bothered about being overtaken, which is a common enough occurrence, but the fact that the cyclist was about my age, or older, and that his legs were revolving in time with mine, got me thinking, and I concluded that his bike must be more efficient than mine. He hadn't spoken as he passed, but on Ballimenach brae, as he was coming down and I was going up, pushing, he stopped in a lay-by. I couldn't understand why and looked behind me in case there was a car I hadn't heard approaching, but when I drew level with him, it transpired that he wanted to speak, and he told me he'd be going to Ireland to ride a hundred miles for charity.

A Royal Navy minesweeper I'd noticed off the Second Water on my way down the Learside was still there when I returned. She began sounding her horn repeatedly, and I wondered why. Then I noticed an Irish trawler, which had been steaming north to pass her, suddenly veer due east, and, when I looked through binoculars at the minesweeper, I saw figures in the water close to the ship, and an inflatable boat attending them. 'Meanwhile,' I jotted in my journal, 'the Highland cows munch contentedly on grass.'

15 May: Ballimenach brae and memories of Tangy

George McSporran and I went to Ru Stafnish for wood that day, but I've got ahead of myself. I'd been wheeling my bike up Ballimenach brae alone – George had been delayed – and paused to rest in the heat of the afternoon. I heard a sedge warbler 'doing its stuff – magnificent – glad I stopped'. While scribbling in my notebook, I became aware of a curious pounding noise on the road, and, waiting and watching, saw George appear round the corner.

We talked about cycling as we pushed our bikes uphill. He told me about his crash on the Lussa road (p 133) and about a double journey he was forced to make to Tangy around 1963. He and Malcolm Cook had gone there to fish from the rocks, and on their way home, at about Drumore, George realised that he'd forgotten his camera. By then darkness had fallen, but he pedalled back for it and, remembering the rock he'd laid it on, retrieved it at once. He also remembered the model, a British-made Ross 'Ensign 82 Special', and told me that he had used it up until the previous year, forty years on from its near-loss.

I'd forgotten how popular Tangy once was. Iain Campbell and I would cycle out there (p 128) and play on the beach. It is an Atlantic coast and high surf isn't unusual even in summer. The most exciting time I remember having there involved braving the breakers. We installed ourselves behind a high rock and would watch the approaching waves, pressing ourselves against the rock when one was clearly going to break over it. But the game turned decidedly scary when we saw a giant suddenly rear and roar towards us. We started running for the beach but were caught and drenched in the wave-burst. We stripped off our clothes and spread them on rocks, and they were dry before we set off home.

Tangy was one of several favoured destinations when neighbours in town would club together and hire a bus for a day's outing, but after road improvements, which bypassed the old bridge and annexed a section of the beach, its appeal declined. While finishing this book, I received a note from the artist Will Maclean, accompanying a letter he thought would interest me. In April 1974, at the beginning of our collaboration on the ring-net project, he came to Kintyre and I introduced him to several retired fishermen. One of them was James Wareham, to whom Will later sent a copy of a photograph of his father, John Wareham. In her thank-you letter, James's wife, Jessie McAllister, mentioned the 'lovely' spring weather and added: 'We are away every day in the Car. We go 5 miles up the Tarbert Road. It is a place called Tangy. We have a flask of coffee and sandwiches. Sometime someone comes in who we know. So we share what we have, and have a chat.'

The Corphin mermaid

While cutting wood under the Ru, George mentioned that we'd been there in the previous year. I couldn't recall the visit, but he pointed out a length of green trawl netting, stretched across the rocks, which he remembered from that day. Note in notebook: 'Find it in notebook.'

We had gone to the Dummy's Port on 28 February 2013. Since I hadn't walked the shore south of the Second Water in several years, I was hoping for a decent haul of quality driftwood, and I wasn't disappointed. We sat near the little ruin which had been Donald McIsaac's fishing station (p 35), counting, until we tired of the exercise, small groups of gannets flying south.

George mentioned that the Learside 'mermaid', sighted in 1811 by Donald's brother John McIsaac, farmer in Corphin, and Catherine Loynachan, a little herd-girl in Ballinatunie, to the north, was currently a hot topic on the internet Kintyre Forum. I wrote about the mysterious sightings thirty years ago in *Kintyre: The Hidden Past* (pp. 191-92), and shan't repeat myself here, but one aspect of the controversy puzzled George: the location of the 'Black Rock of Corphin', a 'fishing rock' referred to by Catherine's father, Lachlan Loynachan. There was no likely 'fishing rock' that we could see between the Second Water and the Dummy's. I asked John MacDonald, a keen angler, if he could think of any rock that fitted the description. He knew of one off Johnston's Point at Feochaig – much too far south – and another between the Bloody Bay and Queen Esther's Bay, but that one is probably too far north.

As George and I were leaving the Dummy's Port, I noticed a 'Fanta' bottle containing a piece of paper. When I opened it, I found a message, which at first glance I was astonished to see addressed to 'Dear Mermaid'. I was mistaken, though. 'Dear Mamaid' was what it said, but the spelling should presumably represent *mamaidh*, 'mammy' in Gaelic. The message, in pink ink, was plainly the work of a child, and said: 'Dear mamaid, where are you? I have been looking forward to see you so I am. Many [words obliterated] think you. From Rilla.' An internet search for *mamaidh* yielded 133 references, but to Scottish, not Irish Gaelic; the phrase 'so I am' had suggested an Irish origin. The name 'Rilla' too is a puzzler. The 133rd internet offering was 'Searching for Mermaids in the Karoo', by one Gary R. Varner, which I decided not to open; it confirmed, however, that I was not alone in confusing the words!

Since that day, I have pondered the nature of that 'mermaid' a man and a little girl both claimed to have observed on different parts of the coast. What could it possibly have been (if not an actual 'mermaid'?) I suggest, not without hesitation, a common seal, which, as nineteenth century local newspaper reports demonstrate, were so rare that specimens were sometimes publicly exhibited, dead or alive. This is merely a half-cooked spud pulled out of a stew of possibilities, but I'll conclude with the following excerpt from a biography of the Arctic explorer Gino Watkins, which I happened to be reading in mid-May. Watkins was on holiday with his father, Colonel Henry George Watkins, at Glengariff, Southern Ireland, in the winter of 1924. 'On one of our sea days,' wrote Colonel Watkins, 'we were paddling along as usual when suddenly a pale and very human face appeared out of the water behind us. Gino's surprise and excitement were intense; it was his first seal, and seemed as interested in Gino as he was in her or him, staring at us, diving and swimming round the boat for an hour. Certainly it never entered Gino's head to shoot at her, she looked so friendly and human.'[53]

16 May: Ru Stafnish

The grandeur of Ru Stafnish is best viewed from the sea. From the shore, the headland somehow lacks presence, unlike the (admittedly higher) cliffs at Largiebaan and elsewhere on the south-west side of Kintyre. Yet, the Norse element of the name is dramatic-sounding: *stafa-nes*, 'point of the precipice'. Norse *nes* is literally 'nose', just as Gaelic *sròn* is 'nose', and both elements are common in place-names attached to a point of land. Ru Stafnish is a truly outstanding promontory, but, again, only when viewed from the sea or from land to the north (Peninver beach, for example).

The Norse part of the name, I suspect, was coined by Vikings and is likely to be more than a thousand years old. *Rubha* – clipped here to 'Ru' – would have been added by Gaelic speakers, doubtless when the Norse influence in Kintyre had declined and the meaning of *Stafa-nes* was forgotten. Since *rubha* is another name for 'point', 'Ru Stafnish' is therefore doubly a point. Interestingly, however, the mid-seventeenth century Gordon map records only 'Staphanich', for *Stafa-nes*, without the Gaelic addition. The *stafa* element is identifiable with the island of Staffa, 'stave-island', from its columnar basalt formations.

15. *Ru Stafnish from the sea, 3 May 1998. The photograph was taken by the author from Campbeltown life-boat, the wash of which is visible bottom left.*

I was sitting below Ru Stafnish prior to sawing a nice branch into logs, but my conscience was troubled because George McSporran, who also collects wood, if not on quite the same scale, had spotted the branch the day before, and here I was about to take it.

I soon forgot my guilt and was describing, in my journal, a phenomenon I'd briefly noted at the Dummy's Port nearly thirty-three years before: 'Very still, so still that – and I want to record this – I could hear, as the tide flowed in, the sea breaking gently on an offshore rock, and then on another, closer in; but back to silence again, broken only by bird song.'

This is the 2014 account: 'Tide is ebbing and a rock, still below the surface, is occasionally breaking a wave, which announces the contact with a muted splash and a whitening of its crest, then re-forms and continues. This reminds me, on a small scale, of William McTaggart's magnificent painting "The Wave". That's basically all there is in the composition, but the power in that momentary response is astonishing. It is virtually the antithesis of a subject he excelled in – violent seascapes – but succeeds by the artist's very concentration on that solitary wave lifting mysteriously to bare its "teeth".'

Walking the shore back to the Dummy's, I noticed something which George and I had examined the previous day. It seemed destined for this book and I almost inserted it into my journal, but superstitious apprehension checked the impulse. It was a laminated 'Novena Prayer' which had somewhere been sent up into the air attached to a cluster of coloured balloons. I now reasoned that, since someone had despatched it into the outer world, it was surely meant to be read, so I copied it into my journal but left the physical remains where the sea had cast them, though I doubted if anyone else would find, let alone read, the prayer on that remote shore. Addressed to 'Mother of Perpetual Help', it is a formulaic composition, therefore I offer only the name 'Margaret', to whose memory it was dedicated, and the observation that whatever spiritual benefits such devotional gestures might offer, the vehicle of the message and the message itself become litter.

Orange-peel

On my way past Corphin ruins to the shore, I had passed some innocuous litter of my own. Five days earlier, I'd rested there on my way back to the road with a load of wood. It was a very warm afternoon, so I groped in my rucksack, found some small oranges I remembered packing days before, and sucked on them greedily. The Ardrossan ferry was on course towards the south end of Arran. I knew my daughter Amelia would be on board, and mused on the strangeness of 'watching' someone who couldn't be seen. Now I was looking wistfully at the orange peel I'd thrown on the grass that day. Nostalgia comes to me in strange forms!

While in Glasgow over Christmas visiting our family, Judy and I caught a nasty cold. After three weeks of it, we felt ourselves recovering, only to be hit by flu-like 'afters' which kept us in bed for several days. One night, at the height of my bout, I became delirious and found myself, in memory, back in the field at Corphin. It was a sunny, peaceful vision of paradise – the grass, the sea, the distant Arran mountains – and I kept returning there, in my fevered state, for solace. Inevitably, that inconspicuous spot has become one of my special places, endowed with spiritual energy.

20 May: Whales

On my way to Kilkerran, I saw the distressing sight of a 26-foot common minke whale lying in the back of a McFadyens' lorry, the flesh above the tail raw from the abrasion of ropes. It was heading for a deep landfill site, after skin samples had been taken for laboratory examination. The creature had become entangled and drowned off Peninver in the prawn-creel ropes of the *Crest* of Campbeltown. The same boat had landed a dead whale, similarly snared, twelve years previously.[54]

Whales and fishermen in earlier generations co-existed harmoniously. The herring-eating species, when actively hunting, would guide ring-net fishermen to shoals. Whales and porpoises herded the herring and fed on the outer fish, and sometimes a whale, bursting clear of a dense shoal, would surface with the silvery herring cascading from her back, a sure sign for watching fishermen. On occasion, a net would encircle a whale along with the herring, but if she failed to escape through the narrowing gap of the closing net, realising that she was trapped, she would break free through the netting.[55] Nets then were spun from natural fibres, and split under pressure. Nets, and ropes, are now manufactured from unyielding synthetic fibres, the crucial difference.

A 'great whale' which beached at Carradale around 1812 was said to have been 'about ninety-six feet long'. Accounts published fifty years later are rather confusing. In one, it 'stranded', and in the other it was 'brought to shore ... scarcely dead ... by some fishermen'.

A second large whale – length recorded as 72 ft., circumference 40 ft., and 'spread of the tail' about 14 ft. – which came ashore at Port nam Marbh ('Port of the Dead'), Westport, in November 1866, was identified as a 'Rorqual'. Its back was broken and it was already decomposing. When news reached Campbeltown, Duncan the town crier went through the streets with his bell, announcing: 'Notice! The Great Whale! Omnibus will start from Argyll Arms Hotel to Westport, at ten, twelve, and two o' clock.' Large numbers of the curious heeded the call: 'Carts, gigs, and carriages were more in demand than all Campbeltown could supply. The wreck of the Charlemagne was not more patronised than the hulk of this big fish.'[56]

The ultimate ownership of the carcass is unclear from newspaper reports, but it appears to have been finally sold for £50. The men who, a week later, were 'busily engaged in cutting up the whale', doubtless had a nauseating time of it earning their shillings. The blubber was sent to Glasgow in hogsheads by Thomas Brown, 'to be melted and converted into oil', and John Lorne Stewart, Stronvaar, the Duke of Argyll's factor in Kintyre and an improving landowner in his own right, took the remains for 'manuring land'.[57] The arch in the garden of Rosemount, Low Askomill, is formed from a jawbone of that whale.

Eight years after the Westport whale, the farmer at Feochaig, Allan MacLean, found a 30-ft. whale on Glenahervie shore. (Coincidentally, the finder of the Westport whale was another Allan MacLean.) *Argyllshire Herald*: 'The whale when found was in a dying state, and is one of the species generally found or seen pursuing fish in our waters.' The Receiver of Wreck, Mr Barnes, was soon 'receiving tenders for the extraordinary visitor, to turn it into sterling value'. MacLean himself succeeded with a bid of £3, though his intentions for the carcass were not reported[58] – perhaps, again, oil and fertiliser, both of which commodities were then in great demand.

21 May: Painted Ladies on Knock Scalbert

I am seldom on Knock Scalbert nowadays, but the hill has been good to me over the past thirty years with archaeological and fungal finds and memorable wildlife sightings. I had hardly set foot on Knock Scalbert until I moved to the Dalintober side of town in 1985. The handiest route was from the Second Walk, through a gate into a field on Bellfield farm, then into the Standing Stone Park and straight on to the hill, but since the field was bulldozed for a building site, I haven't gone near it, and my excursions to Knock Scalbert have been by bicycle, via the Balegreggan or the Whitehill roads.

On that day, I cycled to Auchalochy, left the bike at the anglers' car-park there, and headed on to Knock Scalbert. My mind was troubled, but the mood lifted when I reached the top and encountered my first painted lady butterflies of the year. There were two butterflies chasing each other around the summit, one a painted lady and the other a small tortoiseshell; then a second lady arrived and joined in the fun, if that's what it was.

The painted lady (*Vanessa cardui*) makes herself easy to identify – not only does she tend to charge about the same space for hours at a time, but she also enjoys frequent rests and will obligingly alight close to a human. I was able to study (and photograph) both ladies on the ground and noticed that one of them had bits of her lower wings missing. The upper wings display magnificent splashes of colour, the 'paint' in 'painted', I presume.

They appear to be attracted to windy hill-tops, though I have never seen the trait mentioned in print. Being unable to over-winter in the British Isles, they are migrants from mainland Europe, but in some years they are scarce and only a few are seen, or none. In 1995, they arrived in spectacular numbers, and again in 2009. I have a clear memory of their appearance in the latter year. Our dog Benjie had died, and, without him, Judy and I were cycling more. On 30 May we decided to cycle down the Learside to our caravan, and, before setting off, bought a take-away dall curry at Mota Singh's restaurant and sat to eat it at a picnic-table on Kilkerran road. All the way south that evening, we saw painted ladies arriving on a warm southerly wind.

23 May: The Pirate's Grave

Our visit to the Ru a week earlier had inspired George McSporran and me with a mission: we'd search for the stone, known as the Pirate's Grave, which lay on the shore north of Johnston's Point. We left our bikes at the quarry above Corphin ruins and walked south from the

Dummy's Port. Our expedition had been timed to coincide with low tide, when the rocks in the ebb would be exposed and dry, enabling us to quit the foreshore when the going got rough and step safely from one smooth surface to another.

George had first seen the carved slab in the 1960s during his explorations of the Learside with his boyhood companion, Campbell Macarthur. It was shown to me in 1980 by Jock Smith, who kept a caravan and boat at Feochaig and knew the coast intimately. My niece Barbara Docherty saw the stone on 12 July 1981, noting in her diary that she set out with John MacDonald and me at 9.30 a.m. and that the weather improved as the day went on. At Feochaig she 'met Jock Smith ... very hospitable' and 'saw grave of man; skull engraved on it'. We didn't arrive home until 11.30 p.m., a detail which surprised me. By then, John's mother, Rene, and Barbara's twin, Christine, were 'very worried'. Barbara's final note: 'Had greasy chips and eggs, lovely.'

I have already examined the history of the 'grave',[59] so will try to minimise repetition; there is, however, a good deal to add. The most important record is on a small-scale map annotated by Duncan Colville in 1960 and now in the Kintyre Antiquarian and Natural History Society archive. He stated the dimensions as: length 5 ft. 9 ins., breadth 2 ft. 3 ins., and thickness 8 ins. The slab was red sandstone – most of the rocks on that shore are – and bore a human skull and a shield, both crudely sculpted. His description of its location – marked on the map with a cross – is significant, and I'll quote it in full: 'Lying N. & S. at an incline, with North end 18" higher than South end. Situated on the foreshore where precipitous grassy slopes meet the highest tide mark on beach covered with boulders.' The slab was said to commemorate either a ship's captain or his wife, drowned and washed ashore near that spot in the nineteenth century, and the carvings were attributed to Donald McIsaac (p 35). That there could have been an actual burial there is utterly improbable; there is no suitable depth of soil anywhere on that rocky shore.

Both George and I remembered seeing the stone lying a short distance to the north of Johnston's Point, close to a large metal tank. We searched back and forth along that stretch of shore, further than we need have gone, without finding any trace of it. Our conclusion – the slab was probably broken in pieces by wave action. My last sighting of it was in 1988, when I showed it to Judy during our coastal walk with daughter Sarah (p 44); there is no written evidence, but a slide of the stone, processed on 11/05/88, proves that it was still there, and I reproduce the photograph here.

16. *The author's last photograph of the Pirate's Grave, 30 April 1988.*

We returned two days later to search again, and were again disappointed. I'd suggested to George that we speak to Billy Rankin, who had farmed Feochaig, and whom did we see as we cycled home but Billy himself, out for a stroll on Kilkerran Road? He reckoned he last saw the slab about twenty years ago, when, curiously, it had been turned upside-down and a single rock placed on it. Jock Smith, whom I visited on 17 July, reckoned he was last there about thirty years ago, when he had difficulty finding the stone. It had been covered over with gravel, which he cleared away. He intended to return to clean up the carvings, but never did.

Jock's maternal grandfather, Charles Johnston, appeared as a witness in a poaching case reported in the *Campbeltown Courier* in 1935. He had met the two accused, James McAulay and William McGeachy, 'on the shore between the Second Water and Feochaig Point – at a place known as the Sailor's Grave'.[60] This is clearly a reference to the 'Pirate's Grave', and I believe the earlier name to be the authentic one. The carved skull – which signifies mortality – plus imaginary crossbones, which local legend grafted on to the stone, together created its later identity. (There is also a 'Sailor's Grave' in the Inneans Bay and another, with Kintyre associations, on the Arran coast between Lochranza and Catacol.)[61]

Teddy Lafferty remembers when the big tank – he heard that it was part of a pontoon – was washed ashore on Johnston's Point. Whatever it was, it drifted over from the Irish coast and was being monitored as a shipping hazard. The year eludes his memory, but it was around 1960. On his way to Feochaig Bay one day, he met Hughie Wilson at the farm and stopped for a chat. When Ramsay's milk lorry appeared, Teddy helped Hughie lift the Feochaig milk cans aboard. Then Hughie asked him into the farmhouse for a cup of tea. While they were sitting at the kitchen table with Hughie's parents, there was a knock at the door. This was a Customs and Excise officer, Tom Scott, who had come to ask the Wilsons if they wanted the thing for scrap, but Hughie's father said that its value wouldn't justify the labour. It's still there, but the ends have both disintegrated in rust. Jock Smith recalls an unfortunate wanderer from town sleeping in that tank.

Jock Smith at Feochaig

Jock also recalls an evening spent yarning with Robert Armour and Duncan McLachlan in Duncan's little caravan which neighboured Jock's at Feochaig. 'Robina' maintained that Johnston's Point was named after Jock's grandfather, Charlie Johnston, who fished off the rocks there. Duncan was in total disagreement, and the debate became heated, but Duncan was correct. Johnston's Point appears on the first Ordnance Survey map, surveyed in 1866, and therefore predates Charlie Johnston's birth. The O.S. Name-Book for Southend Parish derives the name from 'the owner of a vessel which struck there some few years ago', information provided by Allan MacLean, farmer in Feochaig.

I first encountered Jock in May 1980, during a hike which brought me into Feochaig Bay from the north. He and his wife, Marianne, occupied a caravan during spells of favourable weather. They created a small garden at the caravan, and, from a spring above the shore, Jock formed a nicely constructed well. He kept a boat and lobster-creels and other gear on the shore and made creels from hazel rods which he cut nearby. I relished my visits to Feochaig in the early 1980s, the tea, the yarns, and sometimes a lift back in Jock's car if he and Marianne weren't staying on. I generally had companions on these hikes, my niece Barbara Docherty and young neighbour, John MacDonald, sometimes one and other times both.

Jock was a captivating storyteller in the old style, and still is. When he tells a story, he is inside the narrative, reliving it, with gestures and facial expressions to bring out the humour or drama. His store of tales is of the anecdotal type, and, as with many raconteurs, the border between the factual and the imaginary is sometimes blurred. But they are his stories, he has preserved them for the entertainment of himself and his listeners, and he is free to enhance them in any way he pleases. The following two, he assured me, are true.

Jock wanted a length of fire-hose to cut into straps for tying down his caravan. He had enquired at Campbeltown fire station, but was told that old hoses had to be returned before new ones would be issued. One day he took a walk towards the Bastard with his dog, and saw an object 'shining out in the water like a tin can'. He continued on his walk, looking back now and again and catching a glint of the flotsam. On his way back, he found the thing beached, and it was a huge roll of fire-hose, tied up neatly and with a metal nozzle on one end. He dragged it back to the caravan and announced to Marianne: 'I don't need to ask any more about firemen's hose.' When she saw the hose, she was sceptical and suspected he'd brought it there himself. A severe gale came days later. The two hose-straps at the back of the van held, but the other two broke, and, with the van's violent motion at the front end, the door steps burst up through the floor.

That same winter in the 1980s, he also needed rope for towing his boat away with an old tractor left in the bay for his use, and was contemplating asking around the Campbeltown fishermen for a length. One day, soon after the hose came ashore, he was walking north of the caravan, when, close to the Pirate's Grave, he found the required rope, and more. It was an inch thick and around 600 feet long. He described these experiences as the most 'amazing' in all his years at the Feochaig caravan.

Jock told me he discovered the location of a shipwreck off Feochaig by the rusty colouration of the lobsters he had fished up from the iron hulk. He subsequently guided a party of U.S. Navy SEAL divers to the wreck, and they came up with clay pipes, bottles and other souvenirs. One officer, before he was posted home, remarked to Jock that the makers of the clay pipes could never have imagined that one of their products would ultimately travel to America 40,000 feet up in the air. The pipes were part of a general cargo bound for Australia and the wreck was the *Charlemagne*.

Wreck of the *Charlemagne*, 1857

Innumerable ships have been wrecked on the Learside, but the most famous of them all – indeed, the most famous of all Kintyre shipwrecks – is the *Charlemagne*. The three-masted clipper ran aground on 20 March 1857, on her maiden voyage from Greenock to Melbourne. Two reasons explain her endurance in local memory – a ballad was written about her, and her cargo included barrels of choice whisky. The following is an account of the wreck from the *Campbeltown Journal* of 27 March 1857.

The new iron clipper ship Charlemagne, 1017 tons, bound for Melbourne, W. Reid commander and belonging to Messrs Cree Skinner, & Co., left Greenock on Thursday last with a fair wind, and was accompanied by a tug as far as Pladda. The pilot left her about 11 p.m. About three hours afterwards she struck on the coast a little below Feochaig, at the Learside coast, and about 7 miles from this port. We believe this can only be accounted for by the fact of her compasses either not having been properly adjusted, or not working properly as they were sailing according to them in the very direction that would take them down the channel. As the rocks were near the shore, all the passengers and crew were saved. 4 valuable horses and 15 sheep were drowned however. When the crew left the vessel there were 7 feet of water in the hold, and as the wind has been mostly unfavourable since that time, the ship has suffered considerably. Large quantities of the cargo have been floating about in the vicinity, and thrown on the shore, and the tug Conqueror and the lighter Rescue are employed in removing as much as they can get.

The passengers left by the Ayr steamer on Saturday morning, and the crew by the Celt steamer on Monday morning for Glasgow. The cargo and ship is (*sic*) insured, and was valued at £110,000. Captain Coppin has arrived at the wreck on Wednesday last, and a number of men are employed in securing the sails, spars, cargo, etc. Hopes are entertained that the ship may be got off if the weather takes a favourable turn. This is the sixth vessel lost within two or three years on this coast.

One of the *Charlemagne*'s passengers was said to have been a Campbeltown flesher, Angus Macdonald. According to Donald McLean's 'Campbeltown Fifty Years Ago', published in 1913, Macdonald had a thriving business in Longrow, which 'with surprising suddenness he sold off and booked a passage to Australia'. Following the shipwreck, he abandoned his emigration plans, bought back his old property, had it pulled down and replaced it with a tenement of shops and houses. He was, McLean recalled, '... a terribly keen business man, and it was a treat to see him weigh half-a-pound of mincemeat. You never got more than the half-pound, but never less. His shop was not haunted by the bargain hunters who wanted a bone given in to the bargain for nothing. If you got a bone you had to pay for it, as Angus argued that he had to pay the same for the bone as the meat'.[62]

Another of the *Charlemagne*'s passengers was still alive in 1924, aged a hundred. He was John Hood, living in 'excellent health' at

Auchencrow, Berwickshire, and his mind 'ever alert and attentive'. He recalled that the ship grounded at about 1 a.m. and heeled over at about 10 a.m. 'All hands were at the pumps' from then until about 6 p.m., when Captain Reid gave the order to abandon ship. Her ten passengers were taken on board the steamer *Scotia*, but the horses and sheep went down with the ship, unnecessarily, according to Hood, who accused Reid of being 'very careless about them'. The cargo, including casks of whisky, was 'floating about', and a family bible, belonging to 'Mr and Mrs Meikle ... late of Lemington Farm, Reston', was washed ashore and taken away by a man on the beach.

Mr Hood, undeterred by his *Charlemagne* experience, took another passage to Australia, on the clipper *Blackhill*, arriving safely in Melbourne after a voyage of 106 days. He was a joiner to trade, but worked as a mail-carrier between Melbourne and two outlying settlements until 1862, when he moved to New Zealand and set up as a builder in Dunedin. In 1894 he returned to Scotland and rebuilt the family house at Auchencrow, in which he had been born in 1824. He was living there in retirement, cared for by two nieces, when the anonymous *Campbeltown Courier* correspondent interviewed him.[63]

A witness to the shipwreck was still in Campbeltown in 1924. He was Angus Kerry, a retired seaman in Saddell Street. In 1857, he was ten years old and living 'at the Feochaig colony'. He viewed the ship, 'wedged in between the rocks', two days after she grounded, and sixty-seven years later volunteered a detail which perhaps only an old seaman would have remembered: 'Her sails were not furled, merely clewed up, but later in the day the crew returned on board to furl'. He found a book washed ashore – a commentary on the 119th Psalm – which he took home. The covers were damaged, but his father had it rebound. He recalled seeing barrels of marbles, barrels of ink-bottles, bales of packing paper and 'much liquor piled up on the shore'. Two boys from Campbeltown broached one of the whisky casks and drank so much they had to be carried to Feochaig farmhouse and a doctor summoned from Campbeltown to attend them.

The bible mentioned by John Hood survived in a house in Longrow, Campbeltown, where it was 'valued as a relic', Captain Reid's binoculars were in a farmhouse 'not many miles away from the scene of the wreck', and in another farmhouse the furniture included a chair from the ship's cabin. A more public relic helped preserve the *Charlemagne* in local memory, her figurehead, which was salvaged intact and mounted at the entrance to McNair's wood yard in Longrow, where it stood, 'in massive impressiveness', until around 1920, when it finally disintegrated.[64]

Angus's parents were James Kerry, farm labourer, and Catherine Lang. In the 1851 census they were in Glenahervie. James was 'McKerry' then, aged forty and born in Ireland. Catherine's birthplace was given as Irvine, Ayrshire, but I have little doubt that she was a Loynachan, the earlier form of the name 'Lang' in Kintyre. On her death certificate in 1879, her father is identified as Angus Lang, seaman, and her mother as 'Armour', there being a blank where the forename should have gone. Since the death was registered by Angus himself, his maternal grandmother's forename was presumably unknown to him, a peculiar failing in those rooted times. And Angus was presumably responsible for the following alterations to the register: from 'Catherine McKerry' and 'widow of James McKerry', the 'Mc' was subsequently scored out.

In 1835, his father was 'James McKarry' when interviewed as a witness to an assault on John MacLean, fisherman at Glenahervie. James was described as aged twenty-five and a servant with John Drain, farmer at Glenahervie. He and companions were in Campbeltown for 'fair day' on 20 November, and in the evening went to the Heatherhouse at Glenramskill, where drinking and dancing were going on. They must have been there until late, because the assault happened between one and two o' clock in the morning at the Merkland on Kilkerran road when they were on their way into town.[65]

James and Catherine had three children with them in 1851, sons Archibald (10), Duncan (7) and Angus (4). Which of the Glenahervie settlements they were in isn't clear, but they must have been somewhere north of the present Glenahervie, which was 'Gartnagorach' in the same census. In Angus Kerry's obituary, his childhood home – 'only the foundations of which can now be traced' – is described as being 'near Corven Glen', a fair way from Glenahervie! Angus was admitted to Campbeltown Poorhouse Hospital on 22 May 1929 and died sixteen days later, aged eighty-two. The greater part of the obituary of that master mariner and 'fine old citizen' was devoted to the wreck of the *Charlemagne*, of which he was the last surviving witness.[66]

The ballad of the *Charlemagne* was composed locally to the tune of 'Hey Johnny Cope', but only fragments remain. The best known of these celebrates Allan MacLean, the Killean-born tenant-farmer in Feochaig, who was supposed to have carried Captain Reid off the wreck. According to Colonel Charles Mactaggart, the 'Feochaig people' brought the crew ashore using a rope, except for the captain, who had been injured, perhaps by 'a falling spar'. This is the verse:

> Allan MacLean he wasna slack,
> He carried the Captain on his back,
> And a gless o' brandy he did tak'
> When he got home in the mornin'.

MacLean was evidently a witty character. One day, the 8th Duke of Argyll was driving round the Learside and stopped, as was his custom, to have a chat with Allan, who was a tenant of his. Noticing a nearby field of beans, the Duke remarked to him, 'That bean crop of yours is very poor'. – "Deed aye,' Allan replied. 'If they were aa' pipers, they wadna hear each other playin'."[67]

The quantity of whisky lost from the *Charlemagne* was incalculable. Some casks were taken from the scene of the wreck, but others were said to have washed ashore all around the coast from Feochaig to Largiebaan. If the traditions are true, some folk had so much whisky they hid it in the hills or in caves, and these caches supplied them with liquor for months and even years. Colonel Mactaggart in 1922 recalled an encounter with an old shepherd, 'Johnnie', while shooting in the Southend hills. Johnnie, who was 'a frequent and a welcome guest at lunch time', subscribed to 'the old Scottish doctrine' that there was no such thing as bad whisky, but always maintained that 'no whisky had ever been drunk in Kintyre, which for flavour and potency – especially potency – could touch that which came out of the "Charlemagne"'.

> It was a beautiful day on our hillside, but a thick bank of fog lay on the sea, and the fog guns on Rathlin were banging, and the foghorns on Sanda and the Mull were hooting merrily. As we rose to go our separate ways, Johnnie waved his hand dramatically towards the Mull and gave vent to his feelings in these words: 'Listen to them (adjective) foghorns; I wish they were all bursted; there's no chance for a body to live on this coast noo"; and then, after a rueful pause, he added, 'I doot I'll never seen another Charlemagne'.[68]

Two Donalds

In the mid-nineteenth century, when the *Charlemagne* was wrecked, Feochaig was a busy little community. It was a farm, but farming was labour-intensive then, and, like most farms, Feochaig had its resident workers, a few living with the farmer's family, but the majority in cot-houses nearby. In 1851, six years before the wreck, the census recorded six households at Feochaig. There was the tenant himself, sixty-four-year-old John McIsaac, with his family and two female servants, and Neil Loynachan, Neil McNaughton, Thomas McCallum and James Quaintain – all described simply as 'agricultural labourers' – with their families. The sixth household consisted of one occupant, Donald McEachran, described as an eighty-eight-year-old retired farmer and widower, born in Southend Parish. His was among the oldest and most distinguished of all Kintyre surnames – *Mac Each-thighearna*, 'Son of the Horse-lord' – and I'd wager he had scarcely a word of English in his head.

Soon after that census was taken, Donald would be the victim of a brutal assault in his 'lonely shieling at Feachaig'. He was wakened in the night by a noise at his door, and 'In a few minutes, the door was broken in, and several severe blows were given him'. His attacker, Daniel Sillars – 'well known to the police, and feels no way tremulous in appearing before a public court' – was arrested in Glasgow and brought by steamer to Campbeltown. In September, at Inveraray Circuit Court, he pleaded guilty to 'assault to the effusion of blood and imminent danger of life', and was sentenced to fourteen years' transportation. Donald died days after the sentence was passed.

An unusual notice was inserted in the deaths column of the *Campbeltown Journal*, suggesting that Donald's age – he was born around 1762 – had earned him a measure of veneration: '... For a considerable time past he had received the kind attention of His Grace, the Duke of Argyll, and we may state that his sudden discease (*sic*) has caused deep regret amongst a wide circle of friends and acquaintances ...'[69]

The other Donald was a little boy whose death occurred twelve years later, in September 1863. He was playing with friends when some gunpowder was found in one of the Feochaig houses. The children started playing with the powder, but one of them put a light to it and Donald was caught in the explosion. 'As there was no adult in the house, the poor little sufferer ran into the sea and, finding no relief there, he ran back again to the house, and sent a little girl to a neighbouring house for assistance.' That afternoon he lost consciousness, but he lingered between life and death for three more days until his terrible sufferings ended.[70]

He was described as a son of John McAulay, 'workman', and is identifiable as the child born in Shore Street, Campbeltown, on 24 July 1855, his father a twenty-nine-year-old fisherman, born in County Derry, and his mother Euphemia McEachran – that surname again – who married McAulay on 12 May 1849 in Campbeltown. They had '2 boys living, 1 boy dead'.[71] New-born Donald would be another son fated to die in childhood.

A flock of sheep

I am still with George on 23 May, and we have passed Johnston's Point and entered Feochaig Bay. There is still a caravan there, on Jock Smith's old site, but it is dilapidated. We looked for the site of Duncan McLachlan's little van and found it, but nothing of it remained there. While searching the shore, lifting bits of smooth sea-coal, we heard a commotion approaching: a flock of sheep was being driven towards the bay from the south. We moved further down the shore so as not to disrupt the proceedings, but, as it transpired, we were not in the way.

There were two men on ATVs, and the first of them to arrive stopped on the foreshore and walked over to us. He was Kevin MacIntyre, son of the farmer in Glenahervie, Iain. I was aware that Kevin and my daughter Amelia were in the Grammar School together and mentioned her by way of introducing myself. He said that the last time he had seen her, she was boarding the *Isle of Arran* at the New Quay (11 May: p 72). We were soon joined by Iain, who entered the conversation for a while, and then they were off on the bikes to complete their business. Minutes after they left, I cursed myself for not having photographed them together.

The SS *Elisabeth*, 1935

Kevin's great-great-grandfather, John MacIntyre, was farmer at Feochaig in 1935 when the Danish cargo ship *Elisabeth* grounded on the same rocks that claimed the *Charlemagne*. It was to be an eventful November night for the MacIntyre family. A gale was lashing the coast, and John's daughter Nellie rose from her bed and went upstairs to check if the driving rain was penetrating the windows. As she peered out at the storm, she was alarmed to see a ship's lights close inshore. Then came a 'dull crash' and she knew the vessel was aground.

Nellie – later to be mother of Billy Rankin (p 77) – at once roused the family. Her brother Jackie drove his car as close to the cliffs as he dared go and flashed the headlights to reassure the crew that help was near. There was no telephone at Feochaig, so Jackie and his brother Jamie drove through the storm to Southend and alerted the Coastguard, who, in turn, contacted Campbeltown R.N.L.I. The life-boat, with Coxswain George McEachran at the helm, reached the vessel at around 6 a.m. Her crew was able to fire two lines across the bow, but weather conditions hampered the operation and rescue efforts switched to Southend Coastguard which was now on the scene. A line was fired aboard the *Elisabeth*, and three of the youngest crew-members were dragged ashore through the surf. When the heavier breeches buoy arrived in two farm carts, the remaining thirteen men were taken off. First ashore, however, had been the ship's dog, which had dived overboard and swum to land; but there was no happy ending for Signore – owing to the stringency of Danish quarantine regulations, he was 'put down, much to the sorrow of the crew'.

17. SS Elisabeth *at Feochaig, taken a few hours after she grounded on 2 November 1935. Newspaper cutting from the author's collection.*

The crew was given food and dry clothing at Feochaig farmhouse.

As Rae MacGregor, on whose article this account is based, remarked: 'As the MacIntyre family consisted of three men and four women, female clothing was in the majority and some of the men found themselves attired in skirts and jumpers!'

The *Elisabeth*, with a crew of fifteen Danes and one German, and under the command of Captain Eric Starke, was on passage from Irvine to Wisbech with 250 tons of coal as ballast. Before salvage operations could begin, the coal had to be dumped overboard to lighten her, 'a benefit which was not lost on the Feochaig inhabitants', as Rae commented, adding that 'to this day pieces of coal can still be found on Feochaig shore'.

The remarkable salvage operation, under Captain C. G. Bonar, V.C., D.S.O., of the salvage tug *Bullinger*, took three weeks to complete. When at last freed from the rocks, the *Elisabeth* was towed to Campbeltown, where a crowd awaited her arrival, and then towed to Copenhagen. When a reporter from the *Campbeltown Courier* approached Captain Bonar to enquire into his Victoria Cross award, Bonar 'absolutely refused to discuss the matter'.[72]

The MacIntyre family has farmed on the Learside for nearly 150 years, first at Auchenhoan, then Feochaig and now Glenahervie, a steady southerly progression. The first of them, Donald, a shepherd, died in 1870 at the age of fifty-three. His widow, Mary Campbell, remained in Auchenhoan, where, in the census a year later, she was with five of her children, the oldest, James, already a shepherd at fifteen, and the youngest, Jessie, just eleven months old. The middle child, John Campbell MacIntyre, would marry Martha Rae, farm Feochaig and die there in 1937. Mary MacIntyre was a daughter of John Campbell, the last schoolmaster in Ballochroy Glen, who went to Canada after the glen was cleared of people. She was an 'interesting conversationalist both in English and Gaelic', and died at the age of eighty-nine in 1917; but see *Kintyre Places and Place-Names*, p 35, for a little more on her.

An abortive camp at Feochaig, 1966

None of my teenage camping trips was a success. The least successful of them, which was also the first, was to Feochaig, and it was unsuccessful mainly because we lacked a tent. There was a tent at Feochaig, but we didn't know where. This predicament came about through Iain Campbell's energetic enthusiasm for the adventure.

The trip had been planned for 19 September 1966 and involved Iain, me and another boy from Crosshill Avenue, Peter Tolmie. I was fourteen years old and still at school, but with a seven-day part-time working week, six days as a butcher's boy with George MacKay, and Sunday as a paper boy with Alistair McEachran. Nineteenth September was a Sunday and the Monday following must have been both a school and a public holiday, because I was entirely free that day, hence the overnight camp at Feochaig. Iain, a year older than I, had already left school and begun a joinery apprenticeship with John McDougall. He, therefore, was free on the Sunday and volunteered to cycle down to Feochaig with the tent and leave it there, a return trip of fourteen miles.

Since my paper delivery involved a halting car journey through Southend, the three of us, loaded with sleeping-bags and provisions, didn't get going until 8 p.m. We met Alastair Thompson and Rab Davison – whether by arrangement, I can't recall – and cycled with them to Auchenhoan farm, where they were to spend the night in Alastair's uncle's bothy. We arrived at Feochaig in darkness, took a wrong road and then found the right one, but couldn't find the tent, which Iain had concealed in a whin bush, and there were bushes everywhere! The consequence was that, as I noted afterwards, with unconscious self-contradiction: 'Slept in open and never slept.' Later in the account, however, I reckoned that I had slept for two hours, Peter for four and Iain for one.

We passed much of the night watching shooting stars until a 'spectacular dawn' broke. Having failed to light a fire to cook breakfast on, we settled for fruit cocktail from a tin. When we finally got a fire going, we heated baked beans on it and had a second breakfast. A third meal consisted of 'fish fingers and chips', after which we were ready to leave. We had discovered by then that our camp was close to a cow's carcass, and the stench was overpowering when the day warmed up.

That corpse would ultimately symbolise the whole fiasco. Alastair recalls my 'reporting sleeping on a soft rock, which turned out to be a dead cow in the morning light'. Neither my memory nor my notebook accords with that version of events, but it may have been closer to the truth than I can now recognise. As we wheeled our bikes uphill to the road, we saw Alastair and Rab coming down to meet us. I remember them, refreshed after a night's sleep in civilised accommodation, surveying our dispirited retreat with smug amusement.

But Alastair's enjoyment would be short-lived. Having retrieved the missing tent from the bush, which Iain was able to identify in daylight, we accompanied him and Rab to Auchenhoan bothy, where Alastair, being familiar with the cooking facilities there, was unanimously elected chef. The imposition still irks him: 'Yes, being designated the cook without assistance was offensive – I should have let you starve.' I can provide, from my notebook, the complete menu from the combined provisions of both parties: ham, beans, pork and beef link sausages, sausage rolls, potatoes, tomato soup and tinned creamed rice. You did a great job, Alastair, and, albeit forty-eight years late, I salute you!

26 May: The Bastard

George and I had returned to the shore north of Johnston's Point to look again for the missing 'grave' slab. While we were sitting there in sunshine, George enquired in puzzlement: 'What's that noise?' – 'A strange bird with smoke coming out of its arse,' I replied. The sound was from my pipe as I sucked on it to get it to draw.

I noted in my journal that day an observation which I had omitted three days earlier – the sudden spectacular appearance of the Bastard cliffs as one rounds Johnston's Point. It's one of the oddest place-names in Kintyre, and probably seems odder to strangers than to natives, who have grown up with it. It's so odd that the name has not yet been interpreted, and probably never will be. Some local students of place-names have suggested it might be corrupt Gaelic, but if the Roy military map of c. 1750 can be trusted, the earlier name was 'Knock Mor' (*Cnoc Mòr*, 'Big Hill'). If 'Bastard' isn't corrupt Gaelic, what is it? Is it English and meaning what it means in modern usage? How could such an improbable name be attached to the landscape and perpetuated in a rigidly Presbyterian society? Questions, but no answers.

I remember my father telling me a story – doubtless apocryphal – of a minister who went out in a fishing skiff from Campbeltown. Passing the Bloody Bay, he asked one of the crew if there was a name for the place. He was told. Further south, looking up at the Bastard, he asked if it had a name. He was told. 'I really don't think I want to hear any more of these names!' was his response. The story, of course, belongs to a time when 'bad language' was widely frowned upon, and I suppose that yarn, and others like it, provided a licence to shock.

A mystery spring and Pursells

In May and June, an e-mail exchange with Duncan Pursell, a mining engineer in Australia, yielded news – very old 'news' on my side of the correspondence! – of a spring on the east side of Ballimenach brae. Owing to the summer growth of vegetation, I haven't yet looked for that spring, but I have identified its location from Duncan's descriptions and will search for it in winter. It's at the first coniferous plantations on the brae, which, when Duncan had a look at the spring in 1964 or '65, had 'just been "contour-drained" above and below the road in preparation for forestry plantation'. On that last visit home, Duncan found the ground overgrown and 'only found the spring by listening'.

The water, he recalled, was 'pure and icy-cold irrespective of season', there was a 'small tin on the right-hand side to drink with', and the outflow from the pipe 'usually had plenty of watercress in it'. The spring was used by the Auchenhoan shepherds, the 'occasional tramp', and Duncan's own family. He was shown the spring by his father, Edward Pursell – Gaelic writer and landscape painter – whose mother, Mary Russell, was connected with Ballimenach farm. Her father, Robert Russell, born in Lanarkshire, was tenant-farmer there for sixty-two years, until his death in 1912,[73] and the five Pursell boys – two of whom, Peter and Bobby, had careers as professional footballers[74] – were often about the farm. As teenagers, they would fish the Second Water for trout, and Edward's job one summer was scything bracken at the top of New Orleans Glen.

'Pursell', like scores of other surnames in Kintyre, is bogus. Since it derives from *Mac an Sporain*, 'Son of the Purse', there is an unusual logic behind the switch, but it failed to catch on; there are still plenty of McSporrans in Kintyre but only one Pursell, Mrs Iona MacNeill. One of the problems with name-changes is that genealogical links can be obscured. An example relating to the MacSporran/Pursell split came up in August. In the Library I met a man who said he'd 'hit a brick wall' with his family research. His mother was a McSporran, but he'd found Pursell a bit further back in the family and assumed that the name had changed from Pursell to McSporran. I explained that it could indeed have gone from Pursell to McSporran, but that it would certainly have been McSporran in the first place. As Judy soon discovered, the individual baptised John McSporran in Kintyre was John 'Porsull' when he married in Glasgow in 1856. I am guessing that the Glasgow registrar wrote the name the way he heard John pronounce it. Bizarre 'Porsull' was that 'brick wall'.

30 May: John Harvey, Gartnacopaig

'Some days there's more happens in one's mind than in the external world.' That's the first note in my journal on an afternoon I cycled to Glenahanty, left the bike there and walked out to Largiebaan cliffs. Re-reading that philosophical jotting, I realise that it doesn't survive scrutiny; but I see the point I was trying to make – until I reached the cliffs, I neither saw nor heard much to interest me.

18. At the silage-pit, Gartnacopaig, 29 May 1982, L-R: Robert Shaw, John Harvey and Angus Martin. Photograph by Donald Docherty.

As I climbed the Bruach Dearg and passed Gartnacopaig steading, which is now unoccupied, my memory drew me back thirty-odd years to John Harvey. I stopped to look at the silage-pit, dense with nettles and its uprights rusting, and remembered talking with John there. He and a friend from Carradale, Robert Shaw, were painting the superstructure of the pit. I photographed them sitting together, and then my nephew, Donald Docherty, photographed me with them. The date was 29 May 1982.

John was killed when a car he was repairing fell on him. I remember hearing that his mother, Peggy, called him for dinner, and, getting no response, went out to fetch him in, and saw the car on top of him. I made a note in my journal to find the date of his death, and my estimate was '87/88'. I remember very clearly the evening I heard of his death. I was staying with Murdo MacDonald in his cottage on Lochfyneside, and was talking on the telephone at his kitchen table and looking through a little window towards the Cowal hills. In memory, I received the shocking news from my wife Judy, and I spent hours searching through *Campbeltown Couriers* from the late 1980s to find that date, but I was years out. The date, when it finally emerged, thanks to the effort of a friend in Southend, Catherine Barbour, was 9 February 1983, before I even met Judy. John was just thirty-two years old, a year older than me at the time.

I had looked in Kilcolmkill graveyard, Southend, for his headstone, and didn't find it, but that's where it is. He is buried there with his father John (died 1962, aged fifty-three) and mother Peggy Ramsay (died 1998, aged eighty-six). His funeral service, in the Highland Parish Church, Campbeltown, was conducted jointly by the minister there, Rev C. M. Henderson, and the Southend minister, Rev W. C. Nelson. The *Courier* published extracts from Mr Nelson's tribute to John, and I'll quote his words, because they seem to me to catch the light of John's departed spirit.

> John's life was unnaturally short. But life is not necessarily measured by length of years. It is the quality of those years that count.
> John had a man's burden placed on him at an early age, and he carried that burden. And in it he found his satisfaction.
> He was at home with his sheep and cattle on the hills at Gartnacopaig. Over the years he could see the results of his work, and he had plans for the future. John loved his work – it was his life. He was a happy and contented person – and a happy person gives happiness to others.[75]

I don't claim to have known John well – we talked when we met, and that was all – but I liked the John I knew. I remember him, at a time when environmental issues were rarely mentioned, talking about the mature deciduous trees in the ravine beside the Bruach Dearg, and the need to protect them from irresponsible wood-cutting. On my way back from Largiebaan on the day the photographs were taken, I met John again and he pointed out ruins by the roadside, 'mid-way between his house and the road-end, and said that his grandfather remembered when the house was standing'. I forget what these ruins were – perhaps Achnaslishaig, an old farm-steading between Glenahanty and the road down to Dalsmirren?

I am struggling here to recover the John I knew, but only scraps remain in memory and in my journals, and the truth is that probably a hundred other people still living remember him better, but I'm not going to interview any of them. He appears briefly in two other books of mine,[76] and it'll suffice to end this meagre tribute with the highest praise I can pay him, that, like most country folk of his time, he would always leave whatever he was doing to spend ten or fifteen minutes with a passer-by, and that his talk was always worth hearing.

Leslie Hunter's Granny

Earlier in the year, I noticed a little book among the local Library's display of unwanted stock and decided to buy it. It was a 1977 edition of *Three Scottish Colourists*, first published in 1950, and the reasons I wanted it were that its author, T. J. Honeyman (1891-1971), was an uncle of Judy's father, Alex Honeyman, and that we didn't have a copy. It consisted of a lengthy introduction and three essays on the artists S. J. Peploe, F. C. B. Cadell and Leslie Hunter.

While leafing through the book at home, I noticed, in the account on Hunter, a reference (p 95) which at once aroused my interest: 'On the maternal side Hunter's forbears were also of good farming stock. His grandmother came from the south end of Kintyre, and after her marriage lived in Glasgow to the ripe age of ninety-two.' Who was she?

Judy began researching her that very day. George Hunter – he later adopted 'Leslie' as his forename, though he didn't own it even as a middle name – was born in 1877 in Rothesay, where his father William was a chemist and druggist. His mother was Jeanie Stewart, born in Glasgow. Her parents, who married in 1831, were James Stewart, blacksmith in Glasgow, and Catherine Gilchrist. Catherine it was who belonged to Kintyre. She claimed Campbeltown Parish as her birthplace in censuses, but Judy was unable to locate a baptismal entry for her. Her parents, who married in 1798, were Archibald Gilchrist, Gartnacopaig, and Mary McIsaac, Feochaig.

The Gartnacopaig link explains this incongruous-seeming account; equally, I could have included it with Feochaig (p 84). The earliest record of a McIsaac in Kintyre is 1505, when 'Lachlan McEsak' stood surety for Gilcrest (Gilchrist) McCor in Kilervan, Southend. McIsaacs were in Feochaig from the seventeenth to the nineteenth century, with a branch in Corphin and a boat-owning branch in Campbeltown. The Gilchrist family was strongly represented in the Largieside and around Clachan from the seventeenth century, but in the Work Horse Tax list of 1797 the one exception in the six Gilchrist farmers recorded was Neil in 'Gartinopaig'.[77]

Little is known of Hunter's grandmother, Catherine Gilchrist. Honeyman, however, remarked that 'This wonderful old lady was remembered by her grandchildren as a great reader with a marvellous memory and a fund of stories about Old Glasgow'. Her husband, James Stewart, had been in the Army and fought at Waterloo, and his medal and discharge papers, signed by the Duke of Wellington, were still in the family (p 96). After James's death, Catherine married again, to a printer William Tafts, and died in 1899. She would almost certainly have been a Gaelic speaker, at least in her youth.

George Leslie Hunter has been described as 'the least consistent of the Colourists yet in some respects the most interesting'.[78] He visited Kintyre at least once, in 1909, when, on 24 June, he signed the Campbeltown Free Library visitors' book. Murdo MacDonald has speculated that Hunter may have come to Kintyre to visit the scenes which inspired William McTaggart's artistic vision,[79] but he may also have been familiarising himself with scenes from his grandmother's girlhood. Dr Honeyman, who knew Hunter, and whose portrait (now in Glasgow Art Gallery) Hunter painted, wrote of full-length study of the painter, *Introducing Leslie Hunter*, published in 1937.

Honeyman, having survived the First World War, practised medicine in the East End of Glasgow before moving to London to become an art dealer. In 1939 he was appointed Director of Glasgow Art Gallery, in which role he gained fame – and notoriety – with his acquisition, in 1952, of Salvador Dali's *Christ of St. John of the Cross*.

A biography of Honeyman, *From Dali to Burrell*, by Jack Webster, was published in 1997.

Largiebaan cliffs

When I reached the cliffs at Largiebaan, I found a reception party of midges, so I headed down to the end of the long spur above Grianan Dheardruin fort, whose mythical giants-in-residence are recalled in *Kintyre Places and Place-Names* (p 172), and remained there for a couple of hours, relatively untroubled. The sea was as calm as it gets on that Atlantic coast, and my attention soon focused on an unusually large patch of sandy seabed just out from the caves.

When the intermittent sunlight poured on to it through the clear water, the sand assumed a turquoise hue, and I began to imagine the appearance there of a school of whales or dolphins, each mysterious creature marvellously defined against the background of pure sand. While the cetacean fantasy was still running in my head, I saw a movement on the sea's surface above the sandy patch and immediately thought – a fish! It wasn't a fish, but a scart – whether cormorant or shag, I couldn't say at that distance – which was doubtless on the hunt for fish. With binoculars, I soon noticed several more, and I'd watch first one and then another plunge with a little leap, and follow it as it scooted purposefully over the seabed. To amuse myself, I began timing the birds' underwater forays, but co-ordinating watch-checking and binocular-direction proved tricky, and I settled for thirty seconds as an acceptable average.

When, from my great height, I saw one bird excrete, the phenomenon was noted as a probable lifetime first. 'The squirt of white, illumined by the sunlight, looked almost attractive,' I noted eagerly; but the aesthetic stimulus was momentary, because the white jet dispersed in seconds, and after five or six visions of spurting bird-shit, my interest too dispersed.

I had been hearing the persistent crooning of fulmars and turned my binoculars to the cliff face above the caves, where I picked out a few nesting. After prolonged scanning of the cliffs north to the Aignish and beyond to the Gulls' Den, a curious perception began to intrude on my consciousness. Since my first visit to Largiebaan almost fifty years ago, my impression of the cliffs has been governed by a sense of awe; but, somehow, the scale seemed to have diminished and, as I noted in my journal: 'It's almost as though I could reach out and scoop up the whole prospect with the sweep of an arm. How strange is that? Normally, the cliffs from here seem stupendous, almost intimidating, but not today. The entire vision seems compact and comprehensible.'

It was time to leave, before the magic of Largiebaan evaporated completely.

3 June: Hillside aglow

Just before sunset, Judy and I cycled to Kilkerran for a walk around the graveyard. As we were meandering back to our bikes, peering at inscriptions in the fading light, I happened to turn and saw a sight which caused me to exclaim: 'Look at that!'

'That' – or a slice of that – might have been captured by a photographer or recaptured by a painter, but a writer has no chance. None the less ... A broad beam of mellow sunlight lit the hill-slope above the graveyard, and the dense flowering rhododendrons glowed exquisitely for about five minutes. The effect was all the more startling because there wasn't a blink of sun anywhere else on the visible landscape.

As usual, when encounters with the spectacular occur, neither of us had a camera. Mine usually sits in a pocket of the jacket I was wearing that evening, but had been removed to recharge the battery, and I missed a photographic opportunity that will probably never recur for me in that particular spot. Would one of those photographs pre-empted by omission have made an eye-catching front cover for this book? I rather think so!

6 June: Second Water

En route to Corphin by bicycle, I stopped at the Second Water and sat on the seaside parapet of the bridge for lunch. The parapet tops are formed of rounded stones, and I sat – as I have sat for the past twenty-five years – on the only one which is relatively flat. The comfort is not only physical, but emotional, or, to project the analysis into hazier distance, spiritual; which is to say that when I'm sitting there, I'm back in past days with companions who occupied those days – and those stones – with me. I was thinking particularly of my oldest daughter Sarah, who was due to give birth to a baby – my first grandchild – that very day. As it happened, Lachlan Gillies, 10lbs, wouldn't arrive until the 20th.

19. Sarah Martin, aged six, with her bike at the Second Water bridge, 18 July 1994. Photograph by the author.

While I was sitting in the warm sunlight, a runner appeared from the south. Few runners are willing to upset their carefully measured self-timing by stopping to chat, but this runner was an 'old timer' in the sport, and, judging by his first remark to me – 'I'm getting too old for this!' – he welcomed a respite. Roddy Girvan is my age – I have known him since primary school – and has been a keen runner for most of his life. I'd encountered him on the Learside earlier that summer, but we were both in motion and merely exchanged a greeting in passing. He now told me he ran once a week from Balnabraid road-end to Feochaig and back.

I was surprised to hear Roddy remark that he finds milestones useful when he is running, because few road-users pay any attention to them, and even fewer notice when they disappear. When my daughter Bella was eight years old and walking with me near Dalsmirren, I pointed out the seventh milestone to her. Her response, 'What's a milestone?', prompted the following meditation: 'The milestone has indeed lost its value in this modern society in which most folk speed from place to place in cars. Not so, of course, when the horse-drawn cart and gig, and, later, the bicycle, were the means of getting around the countryside, not forgetting the humble feet. Knowing how far one was from one's destination mattered rather more then ...'[80]

But back to Roddy, who told me that during one of his runs he found the seventh milestone near Feochaig knocked over – presumably by a verge-cutting machine – and that he returned with a spade and put it back in position. If milestones are out of fashion, traffic signs are very much in fashion, and I drew Roddy's attention to one which must have appeared a few days earlier at the bridge. I'd noticed it just before he appeared, and was astonished by its presence there. It's the one depicting an adult and child hand-in-hand and signifying 'pedestrians in road ahead'. Vehicles are scarce on the Learside, and walkers scarcer, so what was the sign doing there? The only explanation I could venture was that the Learside road was about to be incorporated into the Kintyre Way and that the sign was a legal requirement. Before heading away, I photographed the sign, with, in the background, Roddy chugging up the brae.

Alastair Thompson remembered his uncle Gilbert getting him to round up some friends to harvest a potato crop at the Second Water. 'It was tough picking, as the numerous stones in the soil looked like potatoes,' Alastair said. After he had 'burst' fingers at the lifting, he and his mates were paid less than they believed their effort was worth, and Alastair was elected to approach Gilbert for more money, which he reluctantly paid.

Sandy Helm

Teddy Lafferty remembers Gilbert's father-in-law, Sandy Helm, rotating both small fields on the north side of the Second Water with oats, potatoes and grass. Sandy would invite the 'Coasters' he met there to 'Take a meal of tatties any time you want', but as the shore grew in popularity in the early 1950s, and more cars appeared, some newcomers abused the privilege and took potatoes home with them.

Sandy Helm was the saviour of the day, or night, on Teddy's first camping trip to the Second Water in 1949. He had gone with Pat O'Hara and Bobby Riddell, like himself apprentice tradesmen in town. The tent, which they pitched on the south side of the burn, had no groundsheet. They were prepared for that, because it didn't come with one, but it also lacked poles, which Teddy had somehow forgotten. They were hopelessly searching the shore for sticks they could improvise with, when Sandy appeared from the hill. When the problem was explained to him, he said, 'Come up to Auchenhoan and I'll give you a couple of hazel sticks'. Teddy accompanied him to the farmhouse and received the sticks from Sandy's stock, which he was seasoning for crook-making, at which craft he was an acknowledged expert.

20. *The Second Water, looking north from Corphin brae and showing the two small fields and a heath fire still smouldering, 1989. Photograph by the author.*

Abandoned in the night

The Second Water was the scene of a nocturnal folly which Alastair Thompson had the misfortune to be involved in. Had his companion been other than this writer, the night could have been memorable for different reasons; or it could have been reduced in memory to a few dull fragments.

We had met up with two girls who were holidaying in Southend and had a car. Someone – Alastair, I suspect – proposed a night of fire-lit romance. All four of us arrived at the Second Water after the pubs closed, and a fire was lit; but, far from being a scene-enhancer for the anticipated pairing-off, the fire was where I, in a drunken impulse, decided to deposit my feet. I remember very little of the night, but one memory endures. I am listening to the girls enthusing over a holiday in Spain, and when one of them declares that the highlight of the trip was witnessing General Franco's appearance at some public event, I am overcome by a surge of disgust and stick my feet in the fire. Within minutes, Alastair and I are watching the tail-lights of the car disappear, suddenly aware that we are stranded on a remote beach with five miles of road ahead of us.

After the girls' departure, I remember nothing, but Alastair, who was presumably more sober than I, does. 'We sat and ate some left-over picnic stuff on the moon-soaked headland', he recounted with poetic flair. I'd taken along a transistor radio – another romantic idea, I suppose – which was tuned to Radio Caroline or some other pirate station, and walked the whole way home with my eyes closed and the radio held to my ear. The nearer we got to town, the more the signal faded, until finally there was only 'white noise', which I 'seemed to enjoy'.

I wouldn't have known even the year of the fiasco had one of the letters of mine which Alastair preserved not alluded to it. In fact, the entire letter, which was dated 24 August 1971, was an attempt to justify my conduct that night. I was nineteen, with, it appears to me now, the emotional development of a fifteen-year-old. Re-reading the letter forty-odd years on, I heard the voice of the misfit who still inhabits Angus Martin's psyche, but whose naïve idealism struggles for expression under layers of calculated cynicism and emotional reserve.

In the first draft of this book, I quoted a chunk of the letter, but later decided to leave it, except for the final few lines, where it belongs, in that letter and in its own time. What interpretations Alastair drew from my self-serving pleadings, I never found out, or if I did I have forgotten. We set out on a sexual adventure and returned alone and disgraced. To accentuate the sense of failure, Alastair later heard that a friend of ours had satisfied himself – and the girls, too, perhaps – on precisely the implicit terms I had contrived to reject. Here are these final few lines, upbeat and delusional to the last: 'I only hope that I didn't spoil the evening for you. I hope you were as delighted as I was by that hour's moon-gazing and sea-gazing. That to me was more rewarding than anything that pair could have offered us ...'

Eddie Stone

Worse things have happened at the Second Water, to be sure. Four years earlier, a contemporary, Eddie Stone, fractured his left leg and right foot. He was taking part in an exercise there with the local Army Cadet Force in December 1967, and fell on a slippery rock. Two fellow-cadets, Neil Livingstone and Norrie O'May, ran to Auchenhoan farmhouse to telephone for an ambulance. Meanwhile, the remaining cadets, under Sergeant Peter Scott, applied their first-aid knowledge and assembled a rough stretcher. He was taken to Campbeltown Cottage Hospital and then transferred to the Southern General Hospital in Glasgow.[81]

His complete recovery may be assumed, for he went on to become a sergeant in the Special Air Service and gained celebrity status in his role as a trainer in the documentary series *SAS: Are You Tough Enough*, which, in the pursuit of entertainment, exposed members of the public to the rigours of the SAS selection process.

On 1 October 2004, George McSporran, dog Benjie and I had an evening walk on Ben Gullion. We set out from Narrowfield, and for half-an-hour, on either side of sunset, had a barn owl in view as it hunted over the south bank of Crosshill Loch. On our way home along Kilkerran road, I lifted a yellow 'post-it' note from the pavement at the Paddling Pool with 'FRIDAY AIRPORT 10AM EDDIE STONE' written on it. We conjectured that he had flown in that day and been collected by taxi, and that the driver, having completed the hire, had thrown away the memo.

Bush and bees

I'm back in 6 June. I almost decided to turn back at the Second Water, but there was a botanical puzzle pressing for a solution. George and I had both noticed, back in May, a curious-looking bush at the Ru. Neither of us mentioned it at the time, which was odd, because when we are walking together just about everything gets mentioned, from town gossip to the merest of observations from nature. When one of us did bring up that observation, we discovered we had both assumed the shrub to be juniper, which is rare in Kintyre, so rare, indeed, in our experience, that the Goings, near the Mull, was the only location we could claim with certainty to have seen it. Two guesses from distance don't, however, constitute a botanical record, therefore I spoke to Agnes Stewart, my first resort for advice when botanical questions arise, and she asked me to secure a clipping for identification.

I was now at the Ru, intending only to get the clipping and then head home. The shore was now overgrown and difficult underfoot, and the possibility of breaking a leg on that remote coast – I hadn't met a soul there all year – or stepping on an adder flickered at the back of my mind like a film running on a television screen in the corner of a room; I wasn't watching it, but was aware of it. The bush I wanted to reach was below the cliff, and I set off towards it through dense undergrowth, cutting away brambles with the secateurs I carried in my rucksack; but that route soon appeared unnecessarily long and difficult, so I turned back, continued south for a bit and chose a more direct approach.

The going was much easier, and I was soon at the rock with its overhanging bush. I saw at once that it wasn't juniper, but a species of cotoneaster. I snipped off a sprig, bearing tiny red flowers and clusters of unripened berries, and tucked it into my rucksack. The bush, to my delight, was swarming with bees – close on a hundred, I estimated – which I photographed as they bustled about the flowers. There is an immense carpet of the same shrub on a slope of the headland, and I imagined the numbers of bees congregated there. Two days later, while wheeling my bicycle up Ballimenach brae, I drifted into a reverie, focused on the bush: 'I was reflecting on all the bees that had intimate contact with it, crawling on it, feeding from it, and imagined myself a bee, hovering at one of the flowers, and instead of the flower's being tiny – my human perspective – it was huge, the size of a football.'

On my way back from the Ru, I called at Agnes Stewart's house and gave her the cutting. She at once identified cotoneaster and said she would examine it later and give me her opinion. Two evenings later, in an e-mail, she referred me to M.H. Cunningham and A. G. Kenneth's seminal study *The Flora of Kintyre*, which records (p 22) *Cotoneaster microphyllus* 'south of Johnstone's Point', and notes: 'Not infrequent as an escape, well away from cultivation.' 'My' cotoneaster was north of Johnston's Point, but close enough. She showed the sprig to Ian Teesdale, another local botany enthusiast, but he doubted he was looking at *Cotoneaster microphyllus* and sent the specimen to an expert, Heather McHaffie. On 23 June, he brought Agnes a note he had received from Ms. McHaffie, and she was certain the plant was *Cotoneaster horizontalis*, the common one.

8 June: Balnabraid

Balnabraid is one of a cluster of old farms which successively merged with Auchenhoan into one big sheep-farm. I have a special attachment to Balnabraid because a McKerral family – connected with the John McKerral who entered my genealogy on my mother's side (p 205) – farmed it from 1770 until 1838. 'Malcolm MacKerral', which appeared in my first collection of poems, *The Larch Plantation*, is about Balnabraid, but the poem's catalogue of misfortunes is largely fictitious. The narrative part ends with eviction and the coming of sheep, and the climax – quoted below – addresses the loss of cultural identity, a theme which I have pursued repeatedly in my verse.

> There was no end to the known land.
> You looked, and there were names
> on every shape around you.
> The language had its homes.
>
> Words had their lives in rivers;
> they coursed them to the sea.
> Words were great birds on mountains,
> crying down on history.
>
> Words were stones that waited
> in the silence of the fields
> for the voices of the people
> whose tenures there had failed.
>
> You knew those names, MacKerral;
> your father placed them in your mouth
> when language had no tragic power
> and you ran in your youth.

You ran in the house of the word
and pressed your face upon the glass
to watch the mute processions
of your grave ancestors pass.

Look back on what you cannot alter.
Not a stone of it is yours to turn.
All that you leave with now:
lost words for the unborn.

The poem was written around 1986, and I remember where I wrote it – sitting outside the Wee Man's Cove at New Orleans – and why I wrote it: I was bored. In a sense, the poem came from nowhere – I was trawling my unconscious – but, of course, it was waiting to be born. On another day it would have appeared in a different form and might have joined the pile of dud efforts which has accumulated ever since I began writing.

'Malcolm MacKerral' was one of two poems of mine which Douglas Dunn selected for *The Faber Book of Twentieth Century Poetry*, but I had no inkling of the honour until the anthology was published in 1992 and I received a congratulatory telephone call from a friend in Penicuik, Margaret Macaulay (who died on 5 October 2014, at the age of eighty). Macdonald Publishers had brought out *The Larch Plantation* in 1990, but the proprietor, Callum Macdonald, retired soon afterwards and the business passed to The Saltire Society. The request for permission to publish the poems had gone to that Society, but instead of referring it to me, the copyright-holder, someone had agreed on my behalf and hadn't bothered to let me know, resulting in the first dispute I had with The Saltire Society.

Balnabraid is one of my favourite ruins. Quite apart from the McKerral connection (which, incidentally, Margaret Macaulay shared) the steading, with its added sheep-fank, is in a lovely setting, overlooking Balnabraid Glen and enhanced by a line of mature deciduous trees in the gully of the burn which flows past the ruin. A big sycamore has grown inside the walls of the ruin, rooted under the floor which generations of feet once trod.

Sandy McSporran, as a boy, climbed into that tree and claimed to have seen a hare from there. When his identification was questioned, he explained that 'It was hairier than a rabbit', a neat pun. He was there (30 October 1988) with his father George, Judy, Sarah – a baby at the time – and me. We continued to the top of Balnabraid Glen and sat on high moorland, enjoying, in astonishing clarity of light, phenomenal views to Arran, Ayrshire, the Lake District, and Ireland. On our way home, we watched a short-eared owl quartering the twilit moors at the back of Ben Gullion.

21. *In the hills north of Balnabraid Glen, 30 October 1988, L-R: Angus Martin, Sarah Martin, Sandy McSporran and George McSporran. Photograph by Judy Martin.*

Jimmy MacDonald has photographed short-eared owls and various raptors hunting over the grassy ridge to the east of Balnabraid ruin. In the east-facing gable he constructed an improvised hide, through which he can train the lens of his camera. When I began visiting Balnabraid in the early 1980s, the fire-place, where Jimmy has rigged his cover, was intact, but the lintel-stone later fell. It was still in place on 21 February 1988, a day of sunshine, when Judy and I took Sarah there. I photographed Sarah in her baby-carrier in front of the old fire-place, and reflected on the passage of generations. I now have more cause for reflection, because Sarah is herself a mother.

On 7 June 2013, I spent an hour at Balnabraid and instead of returning by the track to the main road, took the path up the side of the glen until it ran out, then climbed to the top of the hill and descended to the track. I knew I'd be passing a spot with personal associations, and as I approached it I experienced one of those exquisite sensations of re-entering the past. I remembered walking inland from the Second Water with Benjie, to return home by the back of Ben Gullion, and of falling asleep in the heather. I sat and rested at the spot, or as close as I could get to it from memory, and thought back to that day. I couldn't remember much about it, so checked my journals at home. The date was 1 August 1999, and I was walking home from Polliwilline, where I'd sat at a beach fire until two in the morning, drinking Bushmills whisky. Not surprisingly, I didn't feel 'wonderfully fit', and as Benjie snoozed at my side in the mid-day heat, I willingly joined him.

11 June: Minen

I had been working on place-names projects intermittently since 1999, and that work was coming to an end in 2014 with the parishes of Killean and Kilchenzie, Kilcalmonell, and Saddell and Skipness compiled but not quite completed. Many questions, particularly on locations, remained unanswered, and I knew that some of them never would be answered because the knowledge was gone; never the less, I was keen to find out as much as I could before publishing the booklets. Minen in upper Ballochroy Glen was one of the settlements I was keen to visit. There were three sites bearing the name 'Minen', and, to complicate matters, one of these had flirted with two other identities.

My guides for the day were Alex Mackinnon, retired – or not quite retired – farmer at Cleongart, and his wife Margaret, a daughter of Adam MacPhail (p 47). Alex belongs to an old and once numerous Largieside farming family and was brought up at Achnafad, south of Ballochroy. He had contacted me after I published an appeal in the *Kintyre Magazine* in 2013 for assistance with place-names I couldn't precisely locate, and we had already met twice with beneficial results for the project.

We drove up the glen road as far as the present shepherd's house, 'Minen Cottage', a structure of idiosyncratic design. Having parked the car there, we set out on foot along the track to the next Minen, a steading of more traditional character, but uninhabited. The remains of an Iron Age dun, known simply as An Dùnan, 'The Little Fort', occupy a rocky spur south-west of the steading. This is the Minen which attracted two additional names. It is 'Auchabrad' on O.S. Sheet CCXXIV, surveyed in 1867, 'Auchavraid' in the 1898 revision,

'Auchameanach' in 1915, becoming 'Minen' on O.S. Sheet 76, revised in 1924. But I'll leave the matter in that state of unresolved confusion, as I left it in *Place-Names of the Parish of Kilcalmonell*, finally published in November 2014.

Margaret described the steading as 'very neat', but decided to stay outside while Alex and I examined the living-room/kitchen. Murdo MacDonald had been to Ballochroy Glen three days previously with a party of Kintyre Antiquarian Society members, led by Elizabeth Marrison, and had peered into the 'best room', the ceiling of which has collapsed. The minister, doctor and other important persons would be ushered in there when they visited. What he saw intrigued him. The lay-out suggested that entry was through a bedroom, and the fire-place was 'very sophisticated', having late nineteenth century Delft tiles affixed to both sides of the cast-iron surround. A copper smoke-hood, which he had seen in a photograph taken in the 1990s, had disappeared.

22. *Mid Minen, 11 June 2014. Photograph by the author.*

Alex remembered being there as a boy with his father, William Mackinnon, in the early 1940s, when the shepherd was Ewan

Campbell. They went there by horse and cart, with a 'Dux' plough loaded on the cart and a second horse, to make up the plough pair, tagging along on a rope. William was there to plough a patch of land for Campbell to grow oats, potatoes and turnips in, and Alex remarked that they would have been nearly as long getting to Minen and back as the ploughing itself would have taken. William was a Gaelic speaker, and Ewan Campbell's first language, too, was Gaelic, so Gaelic was the language of choice at Minen. I remember reflecting that forty years ago, when I was tape-recording in Kintyre, there were still some native Gaelic speakers around, but that it would be hard now to find many sons or daughters of these Gaelic speakers left alive; Alex Mackinnon is one of them.

The Achnafad plough, by a similar arrangement, also saw service at Courshelloch when James Strang was shepherd there; and William Mackinnon, with his horse and cart, helped the Strangs flit from Courshelloch to Lagloskin. At the same time as the Strangs were moving out, a Gillies family was moving in, from Achnadrian. Whitsun (15 May) and Martinmas (11 November) were the term days when these moves took place, and the saying 'Saturday flitting, not a long sitting' was well known as a superstitious warning, meaning that if one moved into a new place on a Saturday, one wouldn't be there long. James Strang it was who taught Alex's sister Margaret to knit using hen feathers as needles.

Alex remembered Ewan Campbell's having three daughters and a son. I found two of the daughters, Johan and Dolina, in the register of admission for Rhunahaorine School. They both enrolled on 6 January 1942, having come from Clachan School. The third daughter was Kate-Ann, and she was probably the eldest since there is no record of her having attended Rhunahaorine School, which is also the case with the son 'Shonny' (John).

Historical references to Minen are sparse – in decades of research, only two have emerged – but, to be honest, I'm not complaining. There is so much suffering and death in this book, it was a relief to go somewhere which didn't have an historical cloud hanging darkly over it.

In 1810, John MacNab in Minen took Hugh Bell, Low Ugadale, to court for £1 1s, 'the price of a cow which he failed to take away'. Bell counter-claimed that MacNab had 'taken a mare and foal from him which he believed he had purchased from the pursuer', and MacNab's claim was dismissed.[82]

In 1938, a black-faced ewe was found by the Minen shepherd with five lambs lying beside her. 'This is a most unusual thing, and it is very rare that one sheep has so many lambs,' the report commented.[83] The shepherd wasn't named – only Mrs Gladys Pollok, owner of Ronachan Estate – but Alex reckoned he would have been Archie Leitch, who retired to Auchavraid, Clachan, with his sister Mary.

Well, here's the cloud, but not over Minen. Mary Leitch was found dead, at the age of seventy-seven, near Auchavraid, in December 1948. She had gone to Clachan post office on a Saturday to collect her pension, and was seen by Flora MacPhail that evening at Loup road-end, 'making for the path across the fields'. When she failed to return home, police and villagers searched 'the stormswept countryside' all that night and all the following day, and were about to resume the search on Monday when word came that Miss Leitch's body had been found by Angus MacPhail, farm-manager, Kilchamaig Cottage. She had strayed from the path in darkness and died on the face of the hill.[84]

We carried on and cut off the track across moorland towards a large, conspicuous rock on the skyline above Loch Garasdale. Murdo MacDonald, too, had been at the rock, three days earlier, and noticed a feature which, since he walked right around it and I didn't, had escaped my attention – a huge split, which he speculated might have been caused by a lightning strike.

We continued from there until we came in sight of the third and final Minen, which was the original, farming settlement. (The thought occurs to me that each successive habitation was built ever nearer to the coast, with its denser population and amenities.) We didn't venture all the way to it, but sat and looked down on it. It appeared to be a typical late eighteenth/early nineteenth century long-house, reduced to low ruins. The earliest records I could find were in the Kilcalmonell register of births and baptisms: among others, Duncan McGilchrist, tenant in 'Minen' in 1784, and John Turner, 'Minans', whose 'natural daughter', Girzel, was born there in 1799.

Ian MacDonald described that ruin in 1993: 'Meanen … is very strongly built as it lies in a very exposed situation. There are huge stones on the corner foundations and most of the stone lintels are still in position although it is many years since it was last inhabited.' He mentioned a large crannog (lake-dwelling) about 50 metres off the south shore of the loch, not recorded in the Royal Commission on the Ancient and Historical Monuments of Scotland's volume on Kintyre.[85]

But the strongest memory of that day has nothing to do with history. On our way out to the last of the Minens, I noticed fungi growing on the high side of the track. I climbed the bank to take a look and was completely unprepared for what I saw – horse mushrooms! I had never before found any of these delicious big mushrooms in Kintyre before the beginning of July. I was so surprised I questioned my identification, but, having studied and sniffed the specimens, I decided I couldn't be wrong and picked one of them, which Judy and I ate that evening ... and survived.

15 June: The Old Road

Judy had decided that afternoon to walk the Learside road to Polliwilline for an overnight stay at our caravan. I offered to accompany her part of the way and suggested we take the hill track from Glenramskill to Ballimenach brae. Until 1851, when the coast road was extended from Kildalloig to Auchenhoan, the 'Old Road', as it is known, was the only route to the Learside and its string of hill farms.[86] Being traffic-free, it offers a more relaxing route on to the Learside, and the only walker I recall ever meeting on the road was Teddy Lafferty.

On 15 June, a surprise or two was in store for Judy and me. We were still on the Low Glenramskill track when we noticed two walkers approaching from the Old Road. We greeted them and they stopped. My leading question, predictably, was: 'Are you here on a visit?' The question, as well as being predictable, was unnecessary – they looked foreign and were dressed for serious hiking – but I was probing for a little background. I got the information I wanted: a father and son from the Netherlands; the son worked in Edinburgh; the father had visited him there and they had decided to 'go west' for a walking tour and had chosen Kintyre; they had spent several days on the Kintyre Way and were now returning to town to take the Ardrossan ferry that evening. (Just after 5 p.m., from Sweetie Bella's Quarry, where I parted from Judy, we would hear the *Isle of Arran*'s engines pounding as she left Campbeltown Loch, and see her pass Davaar Island.)

One encounter on the Old Road was remarkable enough, but there was another ahead. Having passed the little reservoir, we saw a man and a woman looking around them. Their identity was soon established: Yvonne Wilkin and Alexander Kempshall from Bristol. I had asked the Dutch visitors how they knew of the Old Road, and the son had flourished a map in response. I now repeated the question, and the answer was that Yvonne and Alex had been coming to Kintyre for many years, Alex especially, and knew the area well. The interrogation was now directed exclusively at Alex, who explained that his mother belonged to Campbeltown. Her name was Frances McIver Black and she was a daughter of Alex 'Roarin' Black, a retired fisherman I had tape-recorded in 1978. They had travelled to Kintyre by bus from Aberdeen after a week's holiday in Orkney and Shetland, and would be staying in Westbank Guesthouse for the remainder of the week. I left a note there the following day and we met up for a meal in the Argyll Arms Hotel on the last evening of their holiday. I'd cycled up from Southend that afternoon (p 132), and they happened to be on the bus which overtook me past Keprigan.

Three cows

On the Learside road, Judy and I had a third encounter. We had intended eating at the Second Water bridge and parting there, but the day was well advanced and somewhere nearer seemed more sensible. I suggested we go through the gate above the First Water and sit at the little burn which enters the sea just north of the Water itself.

I have an enduring affection for that spot for one reason alone. I stopped there in June 1981 and photographed three cows lying in sunshine on the ridge above the stream. I came across the photograph recently, and realised why I always stop to look – or, if I'm cycling, glance – at that spot. It holds, for me, the essence of summers past – the green, bracken-clad ridge, the cows resting peacefully on it, and, beyond, a blue Kilbrannan Sound, blue Arran mountains, and, over all, a blue sky streaked with white cloud. Without the image I'd have forgotten that moment and the cows who shared it with me. The poor creatures are long dead, but that photograph holds them in a moment of their lives.

The spot was too windy, so we abandoned the plan and returned to the road. Just as we were crossing the fence, a car stopped. Jimmy MacDonald and his fiancée, Katrina Macfarlane, were returning from an otter search in Johnston's Bay. Minutes later, another car appeared and Katrina had to drive off. Judy and I sat in Sweetie Bella's Quarry, ate our rolls and parted.

Willie Watson and turnip-thinning

Passing the Sheep Fanks at Kildalloig, I noticed a man ahead of me, and I was sure I was seeing Willie Watson. I was also sure that he was heading for his car, which would be parked at the corner, and the prospect of a lift to town prompted an acceleration of pace. He was already in the car and reversing to leave when I came in sight of him and waved my cap. He saw me and waited, and with seconds to spare I had secured the desired lift. Willie, who was brought up on North Muasdale farm, is a regular in summer on that stretch of road, and, in winter, on Kilkerran road, without his car, and I have met him often over the years.

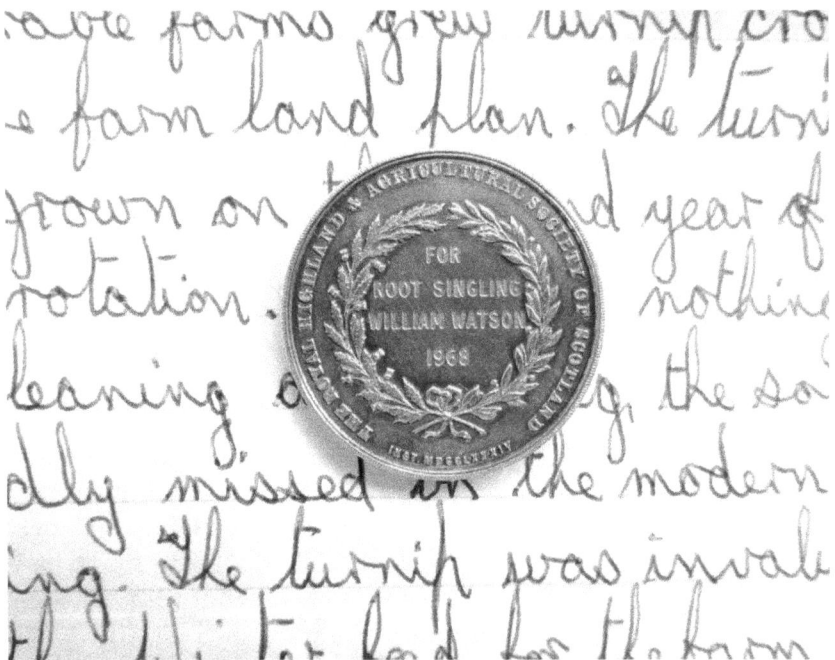

23. *Willie Watson's medal for turnip-singling in 1968, photographed, by Judy Martin, on a page of his 'mini essay'.*

While we chatted in the car outside his house, he produced from the glove compartment a medal he'd been carrying with him, in its little blue case, to show to John McLachlan, farm manager of Kildalloig Estate, next time they met on the road. He'd won the medal, which was awarded by the Royal Highland and Agricultural Society, in a turnip-singling competition for young farmers held in 1968 in the shore field just past the Sheep Fanks. Willie remembered the soil there as being very stony, so that the drills 'wouldn't stand up'. The medal was crafted by Alexr. Kirkwood & Son, Edinburgh, and was neatly inscribed: 'FOR ROOT SINGLING/WILLIAM WATSON/1968.' I reflected on how much it would cost to produce and engrave such a medal nowadays, even if any society considered the encouragement of turnip-thinning skills a worthy cause.

Several weeks after our conversation, I wrote to Willie to ask for further information on that competition, and received rather more of a response than I'd anticipated. He left the medal with me in case I might want to photograph it – I did – and also left a mini-essay he'd written on turnip-growing. I reproduce that too.

In the three decades after the war, almost all arable farms grew turnip crops as part of the farm land plan. The turnip crop was grown in the second year of a seven year rotation. There was nothing better for cleaning and airing the soil and it is sadly missed in modern day farming. The turnip was invaluable for the Winter feed for the farm animals.

During the above period, the farming community was abuzz with young people, farm families, and servants, male and female. Young farmers' clubs were formed and this was a great source of entertainment and rivalry. The thinning competition was one of those events with a stand-off between Campbeltown and Largieside clubs.

Each entrant's challenge was to single out the turnip plants to a very high standard in a given time. Two drills at 100 yards each had to be completed in 1½ hours. The result that was looked for was, leaving the best single plants at 12 inches apart on a high drill, giving the plants a clear start away from the excess pulled into the drill centre.

There were three classes.
1. The Ladies' class.
2. The Junior class.
3. The Open class.

This was normally judged by three judges and the overall winner received a silver medal from the Agricultural Society of Scotland. I was fortunate in my competitive days to win two such medals. Competition was very keen, with around thirty thinners taking part, approximately five ladies, twelve novices and fifteen in the open class.

As the years advanced, farming methods changed, with grass being turned into silage for main Winter keep. The result of this was turnip crops disappeared, as did the next generation of thinners, so turnip singling came to an abrupt end, with the last competition held in 1982 at Archie Clark's South Beachmore Farm, Muasdale. Archie himself was no mean thinner, as he won the Agricultural medal in three consecutive years.

Hope this gives you an insight into the humble 'neep'. Willie.

16 June: High Glenadale

The weather forecast was excellent and I decided to cycle to High Glenadale, where I had unfinished business. I had been there with Judy in 2012 and noticed two intriguing stone pillars, which I hadn't thought to examine at the time.

I set off at 1.15, stopping at Robert Brown's house on the Homeston road to deliver a book. He was in his garden and we chatted for ten minutes, mostly about golden eagles, his lifelong passion. He paid me with a ten pound note and I shoved it into a pocket and continued my journey. Later, I decided the note mightn't be safe there – I'd lost money in the past by pulling something from a pocket and dislodging a note with it – so I folded it and stuffed it into the little zipped pouch attached to the cross-bar of the bike. Still later, I decided to leave the note there indefinitely, so tucked it into a small plastic wallet. This followed a little fantasy which entertained me as I cycled along.

In some future day, Judy and I are cycling together in the countryside and we come to an hotel – specifically, in the daydream, the Argyll Arms in Southend – and stop there. It's a warm day and we simultaneously fancy a pint of beer. Judy hasn't any money with her, since she didn't anticipate a need, and asks me if I have any. 'Only some change in my pocket,' I reply. Then I remember the note in the pouch. We chain the bikes outside the hotel and have our beer.

I sat for a while at the old ruin at Glenahanty, eating a tomato-filled 'barm biscuit' and drinking tea. The last time I'd sat there, my lunch was interrupted by a couple who appeared on the road. I hailed them from my half-concealed resting-place and they stopped to speak. I'd assumed they had come off the Kintyre Way, but no; they had been to the top of Cnoc Moy to claim it as a 'Marilyn', and were now returning to their car to drive to the Mull and climb another Marilyn. 'They' were Eric Young and Anne Bunn, and a Marilyn – a pun on 'Munro', of course – is a hill with a 'relative height' of at least 150 metres (492 feet), regardless of 'absolute height', meaning that any definably independent summit of 150 meters or more qualifies.

That was 11 March, and I'm now back in 16 June. I filled a pipe and set off for the foot of the Bruach Dearg for the long push up to Largiebaan. While free-wheeling to the bridge, a male orange-tip butterfly (*Anthocharis cardamines*) almost collided with me. Jimmy MacDonald once described them as whites which had their wings dipped in tomato soup, and that's as good a description as any. They are very distinctive, yet I can't say I noticed any until two or three years ago. Agnes Stewart identified her first ever in 2004, and documented an 'explosion' of numbers in 2011.[87]

The Bruach is steep, rutted and stony, and is the only hill road I've ever been on where I've had to brake on the way up – to stop the bike slipping back and taking me with it! Mid-way to Gartnacopaig, I heard an approaching engine, and a shepherd passed me on a small tracked vehicle, with a dog on board. Out there, the roar of the engine sounded decidedly sinister emerging through the natural silence.

At the turn-off to High Glenadale, past Largiebaan steading, I noted the time, 4.25. I was curious as to how long the run out to High Glenadale would take me. The answer wasn't long in coming – 15 minutes. It's a good road and downhill most of the way. The return stage was rather more demanding, as I knew it would be, and took almost 45 minutes.

Having reached High Glenadale, I decided to examine the pillars immediately. They stand in strange isolation to the east of the steading and I set off towards them following the burn. Soon, however, I encountered marshy ground, which I had to cross carefully. (I should have approached the pillars along the drier south side of the burn, the route I chose going back.) Having taken several photographs of the pillars from different angles, I turned to the question of what they were doing there.

24. *Stone pillars at High Glenadale, 16 June 2014. Photograph by the author.*

Nothing now, obviously, but when I looked around I saw that a ruined stone wall once joined on to them. It ran uphill to the north, and I could make out the foundation of a continuing wall from the other pillar to the burn. The pillars must have formed a gateway to an enclosure, but the ground is now so damp and overgrown it is difficult to imagine how it would have looked a century ago. Across the burn from the pillars, the bank was as green as a lawn and so closely grazed one might have imagined that a mower had been over it earlier in the day.

I crossed the burn to the grass and then on to a level stony expanse. Beyond that gravel bed, there was a bank which looked as though it had formed an earlier loop of the river. I noticed that the pillars were in direct line with the steading, and then saw the old track, overgrown with rushes and edged by bracken. I decided to follow it, found it reasonably dry underfoot, and carried on until it ran out. There must have been a ford across the river, but I couldn't figure out where.

High Glenadale appears to have been last occupied in 1937, by James and Euphemia McLean.[88] That's approaching eighty years ago, ample time for erosion to do its worst. I sat on the track on the south side of the burn and ate the last 'barm' and drank more tea. Then I looked around the steading itself.

The present steading has four compartments, the largest of which was clearly the living area. It was choked with nettles and I had to content myself with looking in through a window. There is a fireplace at each end, suggesting that there may have been a partition – since perished – creating a kitchen/living-room and a bedroom. The structure on the west end of the steading appears, from its wide entrance, to be a cart-shed, and I suppose there would also have been a byre and a stable; but I'm no authority on rural architecture. Entry at the front, which faces the burn, is through a stone porch, and at the back there is a plain door. There are two windows in the front and one at the back. The priority, when the house was built, was minimising draughts, not admitting light, and certainly not framing a nice view. The porch also has a window, the wooden frame of which remains so sound that a finger-nail I pressed into it made little impression.

Next day, I looked at Ordnance Survey Sheet CCLXI, surveyed in 1866. The 'High Glenadale' on that map is the earlier settlement, to the north-west on higher ground. There is a house, with 'sheep fold' attached, beside the river precisely where the roofless shepherd's house now is, but I suspect it pre-dates the present steading – with its unusual bowed roof – and, from its outline on the map, was a more basic structure. There was indeed a marked ford over which the old road I'd looked at must have passed.

Robert McInnes could have answered many of the questions I asked myself that day. Not only was he a shepherd for most of his working life, but he was born at High Glenadale in 1917, the son of a Gaelic-speaking shepherd. It is an isolated house and its location is difficult to describe, but between Largiebaan and the Mull is close enough. Low Glenadale, in Glen Breackerie, is nearest to it on paper, but the track there, which Robert would have walked regularly as a boy attending Glen Breackerie School, has become overgrown and its fords less fordable.

Judy and I took that way to High Glenadale on 15 July 2012, and it wasn't a comfortable route, especially at the river-crossings. I was researching *Kintyre Places and Place-Names* at the time, and Glenadale was one of the names I was pondering. I wanted to look not only at the glen itself, but also at the steading. More specifically,

I wanted to photograph it. As related in that book, I'd gone there for the first time in May 1982, during a day-long hike from Machrihanish. I had taken photographs of the steading that day for Robert, but when I looked for them in my collection I couldn't find them, and, even stranger, the negatives were also missing. It was vexing, but no matter – I'd replace the images. I did, and one of them duly appeared in the book, but when published it was grey and ill-defined.

High Glenadale is roofless now, but when I first saw it in 1982 the corrugated-iron roof was still on it and the interior was in a fair condition. Visitors had written their names on the plastered walls and I copied these into a notebook and then added my own. The names and accompanying dates were all lost after the roof came off and weathering removed the plaster. Among the names recorded in *Kintyre Places and Place-Names* were Jessie McCallum, J. McCallum and Robert McInnes, 9 June 1968, and when Jan Hynd, Robert's daughter, read the list, she wrote to me to say that she believed she was with her father and her aunt and uncle on that walk, when she was nine years old.

While checking journals and notebooks for material for *A Summer in Kintyre*, I was surprised to find that I actually witnessed the early stages of High Glenadale's ruination. I'd quite forgotten I'd been there with Jimmy MacDonald during a hike which took us first to the Inneans and then to Largiebaan. The date was 3 June 1990 and I noted the following: '16.35. Halted at High Glenadale. The tin [*sic*] roof is breaking away and the interior is dilapidated and dung-carpeted. The inscribed plaster is crumbling in parts, but I'm still there, & so is Robert McInnes.'

Jimmy and I ended the walk at Glen Breackerie School, where I knew Judy would be with our infant daughters, Sarah and Amelia, attending a Girl Guides' camp. The school by then had become an outdoor centre, and Jimmy and I reached it just before a deluge. When we arrived, Judy was helping at an open fire in the old playground, where the camp had been set up. Sarah was asleep – the previous night she had sat at the camp-fire until 10 o' clock – and Amelia was amusing herself in a tent. We woke Sarah, and I took her home with me. A visitor, Donald Hunt, had happened to arrive at the centre by car just before Jimmy and I did, and he drove us to town. It occurs to me now that Jimmy and I must have followed Robert McInnes's route to school almost seventy years before.

3 August 2013: High Glenadale

But to Jan Hynd and 2103 ... She hadn't been back at High Glenadale since 1968 and was keen to return with her own daughter, Iona, who would turn twenty-one in August. Jan had taken her to Gartgreillan in Glenlussa, where her mother, Isobel McCallum, was born, but as yet Iona had not made the 'pilgrimage' to Glenadale.

Jan, who lives in Glasgow with her husband Bob, mentioned in her letter that she'd be coming to Kintyre at the end of July and was determined to reach her father's birthplace during that visit. She asked about a road which wasn't there in 1968. This was the road to Carskey from Largiebaan, a section of which has been incorporated into the Kintyre Way. I offered to accompany them as 'guide' for the day, Jan agreed, and arrangements were made. That route seemed to me the better option, having the merit of being road all the way, even if longer than that from Low Glenadale, following the meanderings of Glenadale Water.

She and Iona collected me by car at 1 o' clock, and we took the Homeston road, passing Robert's old peat-bank at Lochorodale on our way. Having parked the car at Achnaslishaig brae, we set off towards Glenahanty, up the Bruach Dearg to Gartnacopaig, past Largiebaan and thence to Glenadale, reminiscing all the way.

By the time I knew Robert and Isobel, they were living in Stewarton, and I'd stop there for a meal and a dram after an afternoon of helping Robert with his peats. Both had a fund of stories, for they grew up in a time when story-telling was still a popular recreation. Entertainment was home-made – it had to be. They enjoyed telling their stories and I enjoyed listening to them. Jan and I recalled some of these stories, but she, understandably, had more. One of them belonged to her own lifetime, and it came up when we were discussing the sudden, astonishing blizzard which struck Kintyre on 22 March 2013, knocking out electricity supplies and causing protracted chaos.

Her anecdote was set in the time of the 'big snow' of February 1963, when Robert was shepherd at Uigle. One of his ewes, remarkably, survived for fully six weeks under a drift, and, when finally dug out, was found to have eaten all her wool. Even after her ordeal, she gave birth to the lamb she was carrying, but never produced another. As Robert remarked, 'All the goodness in her had gone to the lamb'. None the less, she was allowed to live out the remainder of her days in a paddock behind Uigle Cottage. By then she was 'Molly', and Jan remembered returning daily from school and Molly recognising her and running to her to receive a ration of special fodder.

When we reached High Glenadale, we sat at the sheep-fank beside the burn and had lunch. Jan didn't know how long her father had lived there, and neither did I, but I later noticed, in *Kintyre Country Life* (p 83), that his father was shepherd in High Glenadale from 1911 until 1935, information which I must have got from Robert and forgotten; so he was there until he left to make his own way in life.

25. *Jan Hynd with her daughter Iona at High Glenadale, 3 August 2013. Photograph by the author.*

I don't recall having discussed the place with Robert, which I now regret, since there is no anecdote, however slight, by which to visualise him there. Jan, however, recalled Robert telling her that his mother, Janet McLean, grew what he described as 'white lilies' in the garden. When I mentioned these flowers to Agnes Stewart, she recalled having seen them. It took her a while to reckon when, but she decided finally that it must have been in the early 1950s when she walked there with her father, Willie Mitchell. The species, she says, is *Narcissus poeticus*, popularly called 'Easter lilies'. She described them as 'lovely flowers with a delightful scent'. They come in April or May, so we were much too late to see them, if they still appear in the overgrown garden at High Glenadale.

The 'J. McCallum' at High Glenadale in the summer of 1968 was Jock, who was not only Jan's uncle, but also my half-sister Barbara's uncle. My mother, who was Amelia McKenzie, married Jock's half-brother Donald McCallum in 1934, and they had two children, Barbara and Donald, but Donald Snr., a sergeant in the Royal Artillery, drowned near Aleppo, Syria, in June 1943. Jock married Jessie McInnes after his war, and when Robert married Isobel McCallum in 1958, that was the second McCallum union within the McInnes family, though the two McCallum families appear to be unrelated.

Donald McCallum's widow, my mother, remarried in 1949, to Angus Martin, who had survived the war. Had her first husband survived, I, of course, would never have existed, a quirk of fate which unites me with tens of millions of other souls who perished or were born in consequence of that particular cataclysm.

Jock, like Donald, was in the Royal Artillery (201st Anti-Tank Battery), but unlike Donald, and yet another brother, Gilbert, he returned from the war. Captured on 9 June 1940 at St. Valery-en-Coux and incarcerated in Germany, he was, at the end of October 1943, the first repatriated prisoner to return to Campbeltown and was accorded a civic reception.[89] But he brought the war back with him, and would relive its horrors long after 'normality' had been restored to others.

Duncan MacDonald

Three days before my June visit to High Glenadale, I was in Campbeltown Library looking through back issues of the *Campbeltown Courier* and chanced on a report of a shepherd's death in 1945. Duncan MacDonald was middle-aged, unmarried, had a widowed mother who lived in Inverkip, and died suddenly in an unspecified 'infirmary'. He was described platitudinously as 'a well-known figure in the agricultural community of Kintyre'. No one had ever mentioned him to me, nor had he appeared in any photograph I'd seen, yet he spent twenty-five years as a shepherd in south Kintyre, at Glemanuill, High Glenadale, and latterly Largiebaan.[90] Having scribbled these particulars into a notebook, I sat for a while at the microfilm reader thinking about Duncan MacDonald, and finally, in imagination, watched him striding across the Mull hills, a solitary, faceless figure from the past.

Cars off the road on the Learside

I withdrew to the family caravan at Polliwilline on 18 June, since there was to be a wood-burning cooker fitted at 13 Saddell the next day and I didn't want to be around during the upheaval. Mist had been streaming over the Laggan all day, though to north and south perfect sunshine had been reported. I was cycling south, anyway, and had left the mist behind by the time I reached the Second Water.

Near the bottom of the hill past Auchenhoan steading, I encountered a car in a ditch. A girl in the front passenger seat averted her face as I approached, but there was a second girl, with a baby under an arm, at the back of the car, and I stopped to speak to her. I asked her if help was on the way – yes, it was – and then asked her if she had met another car. That, too, was a 'yes'. I didn't pry further – she obviously had enough on her mind – but I surmised that she had been reversing towards the lay-by at the bottom of the hill when the car slipped into the ditch. My parting comment was that some drivers can't reverse. It wasn't directed at her, but she readily admitted that she was one of them!

Cars in ditches are increasingly common sights on that stretch of the Learside. The explanation, I suppose, is increased traffic, though I have to qualify that observation. Compared with most Kintyre roads, the Learside remains relatively traffic-free, but it is single-track all the way, aside from a short section between Feochaig and Glenahervie, and even if, say, an average of merely six vehicles an hour are on it in summer, some are bound to meet where overgrown ditches wait to trap the unwary. Road signage can be overdone, but perhaps a cautionary notice at either end of the Learside – Ballimenach sheep-fanks and Polliwilline – would save a few drivers from embarrassment and expense. These, to my mind, would make more sense than pedestrian warning signs (p 98).

The first car I recall seeing in a ditch on that road was in exactly the same spot as the one above. The date was 23 August 2013 and I was with George McSporran on a mushroom-gathering outing to Auchenhoan. It was an evening of mist and drizzle and we drove there in George's car. He managed to pass the off-road car, and, an hour or so later, as we walked down the Ballinatunie track in darkness, we saw the flashing lights of a vehicle recovery truck on the scene. By the time we were on our way home, both vehicles were gone. Ironically, earlier in the day I had remarked to my sister Barbara that I'd never seen a car accident on the Learside!

On 26 April, while chatting to Peter Docherty on Auchenhoan brae, a van passed us, heading south and driven by a local man I'd seen occasionally on that road and given up acknowledging, because there was never a response from him. Minutes later, having parted from Peter, I saw the van again, on the north side of Sweetie Bella's Quarry. It was parked in the middle of the road and there was a car in front of it, its offside wheels stuck in the verge. I dismounted and wheeled the bike past the vehicles, undecided as to whether I should volunteer assistance. A woman had got out the car and was trying to direct the male driver back on to the road, but he clearly resented her advice and shouted irritably, 'I know!', which elicited from her a screech of frustration. Van Man was standing beside his vehicle observing proceedings, his face expressionless. At that point, I decided to leave them to it. As I was wheeling the bike up Corphin Brae, I was overtaken by the van and concluded that the car was out and away. I nodded to the driver, supposing he might, for once, respond, and perhaps convey, with the lift of an eyebrow or a wry smile, something of his feelings about the mishap, but he ignored me yet again.

Agnes Stewart, driving down the Learside for a walk on 11 June, encountered a camper-van off the road between the Second Water and Sweetie Bella's Quarry. The van was well into the ditch, but there was another vehicle present – possibly the one that contributed to the accident – and its driver managed to tow the van out.

Bicycle accidents on the Learside

I hadn't given much thought to bicycle accidents on the Learside until Alastair Thompson included one in his memoir for this book. The accident happened during his 'wilk-picking phase', as he described it. He was working as a message-boy for Willie Mitchell, the butcher, full-time during the summer holidays, with Sundays and Wednesday afternoons off. On this particular day, his companions, Derek and Rab, had gone ahead of him to catch the tide, and Alastair was 'making great haste to avoid arguments about effort and therefore share of the money'. At the bottom of the hill below Auchenhoan farm, he lost control of the bike, crashed head-first into the bank and was knocked unconscious. Just as he was coming to, his uncle Gilbert, who was shepherd at Auchenhoan, appeared. He had been at the steading and seen Alastair's legs 'fly through the air'.

26. *Derek McKinven (L) and Alastair Thompson with bikes on Ballimenach brae. The bike between them belonged to Robert Davison, who took the photo, c. 1966. Courtesy of A. Thompson.*

Gilbert wanted to drive Alastair to the Cottage Hospital for a check-up, but Alastair resisted his arguments and continued to the shore, where, to his relief, he discovered that Derek and Rab had spent their entire time there 'gathering up a mass-escape from our stash'. The 'stash' was a previous day's haul – it might take several tides to fill a sack – which they'd deposited near low water mark, both to keep the shellfish alive and to conceal them from rival winklers. BRS (British Road Services) supplied the sacks, along with metal tags with a Billingsgate address, and when sufficient wilks had been collected, the sacks would be left at the roadside to be uplifted by lorry.

The front forks of Alastair's bicycle were irreparably damaged, and when his boss, Willie Mitchell – a passionate cyclist – enquired about his 'lack of wheels' and was given the explanation, he reached for the keys of his store in Kirk Street and invited Alastair to go and pick one of the 'Flying Scot' bikes which were kept there. Alastair remembered seeing four or five bicycles, from which he selected a green one which appeared to be the oldest. He converted it from 'fixed wheel', which Willie preferred, to a three-speed model, using a Sturmey-Archer hub. Alastair cherished that bike and kept it until 1977, when he emigrated to Canada. He passed it on to his brother Ernie, who later exchanged it for something else.

Alastair asked me to find out from Agnes Stewart, Willie Mitchell's daughter, if any of the other bikes in the Kirk Street store had survived, and, if so, would she sell him one. He was out of luck, but I was in luck, because the enquiry stirred an anecdote from Agnes's memory. Willie, when elderly, ordered a new 'Flying Scot' from Rattray's in Glasgow. It was taking so long to come that his daughter Cathy and her husband, John Kerr, visited the shop during a trip to Glasgow. 'You know,' Cathy remarked to the assistant, 'my Dad's nearly seventy-eight – he can't wait forever.' The assistant disappeared into the back shop to enquire about progress with the bike, but left the door open, and John and Cathy overheard him explain the customer's age. Another voice, this one irate, was heard to remark: 'Well, what the hell does the old bugger want with a new "Flying Scot"?' When the assistant returned he was apologetic about his colleague's response, but Cathy reassured him that these were precisely the family's own sentiments. Willie got his bike the following week.[91]

My own cycling accident was rather more mundane. It happened on 22 May 1983 with John MacDonald. When we set off for the Learside,

John was on an old bike of mine, but it wasn't performing well, so, at my cousin Stuart Martin's house on Kilkerran road, he borrowed a bike of Stuart's. That one wasn't much better, so I gave John my good bike and I took Stuart's. The brakes were defective, as I discovered during their first test, on Auchenhoan brae. I had them fully on at the start of the hill, but despite that the bike gathered speed until finally it was out of control and, at the foot of the brae, I couldn't get the wheel round at the turn and shot into a ditch. Fortunately, both bike and I bounced back on to the road and I was unharmed. That would have been the spot where Alastair had his accident sixteen or seventeen years before.

My friend Iain Campbell had an accident in the mid-sixties on the winding road down to the Second Water. I was ahead of him on the descent when he suddenly overtook me at great speed. I was momentarily awed by his courageous impulse, but quickly realised that he was out of control, the handlebars jolting back and forth and his feet flailing. Inevitably, he failed to take the first bend. Having satisfied myself that he had survived the crash, I succumbed to convulsive laughter. Needless to say, this was not the response Iain expected, and my punishment was to accompany him on foot back the way we had come in search of the brake-blocks, which had dropped off.

Recently, when I spoke to Iain about the incident, he remembered it all too well, and added a few details I'd forgotten. His bicycle was a Triumph 'Palm Beach Tourist' – an almost identical model to my Raleigh 'Trent Tourist', which I didn't remember owning! – and was almost new from Jock Shields's bicycle shop. The brake blocks presumably hadn't been properly tightened in the factory, and Iain's main concern during the emergency was that the new bike would be damaged.

We had a game at the Second Water which we both enjoyed, though it probably didn't last even a year. On the north side of the burn we laid out a race course around rocks on the grassy foreshore, and took it in turn to cycle round it. The one who wasn't on his bike held a watch and logged the time taken to complete the circuit. I forget who clocked the best time, but the competition was always close. It was good fun, but must have been sore on the bikes, which, unlike the mountain bikes of today, were not designed for rough-riding.

I have a distinct memory of returning home with Iain from one of those outings to the Second Water. It was a bitterly cold day in winter and I had no gloves. By the time we reached Crosshill Avenue, my hands were freezing. The first thing I did was warm them at the fire, which produced a most excruciating pain, penetrating, it seemed, right to the very bones. I'd felt pain like that before – after playing gloveless in snow, most likely – but not since.

My brother Donald saw a friend fatally injured in a cycling accident. He and Duncan McMillan, who was twelve years old, and a near-neighbour in Crosshill Avenue, were returning from the Learside one evening in July 1950. They were descending Ballimenach brae – no doubt enjoying the exhilaration of the long free-wheel – when two other cyclists, who had dismounted near the foot of the hill, appeared in view. Duncan crashed into one of the stationary bicycles and was thrown off and suffered a serious head injury. He was taken by car to the Cottage Hospital, then by air ambulance to the Western Infirmary in Glasgow, whence he was transferred to Killearn Hospital. His father, Charlie, visited him there and set off home reassured that he was 'on the way to recovery', but by the time he reached Campbeltown Duncan was dead.[92]

In Norman Morrison's *My Story*, there is a dramatic account of a bicycle accident in which he is knocked unconscious and then 'awakened by a tickling sensation'. This was an adder he had captured and confined in a tin box tied to the handlebars; the box had broken open when Morrison crashed his bike, and the snake was now crawling over his face.

His account lacks a date as well as a location, but offers a couple of clues. He was cycling through a district 'new' to him, which could have been somewhere in Kintyre after his first posting there in 1892; and he described the scene of the accident as a long brae, down which he free-wheeled at 'high speed': 'As I was nearing the bottom of the incline, I saw that the road took a sharp turn over a bridge, and to avoid crashing into the wall I suddenly turned my machine. The jerk caused my rear wheel to skid, and I was bodily thrown over the handlebars, with the result that the right side of my face came down full tilt on the hard road, about a foot from the parapet of the bridge ... I was badly cut about the face and bruised all over the body, and I was in the hands of the doctor for three weeks.'

He could well be describing the brae on the north side of the Second Water and the bridge over the burn there. Certainly, from other evidence, Morrison was fond of the Learside, and the Learside is still a good place to seek adders, should that be one's desire. When I checked Morrison's police record, however, I found two absences owing to bicycle accidents, but neither of them was in Kintyre. The first happened in June 1908, while he was stationed in Islay, and he was off work for five days; the second was in June 1917, while he was at Oban, and kept him from his duties for twelve days.[93] The latter is probably the one he described.

18 June: Polliwilline and 'Queen Esther'

I cycled off alone at 4.30, heading for a night at the family caravan at Polliwilline. By the time I reached Glenahervie, I was longing for the Linda McCartney vegetarian sausages, Ayrshire potatoes and spinach which would form my meal. My thoughts drifted back to childhood cycling expeditions with Iain Campbell. When heading for Tangy shore, and other points west, we'd stop at Cathy Thomson's wee shop in Longrow and buy a bottle of 'skoosh' (lemonade) and a few snacks, or 'snashters'. On the way home, hungry from those outings, I'd obsess on one meal, and one only – a McKellar Watt meat pie topped with Heinz baked beans – and as soon as I arrived back, I'd be running to McRoberts' shop on Ralston Road to satisfy my cravings.

My sister Barbara Docherty and her son, Malcolm, were already in the bay, installed in Barbara's caravan. After I'd cooked and eaten my meal and had a smoke, they came over and sat with me for a couple of hours around a bottle of malt whisky. Malcolm mentioned that, while photographing the big cave north of the bay, he had disturbed a small tabby cat, which disappeared into bracken (pursued by a pair of agitated pied wagtails). The name of that cave is the Cats' Cove.

It was occupied in the mid-nineteenth-century by Irish-born Esther Houston, who lived by gathering winkles, fishing from her boat, working seasonally on farms, and, when in greatest need, charity. Esther is commemorated in two place-names on the Learside, Queen Esther's Bay (p 12) and Esther's Bay, on Glenahervie shore. The cave itself took its name, the Cats' Cove, from her pets, which remained there, in a feral state, after her death. A photograph of 'Pullywillan', published in the *Campbeltown Courier* on 11 February 1939, carried the following caption: 'The Witches Cave is among these rocks. Some years ago a woman lived there with about twenty cats.' So, poor Esther had turned into a 'witch' by then!

Macharioch House, along the coast from Polliwilline, was gifted by the 8th Duke of Argyll, George Douglas Campbell, to his son John, Marquess of Lorne, when in 1871 he married Princess Louise, the artistic fourth daughter of Queen Victoria. The newly-weds stayed for a fortnight in the mansion during their marriage tour that year, but never returned.[94]

During their stay, the Lornes visited Esther, who claimed titular superiority over the Princess, having styled herself 'Queen' and her rocky cave a 'castle'. The Marquess's father, when he took possession of Macharioch Estate, had provided money to send Esther back to Ireland, but she soon returned to her cave. The Marquess and his Princess were 'much pleased and amused by their visit' and ordered 'a large quantity of provisions' to be sent to Esther.[95]

Just north of Esther's cave, a hollow in the conglomerate cliff is still known as the Duke's Seat, after the 8th Duke, for whom, when in residence at Macharioch House, it was a favourite vantage point. After his death in 1900, an imposing Celtic cross was erected to his memory by his widow, the reclusive Ina Erskine MacNeill, on Dùn Dubh, the headland below Macharioch House.

These are the final lines of a poem I wrote about Queen Esther:

> She had two snug bays named after her
> Queen Esther's and Esther's miles apart
> which is more than can be said for Sir William MacKinnon Bart
> an eminent native who excelled in commerce
> which proves that history is fickle
> and that in the annals of the people
> the lowest may be honoured of a dead generation.[96]

Towards the end of the year, an e-mail correspondent in Minnesota, U.S.A., Charlotte Brodie Eastin, mentioned that she was about to start work on a portrait of Esther, inspired by the poem and an account of Esther in *Kintyre: The Hidden Past*. Later, however, she reported that the project had stalled because Esther was demanding a 'white fur cloak' and Charlotte couldn't locate a suitable material. The strange problem was solved here in Kintyre. My wife Judy had taken up spinning, using wool from the three alpacas her daughter Doreen keeps at Baraskomill farm, and I posted a handful of white fleece to Charlotte just before Christmas. The accompanying photograph shows a rather more glamorous Esther than I could have imagined;

but here is Charlotte's explanation: 'I became intrigued by the story of this woman who had escaped the conventions of her time and I imagined her as a crazy old cat lady, living on the edge but free. But as I explored her image, I came to see her as she might have seen herself: not as an old hag, but as a beautiful young queen.' The painting is festooned with 'found objects', such as glass and shells, attached by wire.

27. *Portrait of 'Queen Esther' by Charlotte Brodie Eastin, 2015. Courtesy of the artist.*

(Charlotte's paternal great-grandfather, Robert Brodie, emigrated to Middlesex County, Ontario, from Lochgilphead, in 1832. Given the undoubted Gaelic background of that family, we suspect that the name represents Brolachan (p 63), which was Anglicised in Kintyre as 'Brodie'; but so far the link has proved elusive.)

19 June: Homeward

28. *Malcolm Docherty's assemblage at Polliwilline, photographed by the author, 23 July 2014.*

Malcolm Docherty, who has lived in Skye since 2004 with his artist wife, Caroline, and three children, was occupying his time, and exercising his creative talents, in making assemblages. He left one with his mother, and it sits in her van. The work, glued on board, includes a fragment of oyster-catcher eggshell, a bird's wing, a sea-worn plastic net-float, a triangular piece of drainage tile, seaweed, wood, and a little painting of Ailsa Craig with two gannets flying in the foreground. He describes these arrangements of 'incidental and selected items from the littoral' as attempts to 'capture the spirit of the place', and remembers exploring the medium for the first time at Glasgow School of Art in 1979.

Nineteenth June was the first anniversary of Malcolm Senior's death. He was fond of Polliwilline, and paid for the petrol which took him there by wilk-gathering on the shore to the north. He also kept the shore track clear by cutting back vegetation. He is missed at Polliwilline, and Barbara would have missed him especially that day.

Rather than cycle back up the hilly Learside, I decided to head for Southend village, spend a few hours there and then choose a route home. I stopped at Kilcolmkill, ate lunch and filled my pipe, then browsed among the gravestones. I was searching for the grave of John Harvey, but failed to find it (p 92). The day was pleasant and sunny and there were visitors about, but few of them spoke. I set off again on the loop-road which would take me on to the main Campbeltown road at the War Memorial. The prospect of the World Cup qualifier between England and Uruguay, which was to be televised that evening, was clearly impinging on my thoughts. Just before Dalbuie road-end, I saw an English flag fluttering from the upstairs window of a cottage, and wondered who could be so bold as to display such a patriotic banner here in Scotland. As I drew level with the cottage, however, the 'flag' turned into a red and white curtain which wind had sucked through the opened window.

23 June: To Lussa Reservoir

By the time I rose and ate a breakfast, Judy had already put in a couple of hours' work at her organic allotment in Lady Mary Row. When she returned for lunch, she said she fancied a cycle up to Lussa Reservoir, which was an amazing suggestion for two reasons: that destination had already suggested itself to me, and we had never gone there before by bicycle. In fact, I've seldom been there at all, and only by car for a short walk on arrival. The place doesn't appeal much to me. The reservoir itself is attractive enough if one enjoys large artificial bodies of water, but the surrounding conifer plantations bore me. Judy reckoned we should see plenty of butterflies there, but I reminded her that Agnes and Allister Stewart monitored that area. (As it transpired, we saw only two butterflies all day, owing to cloudy conditions.) There were, however, two ruined steadings I was keen to revisit, so we decided to go, and set off just after 2 p.m.

We knew that since Lussa Reservoir is in the hills, we'd be pushing our bikes for most of the way, but there was much to occupy our interest – the delightful views back to Ben Gullion and the Mull hills in the south, and the roadside botany – so the journey passed pleasantly. It was on one of these braes that George McSporran had his cycling accident (p 67). He was returning from a day at Lussa Reservoir with friends, was going too fast and ran off the road and into a ditch. He was unhurt, but the handlebars, front forks and front wheel of the bike were badly twisted and he had to push it home.

At Skeroblin, we saw Christine Duncan at work in her garden and stopped for a chat with her. The subjects ranged from the midges that were abusing her, on and off, to the abuse of bus passes, a bugbear of mine. Her Jack Russell terrier appeared from across the road, and when she mentioned that his name was 'Lachie', we told her that our grandson, born two days earlier, had been named Lachlan, which would probably end up shortened to 'Lachie'. Christine and her husband Hector farm East Skeroblin, and the neighbouring farmsteading, West Skeroblin, which is owned by Paul McCartney, is on the opposite side of the road, a very unusual proximity.

George Campbell Hay and Annie MacDougall

Sandra Black lives at West Skeroblin, and I recalled that the poet, George Campbell Hay, befriended her paternal grandparents, Donald MacDougall and Annie MacLean, in Arran. After the MacDougalls moved in 1936 to High Park – close to West Skeroblin, and McCartney's first property acquisition in Kintyre thirty years later – George would lodge with them there, exploring the countryside by day, with maps and a sandwich, and returning to share the MacDougall family's evening meal.

He was particularly drawn to Annie and would sometimes sit up late with her, discussing Gaelic at the kitchen table, 'with the hams hanging at the roof'. She was a native of Sleat, Skye, and for some reason George preferred her Gaelic to her husband's Lismore variant. Their late hours exasperated Donald, and he remarked to George once: 'You don't take my Gaelic, but you'll wear my tartan.' This was a reference to George's custom at the time of wearing a kilt of the MacDougall tartan, adopted through his paternal grandmother in Tarbert, Mary MacDougall.

George's regard for Annie was reciprocated. They corresponded – regrettably, no letters appear to have survived on either side – and she kept a framed photograph of him, and would explain: 'He's just a young lad and he's very keen.' The friendship ended suddenly in 1940 when Annie suffered a fatal heart attack at the age of forty-two. The call-up for military service of her eldest son, Iain, had affected her badly, and she wrote to George with news of it; but George himself, by then, was confronting his own trauma in the face of war (to avoid military service, which conflicted with his extreme nationalistic convictions, he hid out in the Argyll hills from October 1940 until May 1941, when arrested at Arrochar). After Annie's death, the MacDougall family moved to West Skeroblin, and lost touch with the young man who would become one of the finest Scottish poets of his generation.[97]

George was born on 8 December 1915, at Elderslie, Renfrewshire, where his father, John Macdougall Hay, author of the once-controversial novel about Tarbert, *Gillespie*, was minister – 2015 is therefore the centenary of the poet's birth. His poems deserve a wider readership, not least in Tarbert, which nurtured his love of Gaelic and inspired many of his finest lyrics.

East Skeroblin Cottage

A little further up the hill, we stopped to look at a small ruin. It's on the west side of the road, but belongs to East Skeroblin and was a farmworkers' cottage. There is a fire-place on each side of the living area – which was presumably partitioned into a kitchen and a bedroom – and a byre on the north end of the building. I was told that Donald McKerral, ninety-one years old as I write, was brought up there, and I wrote to him at once, asking for his memories of Skeroblin. My informant, however, was mistaken. It was Donald's mother, Mary Buchanan, who was reared there. She was one of nine children born to Thomas Buchanan and Agnes Reid. When I checked the 1901 census, East Skeroblin Cottage was unoccupied, but I found the family there in 1891: Thomas Buchanan, thirty-one-year-old ploughman, wife Agnes, and four young children, the oldest of them, Helen McL., aged nine. Helen's name points to her paternal grandmother, Helen McLean, down the hill in East Skeroblin farm. She was the native wife of the farmer there, William Buchanan, who belonged to Lochwinnoch, Renfrewshire.

An unexpected meeting

Our destination was Bordadubh, beyond the northern end of Lussa Reservoir, and we had intended stopping there for lunch, but, though there was a wind, it varied in strength according to where one happened to be, and we judged that Bordadubh might not receive enough of it to counter the midge threat. Judy remembered having seen a picnic bench near the head of the loch on an earlier visit, and when it came in sight we decided to eat there. Just as we were about to move, I remarked to Judy that we hadn't seen another person since arriving at the reservoir; but minutes later, as I rose from the table to start packing my rucksack, I saw two figures approaching along the road. This was, literally, a 'turn up for the book', and I lifted my binoculars for a quick look while they were still far enough off not to detect the scrutiny.

29. The author, Nicola Coffield and John MacDonald at Lussa Reservoir, 23 June 2014. Photograph by Judy Martin.

I saw a man and a woman, and wondered what stories, if any, they might have for me; but the closer they approached, the more I thought I recognised the man's gait. Judy, too, was watching, and almost simultaneously we realised that we were seeing John MacDonald, a friend, and his friend, Nicola Coffield. I had a good idea why he was there and shouted to him jokingly that he was banned for poaching. By then, he had identified Judy and me. John had a fishing rod with him and we accompanied him and Nicola to the stream he intended to fish at the end of the reservoir. Coincidentally, on the Sunday before, we had met, by chance, and at about the same time of day, John's brother Jimmy on the Learside (p 111).

Bordadubh

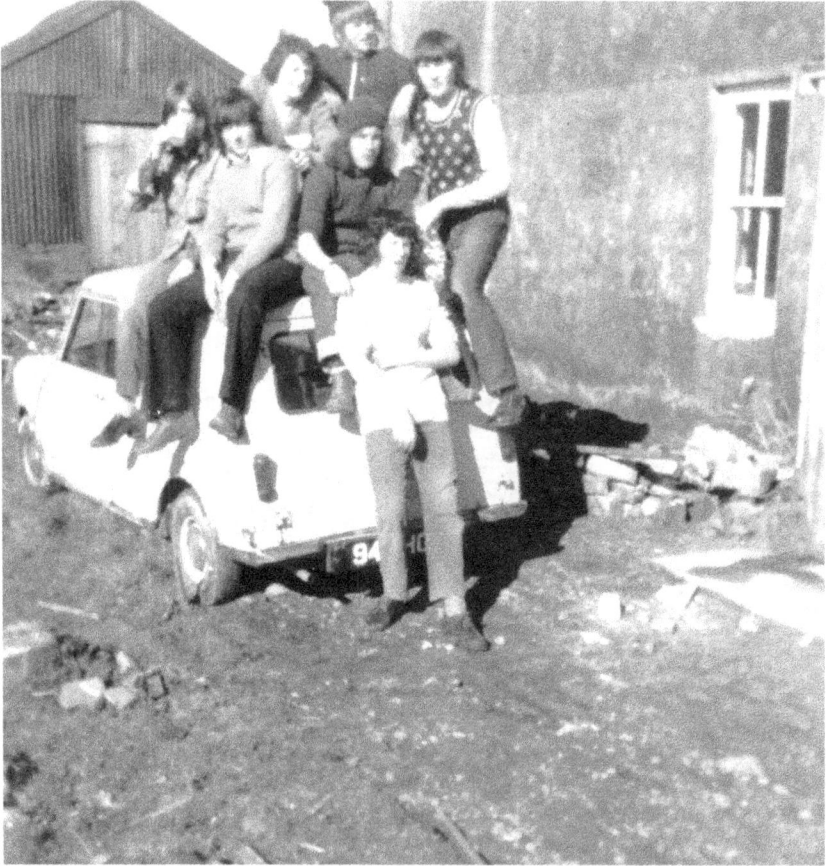

30. *Campbeltown Grammar School work force at Bordadubh with mini-van, 1973. L-R: David Allen (drinking tea), David Campbell, Derek Stewart, Jim Blackstock, David Robertson (in 'toorie' hat), Kenneth Anderson (in tank top); Douglas Galbraith (standing). Courtesy of D. Robertson.*

We left John and Nicola at the bridge and cycled on towards Bordadubh. In 1973-74, after its desertion, the steading was converted into an outdoor centre. Davie Robertson (p 165) remembers working on the renovation in 1973 as a teen-aged pupil at Campbeltown Grammar School. The year lodged in his memory because he was at Bordadubh on the day the Campbeltown trawler *Harvest Hope* blew up at sea (28 August 1973). Davie was one of a group of boys from 'Technical' who spent Wednesday of every week at the cottage, under the supervision of the late Donald Leys. There were no cooking facilities at Bordadubh at that stage of the renovation, and the boys took flasks and 'pieces' with them. Davie supplied a little colour snapshot for the book. Composition and quality are poor, but I publish it, anyway, in the belief that something is sometimes better than nothing.

Davie's main job was filling pot-holes in the road with gravel, while his classmates worked all over the building, inside and on the roof, doing repairs. 'Health and safety' considerations were minimal – not a steel-capped boot or a helmet in sight! – but Davie has no recollection of any accidents. The boys were driven to Lussa Reservoir by Donald Leys in an old school minibus, from which they transferred to a minivan which was kept in a Forestry Commission shed. That vehicle had belonged to a teacher in the Grammar School, Mr Fraser, who donated it to the project after it failed its MOT, but it was fine for driving about the forestry roads, and Davie was allowed to use it for his road-mending duties.

Bordadubh centre was opened in June 1974 by E. T. F. Spence, convenor of Argyll and Bute County Council's education committee. In his speech, he acknowledged Kintyre Rotary Club's initiative in acquiring the property, which would be 'most helpful for hill walking, nature study and camping'. An illuminated scroll was presented to Donald Leys for his efforts, and local tradesmen were thanked for their free assistance. The listless *Campbeltown Courier* report – which disappointingly lacked photographs – ended with a trite editorial: 'All in all Bordadubh is a centre involving the whole community. It is indicative of the new spirit that is abroad in Scotland just now. It is an exciting Highland development.'[98]

The year after the centre opened, Agnes Stewart spent a Saturday night there on a course for leaders of outdoor groups. She remembers the accommodation as rather basic, with bunk beds in the attic for the women and beds in an outhouse for the men. Doreen Coulson came up that evening to demonstrate how just one curried chicken could feed 'a huge number of people'. Agnes's husband Allister joined her on the Sunday, and, with the late Margaret Pate (née MacKay), they enjoyed a long circular walk to Beinn an Tuirc, the highest hill in Kintyre.

Davie Robertson was one of a group which walked from Ifferdale Glen across Kintyre to Bellochantuy one day in 2002. They stopped at Bordadubh on the way and found the interior absolutely wrecked – vandals had been busy reversing the restoration of thirty years earlier.

Nothing now remains of the steadings but a stump of gable beside the Kintyre Way, a memorial to the shepherds and their families who lived there. But there is a more explicit memorial just before the cleared site, at a clump of deciduous woodland. It is a plaque with the following on it:

Hughie's Wood
Hugh McMillan
1927-1990

Hugh McMillan was brought up at Bordadubh, his father being a shepherd there from 1936-1952. Hugh went from farming to forestry and spent most of his life in forestry as a ganger with the Forestry Commission, living in Grogport. Well-respected and well-liked, his advice helped many through difficult times. Sadly Hugh died while erecting a fence at Bordadubh on Wednesday 7th November 1990, and this small wood was planted in his memory.

There is another memorial near Bordadubh. It was erected by the Rotary Club in 2006, to mark 'the graves of three children of the McConnachie family who lived at Bordadhu around the period 1880-1910', but the commemoration is puzzling. No evidence of child deaths there has been discovered within the stated period, and, in any case, as late as that any burial outwith a graveyard would be irregular, to say the least. Yet, the tradition is persistent. Malcolm MacMillan, who went to Bordadubh in 1926, had this to say on the subject: 'A former shepherd in Bordadhu had 21 of a family; they were known as "The Wee Twenty-ones"! There are three graves of their children at the foot of the glen dividing Strathmolach from Altentarve.'

Malcolm MacMillan

MacMillan families in Bordadubh had been puzzling me. Had there been two or just one? The answer arrived from Christine Duncan (p 133), in the form of a typewritten page with 'Bordadhu' at the top and 'Written by Malcolm MacMillan 1974' at the bottom. From the evidence of the text, however, Malcolm didn't write it, but dictated it to someone who then had the notes typed up. It's a fascinating and well-written document, and the following paragraphs are based on it.

Malcolm replaced John McCallum as shepherd at Bordadubh in 1926. He was single then, but two years later he married Agnes MacKay. The weekly wage at that time was about 30s, with perquisites: the keep of three cows and four 'followers' (calves), three-quarters of an acre of ground for growing potatoes and vegetables, and 'as many peats as he wanted to cut'. Additionally, he kept 50 hens and two pigs. Bordadubh, he said, marched with Strathmollach, Corrylach, 'Arihearaig', Colluska, Ifferdale, Low Ugadale and Ballochgair, and the hill carried about 630 ewes and 200 hoggs (yearling sheep). Malcolm and Agnes had four children, John (born in 1929), Archie (1930), Isobel (1933) and David, born at East Skeroblin in 1937.

There were two annual clippings, attended by about forty Argyll Estate shepherds, who 'got dinner at Strathmolach and tea at the fanks'; the women would rise at 3 a.m. to bake and cook for the gathering. There were dippings in August and October, which brought about seven shepherds to Bordadubh to assist. At 'musical evenings', when other shepherds came to Bordadubh, 'Malcolm gave a free hair-cut to those needing one'. Occasional other visitors to the isolated steading included 'Drinks' Brodie, who sold kippers, 'Morris the Jew', who sold drapery, and would walk the length of Collusca with his wares, and 'McPhee the hawker', selling haberdashery. 'They all carried packs on their backs and each one got a meal.'

There was no road from Bordadhu to Strathmolach and the children had to walk to Strathmolach to get to the school car leaving at 7.30 in the morning. One time the burn was frozen and Malcolm had to carry a ten stone sack of flour on his back from Strathmolach to Bordadhu. Visits to Campbeltown were from four to six months apart. Provisions in bulk, e.g. sugar, flour and oatmeal, came with the cart, which had to cross the burn five times. In 1930, the snow was so deep they were walking over the fences and hedges and Archie's birth could not be registered for three weeks ...

When Malcolm's mother died at Bordadubh, a cart was used to carry her body to Strathmollach, and from there a 'proper hearse' conveyed her to Kilkivan for burial. On the day of her funeral, 'the peat shed at Bordadhu went on fire'. She was Isabella Shaw Gilchrist, widow of John MacMillan, and died in August 1932, aged sixty-seven.[99]

Betty McMillan

In 1949, an admiring article was published in the *Campbeltown Courier* about 'Betty of Bordadhu'. Her full name was Betty McMillan, and these McMillans – Hugh was her brother – succeeded Malcolm in Bordadubh. It is an informative account, which I'll later quote in full, but I'm certain that without the novel 'shepherdess' tag it would never have been published. I asked Malcolm Speed, whose distinguished career in Scottish newspapers began on the *Courier*,[100] if he knew who the writer was. He started as a junior reporter in 1947 and would have been there when the piece was published, but it wasn't his work and he couldn't suggest whose it might have been.

The article contains sufficient insights into life on a mid-twentieth century Kintyre sheep farm to make it an interesting social history document, but it also contains exaggerations, calculated, I suppose, to increase the reader's admiration of the subject. The wind did not howl round the hills of Bordadubh 'without a halt' (paragraph 4); her 'hirsel' (or daily beat) would not have been considered 'difficult, dangerous and desolate' by 'the most seasoned shepherd' (paragraph 4), and one might be forgiven for suspecting that alliterative flair took precedence over factual care; Betty's walk to school was not 'impossible' and needn't necessarily have kept her from further education (paragraph 8) – it was about two miles to the nearest farm for a lift to town in a car, and the same back home at the end of her day, which she did throughout her mandatory schooling. But these are quibbles. Here is Betty's story.

Few people meet Betty of Bordadhu, who is Kintyre's only shepherdess and the loneliest in Scotland. In snowstorm, in sunshine, from daybreak to dusk, Betty, crook in hand, a whistle in her pocket, plods through the swampy black moor, jumps ditches, climbs over rocks and hills to tend her 300-odd blackface sheep roaming over one thousand feet above sea level.

Betty gives commands to her dogs on the whistle, for she hasn't yet acquired the 'knack' of giving a shrill whistle through thumb and finger, like her experienced shepherd father.

Depending on the state of the weather, Betty may be seen wearing her MacMillan kilt, or in breeches or shorts – the latter only in the warm summer days.

She is more often in breeches, for the wind howls round the hills of Bordadhu without a halt and the rain sweeps in wide gusts through the valley. Around her cottage home the burns, the bogs and the bracken make her job no sinecure. Even to the most seasoned shepherd, it would be difficult, dangerous and desolate. But for Betty it is a job that has got to be done and it is a job into which she puts her heart. It has got to be a stout heart to face morning and night those five hundred wind-swept acres spread over her hirsel of Auchenariff,* which includes a rocky hill face and miles of marsh and peat bog.

Yet Betty McMillan only celebrated her 20th birthday on the 10th February. She is strong of limb, fresh, pink-complexioned, with blue-grey eyes and fair brown hair. Perhaps her mother's home baking, eggs from her hens and her geese, and fresh milk from the family cow, plus an open air life, give her that vivacity.

Since she left school at Campbeltown at the age of fourteen Betty has assisted her father as shepherd. Together they look after some six hundred sheep. She has one hirsel and her father the hirsel opposite.

Her father has sheepdogs Betty and Frank to help him, but Betty goes out with Moira and Callach (the Gaelic name [Caileag] for Lassie). She prepares a tasty dish of maize-meal porridge for the four dogs and then milks the cow before she goes out to bring the flock down from the hills.

At school in Campbeltown, twelve miles away, she was a bright, intelligent scholar and would, perhaps, have risen to higher education and a job in the city, which she often feels she would like, had it not meant an impossible walk. When she was at school, Betty used to have to walk nearly two miles over the moor to the nearest farm and next-door neighbour, as it were, and from there she got a car to school.

Betty still has to take a daily walk to this farm but it is to gather the mail and the groceries, for there are no callers at Bordadhu. But further down the valley nearer the town there is more activity than ever. A tunnel is being churned out of the hill face and new roads are appearing over the sheep tracks, and girders of iron and concrete are being thrown over the trout fishing Glen Lussa river – the embryo of the Hydro-Electric Board's Kintyre electricity scheme. But this seems far away from desolate Bordadhu, where Betty comes home on a winter night to knit by the paraffin lamp.

As she knits her mind goes back to the clipping, when several hundred ewes and hoggs from her own and her father's hirsels will be brought down into the clipping-pens, twice during the summer. The hoggs and the eild [barren] ewes are clipped during June and the ewes during the second or milk clipping in July.

The clipping is a hill festival. The neighbours come to lend a hand. There's an al-fresco lunch and the gossip of many months is stored up for that grand get-together with the sheep-shearers. Every 6 lb fleece will be heavily trampled into the long bags and over two ton of wool will be taken away at each clipping by motor lorries for the manufacture into the same wool that is, perhaps, so deftly fashioned by Betty's knitting needles. Betty is a good all-rounder at the clipping. She can look after the food and clip a few sheep too.

Then another job that falls to Betty is the marking of the lambs – every hirsel in the country has an official lug mark, so that if a sheep from Bordadhu turns up at Buckie or Ballantrae and it has the correct lug mark, it can be identified immediately from the official records. In August there is the dipping. Betty does not do much there apart from informing the Police that the job is to be done on a certain date and then rounding up the sheep for the dip.

Her most anxious time is from the 20th April until 28th May, when she becomes a nurse as well as a shepherdess. Besides her crook and her whistle she carries lambing-oil and disinfectant – in case there is a casualty.

Betty, who came to Kintyre from Balfron near Killearn (Stirlingshire) eleven years ago, has the skill and stamina of a veteran shepherd. By her skill she knows every one of her three hundred sheep and her dogs obey her bidding and by her stamina the hazards of the moor and hill, even in winter, present no fear. She crosses them at work and for pleasure. It is all in a night's fun for Betty to cross four miles of ankle-deep bog and mud and climb the hills to Saddell to attend a dance in the village hall of Carradale. She dresses for the dance in a friend's house in the village.

Betty is fond of dancing [and] likes to go to Glasgow occasionally – to see the Rangers. Betty, the shepherdess, is a fervent Willie Waddell fan. She follows the Light Blues with the enthusiasm of a Govan supporter and if she is in Glasgow on a Saturday and the Rangers have a home game, Betty is sure to be making for Ibrox. When at home nothing would keep her away from a Rangers broadcast – except a sheep in distress.[101]

A corruption of Allt an Tairbh, 'Stream of the Bull', a farm shown on the 1801 Langlands map as 'Altenterve', south-east of Bordadubh.

Bordadubh, like most place-names in Kintyre, is Gaelic – *Bord Dubh* or *Bord Dubha*, 'Black Table' – and it described, I guess, a plateau of dark-coloured moorland. The lower stretch of Bordadubh Water forms the boundary of Kilchenzie and Campbeltown parishes, but the steading was on the north side of the burn and therefore in the former parish. The earliest appearance of the name so far found is 1556, when 'Bordadow' was described as a one-merkland holding. Until the early nineteenth century, Bordadubh would have been worked as a farm, combining crop-growing and cattle-grazing, but in 1810 John McCallum was recorded there as a shepherd when his son Gilbert was baptised on 7 October.[102]

Sheep had arrived, and the main produce of the farm would henceforth be wool and mutton. By then, many of the small farms round about had already been deserted. The 1801 Langlands map contains their names, if not precisely their locations, because all small-scale maps, until the arrival of the Ordnance Survey in 1866, were topographically inaccurate. The following (all in Langlands spellings) were farms which, unlike Gobagrennan, Corrylach, Strathmollach, Collusca, and Bordadubh itself, were not occupied for sheep-farming: Ahalochie, Ariharage, Lecknalarach, Mulbuy, Altenterve, Drimfin [for Clachfin], Bogwilly and Easka.

By the mid-twentieth century, sheep farms themselves were already going the way of the little arable farms they had gobbled up, because shepherds with families were no longer prepared to live in remote cottages which had begun to seem desperately primitive compared with the accommodation in towns and on low-lying farms which the transforming energy of electricity had reached.

In Betty's story, the stains of discontent are there to see at the edges of the romantic portrait, and their source is isolation, both geographic and social – the sense of being cheated of educational advancement; the hills and moors which had to be traversed for a few hours of dancing and youthful companionship, 'all in a night's fun' the *Courier* writer suggests; but increasingly, perhaps, for Betty, as for others in her position, the 'fun' would come to seem more like downright inconvenience.

The hydro-electric scheme

But as she sat knitting in the dim glow of a paraffin lamp, the future had already arrived in the form of 'the embryo of the Hydro-Electric Board's Kintyre electricity scheme', which would culminate in the inundation of the valley-bottom to create Lussa Reservoir. Outwith contemporaneous newspaper reports, remarkably little has been written about that project. I know, because when I looked for information for this book, there was nothing available that remotely did justice to the scheme, which took a decade to complete, and at its peak employed around 200 men, most of them local.

Details of the scheme were announced on 3 May 1947, and published in the *Campbeltown Courier* that same day, with the headlines: 'Hydro-Electric Project in Kintyre/ Glen Lussa Scheme to Cost £480,000: Work for 400 Men/ Rates to County Council Will Increase from £4 10s to £1,000.' The announcement, an editorial commented, 'should be balm to the tortured minds of several of our local councillors who have been writhing in a state of impatience and misgiving for some time'. The editorial continued: 'In serving the sparsely populated area from Campbeltown to Lochgilphead, there will be a considerable mileage of transmission lines, distributing power to crofts, isolated houses and a few hamlets ... It will be difficult to over-estimate the boon that electricity will be to people living on farms and in country cottages where the paraffin lamp is taken from room to room and the old storm lantern is hung, at great inconvenience, in the byre or stable.'

Compared with the scale of many engineering achievements in Scotland, let alone worldwide, I suppose the Glen Lussa scheme was modest. None the less, what was accomplished in the hills above Campbeltown, like it or not, should be better known locally. As well as the visible dam and aqueduct to the power-station at Gartgreillan in lower Glen Lussa, a two-and-a-half mile tunnel was blasted, years later, through the hill between Collusca and Arnicle, to divert into Lussa Reservoir water which would naturally have run into the sea at Glenbarr.

This connection required the construction of a light railway from Corrylach to the tunnel entrance, about a mile-and-half north of the farmhouse. A hillside was bulldozed, three temporary bridges laid across Collusca Water, and the railway would ultimately extend to four-and-a-half miles.[103] The tunnel was finally completed, with a 25 lb. blast of gelignite, before a small party of invited guests, in February 1958. Afterwards, the guests were taken through the entire tunnel, the men on foot and the women by rail in a 'mining car' fitted with improvised seating. Eighteen tons of gelignite had been used in 11,000 explosive charges, mostly blasting through mica schist.[104]

Jimmy Allan

This book was practically finished before I heard about a man still living in Campbeltown who had worked at the Lussa hydro-electric scheme. He is James Stevenson Allan, who was born in Airdrie, Lanarkshire, but came to Kintyre at eight years of age and has been here ever since, a connection cemented by his marriage in 1949 to Flora 'Florence' Campbell from Carradale. Jimmy began work in 1950, with Glasgow contractors Wilson, Kinmond & Marr, in the tunnel from the dam to the start of the overland pipeline. On entering the tunnel for the first time, his immediate reaction was, 'Never will I suffer this here', but he quickly adapted to the confinement and spent a year working in the tunnel. There were three shifts, rotated weekly – day, back and night – to which he also adapted. The Campbeltown bus company, A. & P. McConnachie, transported the town employees in lorries with benches fitted in the back and a canvas cover for protection from the elements.

31-34. Work scenes at the hydro-electric scheme, Lussa, c. 1951. 31. The power station at Gartgreillan showing, far left, the railway, and, mid-left, the temporary workers' accommodation and canteen.

32. A digger, used for excavating the foundations of the pipeline supports.

33. A 'puggy', being driven by Peter McKerral, Peninver, on its railway, moving a section of pipeline.

34. A traditional load-pulling 'machine'. The chain-traces of the horse, name unknown, are visible. Photographs courtesy of James Allan and Duncan Westerman.

On completion of the pipeline tunnel, Jimmy moved to the pipeline itself, and for a year drove a little railway engine, known as a 'puggy', pulling pipes. Latterly, he drove a lorry, which involved a range of tasks: taking squads to and from the canteen for meals, shopping in town for the canteen requirements, loading sand at Peninver beach for building work, and, on Wednesday and Saturday evenings, driving the workers billeted at Gartgreillan into town for a recreational break, and back again at 10 p.m. When he started work on the pipeline, his wage was 2s 8d an hour, but with overtime he could earn up to £30 a week, a substantial wage at that time. Saturday afternoons were paid at the rate of time-and-a-half and Sundays at double-time.

When his employment at Lussa ended in 1953, Jimmy took away, as well as memories, a packet of 68 small black and white photographs, four of which are reproduced here. They had been taken by one of his work-mates, an Islayman he thinks, who was going to throw them away; but Jimmy intervened, and that collection, which he passed on to a nephew, Duncan Westerman, constitutes a valuable record of a fascinating and near-forgotten era in Kintyre's industrial history.

Blues in Collusca

Collusca, another abandoned sheep farm, is north of Bordadubh. The name may not be especially old and its meaning is rather obscure. The first record I have found is for 12 May 1791, when Duncan McCallum, a son of Gilbert McCallum in 'Coliska', was baptised.[105] By the 1841 census, Malcolm Blue is in 'Colisca' with his wife Euphemia, daughter Agnes, and four sons. These sons – Robert, Duncan, Malcolm and Neil – became shepherds, and sixty years later, in the 1901 census, three of them are still there, with sister Marion as housekeeper. The fourth brother, Robert, who married, was a near-neighbour, but not in the present-day sense. He was down the glen in 'Stramollach' with wife Christina, son John, also a shepherd, and an elderly drainer, John McNeill.

The Blue family spent seventy-two years in Collusca, after moving there from Low Ugadale. Duncan, the second-oldest of the four brothers, herded there for no fewer than sixty-nine unbroken years. He was retired in Saddell, and bedridden, by 1915, when presented with the Highland and Agricultural Society's long service award, a certificate, 'in a fumed oak case, bearing the Sempar Arms', along with an inscribed silver medal. He worked first for Hugh and William Maxwell and latterly for Colonel J. W. Macleod of Saddell. In 1901, when Collusca was advertised to let by Saddell Estate, its capacity was reckoned at 700 black-faced sheep and 15 head of Highland cattle, and Duncan Blue was to 'point out the boundaries' to interested parties.[106]

'Blue', despite its appearance, belongs to that numerous class of old native Kintyre surnames which for a complex mix of reasons – social, economic and cultural – underwent an Anglicisation process which, in many cases, totally disguised their Gaelic origin. The name 'Blue' began life in Kintyre as *MacGilleGhuirm*, taken to mean 'Son of the Blue Lad', became 'McIlgorm' – in which form, as an import from Kintyre, it survives in County Antrim – and finally, and mundanely, settled down as 'Blue'.[107]

It is worth pointing out that the entire population of what I'll call 'Strathduie' was Gaelic-speaking in 1901, at the dawn of the twentieth century: McNicols in Corrylach, Blues in Collusca, McConnachies in Bordadubh, Campbells in Gobagrennan, and Blues in Strathmollach, twenty-five souls in all.

35. *The bed of Lussa Reservoir exposed during drought, c. 1974. The photograph, by George McSporran, was taken from the Kintyre Angling Club boat-shed and shows the remains of an old bridge over the drowned river.*

As the waters of Lussa reservoir rose, the steading of Gobagrennan sheep-farm disappeared from view, though the name survives attached to a Forestry Commission bungalow. During spells of drought, the old place reappears, as though in a dream of history. On 15 August 1861, at 'Gobagraninan', the death took place of 'Christina McNeil in the 95th year of her age'.[108] If the old lady were to return there tomorrow, she wouldn't recognise the place, and if she were to approach anyone for help, her language would be incomprehensible.

McConnachies in Strathmollach

Judy and I had decided to cycle along the east side of the loch to another abandoned shepherd's house, Strathmollach, on the shore of the reservoir. She had already been along that forestry track in June 2011, while 'in training' to walk the West Highland Way later that summer. She had taken a bus to Saddell and walked the Kintyre Way from there, but timber extraction on the west side of the reservoir had closed that stretch of the Way, and walkers and cyclists were diverted on to the east side.

I had looked at Strathmollach's gaunt ruins from the opposite shore and was keen to explore them, but, when they appeared in sight below the track, we could see no obvious route down to them through the intervening forestry plantation, and deferred the attempt. But even from a distance, the ruins are impressive. The immediate impression is one of solidity. There are two parallel buildings, and the main one – from its chimneys, the dwelling-house – is two-storied, which is unusual in shepherds' houses and suggests relatively modern construction.

From our vantage point on the track, we could see the revolving turbines of two wind-farms, Tangy and Beinn an Tuirc, and the contrast with the reservoir below was immediate – the new and the old, both working to generate more and more electricity for a society which will exercise no restraint in its insatiable demand for comfort and convenience.

Strathmollach is Gaelic *Srath Molach*, which can be translated simply as 'Shaggy Strath', but there is more to the name than that, and a picture emerges of a wide valley-bottom, bristling with vegetation, and a stream running through it. Where was the strath from which the farm Strathmollach took its name centuries ago? It appears not to have been the valley in which the steading was built, and which is now underwater – that was Strathduie (*Srath Dubhaidh*, 'Gloomy Strath').[109]   The answer is that there is no answer.

Two shepherds at Strathmollach died from exposure in the hills within fifteen years of each other, and both were named McConnachie. I had attributed this coincidence to plain misfortune, but later heard an old rumour that alcohol was involved in one case at least.

The first fatality was Gilbert McConnachy, who went out on New Year's morning of 1908 to tend his sheep. He failed to return and, when found by a search party, was 'standing almost erect', but dead, at the side of a burn, the bank having collapsed under his weight. He was a widower, aged about fifty, and left one son.[110] The Gilbert McConnachy in Bordadubh in the 1901 census was probably the same man. With him in Bordadubh were two brothers, Peter and John, and two sisters, Margaret and Julia, all of them, except the latter, born in Saddell Parish. Gilbert's son Archie, born in Campbeltown Parish, was also there, but at eighteen years old in 1901 he couldn't have been the second fatality.

Archibald McConnachie's body was found in a field at High Ranachan in February 1922. He apparently died from exposure, but there was no mention in the newspaper report of how he had arrived there. Had he been in Campbeltown for the day, then High Ranachan is close to the road that would have taken him home to Strathmollach. He was aged sixty, unmarried, and – presumably the finest tribute the *Courier* reporter could elicit from anyone – 'an old and experienced servant of the Argyll Estate'.[111]

On my grandson Lachlan's first visit to Kintyre in July, he was introduced to his great-grandmother Margaret. She is a Mitchell who married Archie McAllister – an uncle of Archie, the fiddler (p 23) – and whose daughter Isobel married Donnie Gillies, whose son Neil is Lachlan's father. Still there? One afternoon, I accompanied Neil, Sarah, Judy and the baby to Margaret's house in Argyll Street, where we enjoyed a cup of tea (mine in a china cup, at my request and to her amusement) and a blether about the 'good old days' (actually not so good). As we were leaving, I noticed two clan shields displayed on a wall. One was MacAllister, with its obvious connection to Margaret's late husband, but the other was MacConnachie, and I asked Margaret what its significance was. She told me that was Archie's mother's surname, and when Judy researched her, she found that she was Jeanie McDonald McConachy, parents Duncan McConachy, shepherd, and Catherine Milloy, and that she was born on 3 July 1905 at Strathmollach.

36. Lachlan Gillies with his great-grandmother Margaret McAllister and father Neil Gillies, Campbeltown, 10 February 2015. Photograph by Sarah Martin.

27 June: Thoughts on Ballimenach brae

As I was pushing my bike up Ballimenach brae, I was thinking about thinking. These cycling meditations frequently yield half-forgotten stories, entertaining fantasies and nuggets of crude philosophy, and sometimes I amuse myself with memory games. My memory appears to be losing its efficiency, and I hear the same complaint from some contemporaries, who express alarm at the familiar facts they have become capable of forgetting. My apology on behalf of the brain is that as one grows older the poor instrument has increasing volumes of data to store, so it's hardly surprising that some items may be temporarily mislaid.

On 8 April, while cycling back from Queen Esther's Bay, I experienced one of these baffling memory lapses. I'd met Les Oman in G10 Bistro that morning and we discussed the commercial transfer of music from LP to CD. I observed that some albums I value aren't yet available on CD. Les, in turn, complained about the addition of inferior 'out-takes' to albums reissued on CD, and I agreed with him.

I had been pondering his case all the way from the First Water to the road, as I lugged my rucksack full of logs, and by the time I reached the road I had identified a personal exception, Isotope's *Deep End*. I'd bought the album when it appeared in 1976 and it gave me occasional pleasure until lack of equipment to play it on relegated it to oblivion. About ten years ago, however, while browsing in Fopp's in Byres Road, Glasgow, I found a stack of *Deep End* CDs at 50 pence each. I could hardly believe my luck and bought several. I kept one and distributed the rest among friends whose musical tastes corresponded to my own. My own copy later suffered some surface damage and I decided to replace it, but by then it had become a rarity and was astronomically priced. I'm getting by with the cheap copy!

Here, at last, is the point. That 2001 reissue contains five 'bonus tracks', one 'new' and the other four digitally re-mastered by the band's guitarist, to provide, the sleeve-notes promise, a 'tantalising glimpse' of how Isotope might sound had the band still been recording. After listening several times to the CD, I had to admit that I preferred the extended guitar solo on the re-mastered version of the title track. But who was the guitarist? His name wouldn't come to me, though it should have been as familiar as that of an old friend. As I cycled home, I ran through the alphabet several times, trusting that the vital prompt would emerge. About a mile on, when a raptor I couldn't identify rose from a field, I interpreted that as a sign that the revelation was imminent, and it was – Gary Boyle.

A little later in April, I was looking for another name. This time it belonged to a plant I was seeing in roadside ditches. I could remember the name as being a long one, maybe the longest I know, but not what it was. The tiny yellow flower itself is inconspicuous, but the plant grows in such dense mats that it cannot fail to attract the eye. I have difficulty every year in remembering the names of certain flowers, usually the same ones, and this one is among them. The problem for me is that some flowers appear and then disappear after a month or two, and by the time they're back the next year, I've forgotten what some of them are called. It isn't really a 'problem', because the 'value' of a flower doesn't depend on my being able to name it, and, anyway, all that's required to recover a name is a book on botany, or an internet search, if one prefers. This time, however, in accordance with the rules of the cycling game, I wasn't going to reach for a book. It took me a fortnight to recall the name, opposite-leaved golden saxifrage (*Chrysosplenium oppositifolium*), and now that I've written about it, perhaps it's secure in memory – but I wouldn't bet on that!

Adders

While pushing the bike up Ballimenach brae, a car on its way downhill stopped and the driver's window opened. This was John Menzies, with his son Gregor. I remember John from Millknowe School, and, like me, he has lived in Kintyre all his life. His father Archie was a farmer, and John was in Knockbay when I first knew him. I have a disjointed memory of a walk my brother Donald took me on when I was small. I was exhausted at the end of it, had fallen into a cow-pat and had spoken to John Menzies or at least seen where he lived.

After a few pleasantries were exchanged, John told me that he and Gregor had decided that day to walk to Balnabraid and from there down to the Second Water and back by the road to the car. They reached Balnabraid by the track from the main road, and were then on rough ground. They hadn't gone far through long grass when Gregor, who was ahead, advised his father: 'I think we'll need to turn back.' John, who admits to a 'lifelong fear of snakes', knew at once what Gregor had seen.

I reckon most folk who enjoy the outdoors would admit, if they are honest, to sharing that fear. I am relaxed for as long as the snake-image doesn't slither into my consciousness, but if I find myself in a spot where I have seen adders in the past or which suggests itself as an adder habitat, a nervous reaction seizes me and each step I take is governed by intense caution until I am back on open ground.

Gregor had seen his first ever adder that day and was fascinated, but it disappeared into the grass too quickly to allow him to photograph it. The creature was about a foot in front of him when it wriggled for cover, and John asked him later for a description. Gregor reckoned it was about two feet in length and of a black-brown colouration, with the characteristic yellow zig-zag pattern along its back.

John attributes his fear of adders to a story his mother told him about his grandfather being bitten. He said he would ask his mother for the story and was as good as his word. Mary Menzies is a daughter of John Macalister, who was head gamekeeper at Limecraigs on the Argyll Estate. She remembered the date, 10 April, and the year was either 1947 or '48. Her father was in 'Glenramskill Glen' with a friend, going about his business. While climbing through the glen, John stood on an adder and was bitten. He and his companion returned at once to their bicycles and hurried back to Limecraigs. He was attended by a nurse and was confined to bed for six weeks.

Coincidentally, on the evening John left his and his mother's written account at my house, I was out visiting Alastair McKinven (p 171), who mentioned that he too had suffered an adder bite. He was aged about twenty at the time and hadn't long returned from National Service. John Armour in Ballybrennan had hurt his back and wasn't fit to do the lambing on the farm, so Alastair agreed to cover for him. He was walking home to Dalbuie from Ballybrennan through heather one day and felt an ankle start to hurt. By the time he reached Dalbuie, he could hardly walk. A woman doctor came from Southend to attend to him. He didn't remember what treatment he received, but he recovered after rest.

27 June: Corphin

On my way into the quarry above Corphin to leave my bike, I saw my first common blue butterfly of the year winging by, and when I took out my journal to record the sighting, I put down 'Bike Quarry' as the location. I'd just coined the name, without giving it any conscious thought.

I had two little projects that day. The first was to look at Corphin ruins, since I've referred to the place and its McIsaac associations (p 35). I'd prowled around them in the 1980s, but since then had tended to pass them with hardly a glance. I remembered on my way down that in the 1970s a nephew, Malcolm Docherty, had found the blade of an old shearing hook in the drystone wall of one of the Craigaig ruins. The wooden handle had rotted away, and the blade itself was rusty and thin. I had wondered how old it might be, since it's unlikely any corn was grown at Craigaig much after the eighteenth century.

There was no relic to be found at Corphin, but as I approached the ruins I noticed a cluster of tall pale flowers sticking out of the only surviving gable. I couldn't remember having seen these flowers before and, in my excitement, thinking I'd discovered a rarity, took several photographs, but failed to check the leaves. I didn't notice these until I walked around the sheep-fank, where the flowers were also growing from the walls. I'd first noticed the plant, which was not in flower at the time, on the dun at Kildonan many years ago, and someone with me identified it as pennywort (*Umbilicus rupestris*); but an alternative name, navelwort, is just as apt, and that's what Agnes Stewart called it when I stopped at her house with a sprig of cotoneaster from Ru Stafnish, and took the opportunity of showing her the photographs I'd taken. 'Penny' is from the coin shape of the leaf and 'navel' from the dimple in its middle. The flowers, which tower above the low-growing flat leaves, are bell-like and drooping, and yellowish in colour, though I noticed some with a pink tinge.

37. Pennywort growing from gable of ruin at Corphin, 27 June 2014. Photograph by the author.

The ruins consist of two long parallel steadings aligned south-west to north-east, with the little square-shaped sheep-fank at the south-west end. At the seaward end of the southernmost steading, of which little remains, I found a raised platform which, from the several stone rings within it, must have been the stack-yard, where corn was stacked and thatched for the winter. I sat there and had my filled roll and tea, enjoying the sun, after which I headed to the shore.

I'd last been down on 6 June – three weeks earlier – and, in the interval, the path had become so overgrown with grasses, bracken, nettles and brambles I was soon wishing I was somewhere else. Had I not been using that path down to the Dummy's Port all spring, chopping bracken and snipping briers, I believe I wouldn't have found it. Mid-way down, my left foot slipped off the track and I tumbled backwards into the thick vegetation, stinging a hand on nettles. I looked for and found a docken, and rubbed a leaf over the sting. I have no idea whether the remedy is effective, but I believe it to be, and that, I suppose, is enough.

As I walked the coast towards the Ru and – project two – the shrub I had come to examine (p 101), I encountered a particularly tangled section of the path, and decided to avoid it by using the lower shore. I'm glad I did, because as I turned down I caught a whiff of fragrance, which drew me to a small dog-rose bush, with its lovely pink flowers, growing among boulders almost at the high tide-mark. It was festooned with dried seaweed, reminders of the past winter's storms.

Whenever I encounter dog-rose (*Rosa canina*) I think of old Hugh MacFarlane in Tarbert (p 57). He had an abundance of knowledge and a rich local vocabulary, and I tape-recorded him assiduously in the last five years of his life. The dog-rose for him was always Gaelic *earradhris*, and he had reason to remember it, because in his earliest years as a fisherman its wood was preferred for carving net-mending needles. Its fruit, the hip, for him was *mucag*, Gaelic again. When my daughter Bella was going to *Bogha-frois*, the Gaelic play-group in Campbeltown, I'd give her words I remembered, and I gave her these two time and again, when we'd meet with fruiting dog-rose on our walks. If she hasn't forgotten them, I'll be surprised and delighted.

1 July: Creag nan Cuilean

This outing began with a taxi fiasco, the aftermath of which marred the entire day. I'd intended travelling to Machrihanish by bus, visiting the Inneans and returning to Machrihanish by the coast. Judy, too, had a notion for a hike, but had several tasks she was keen to finish at her allotment. It was a day of uncommon heat, and we decided that a later start would be sensible. I suggested taking a taxi to Ballygroggan at 4 p.m. and returning from Machrihanish by the late bus, and we agreed on that. She would return to her allotment, work there until 3.30, and in the meantime I would get on with some writing. She duly returned, I phoned for a taxi, and at 3.55 we stood outside on the pavement to await our transport.

Just before 4, a bus for Machrihanish drew up at the stop across the street, and we reproached ourselves for not realising there was a bus at that time; we could have been boarding it with travel passes in hand. Still, we reassured ourselves, by opting for a taxi we would eliminate an hour-long slog in the heat up Lossit brae to the true starting point of the walk, Ballygroggan. The bus drew away and the wait for the taxi began. By 4.30, we were still on the pavement, certain now that something had gone badly wrong with the hire.

When the taxi finally appeared, an explanation appeared with it – it had already been to Ballygroggan! The problem had been entirely semantic. I couldn't recall precisely the words I used in ordering the taxi, but I probably requested 'A taxi for Ballygroggan' instead of '... to Ballygroggan'. I blithely accepted blame, though the driver did admit that she had been caught out in the past by similar ambiguities.

I hadn't ordered a taxi for decades; indeed, I have often been heard to vow that I'd rather walk, no matter the distance involved, than pay for a taxi, which brings me to the cost of the taxi and the ensuing angst. At the top of Lossit brae, I told the driver that she could drop us there and turn, since she'd already been to Ballygroggan; we'd walk the rest of the road to Ballygroggan, a short distance anyway. I asked her how much I owed her and she said, 'Sixteen pounds'. – 'Did you add on anything?' I queried. 'No,' she replied. Judy had earlier pressed her to charge us extra as compensation for the double journey and a lost hire from a pub in town. I'd later wish that she'd just stated what she considered a charge fair to both parties, but the issue was left to me to deal with, and I was the wrong person. In my ignorance of taxi fares – the last one I paid was probably around twenty years ago, a couple of quid to Narrowfield – the basic £16 itself seemed punitive for a twelve-mile round-trip, and in my turbulent mental state I decided to add £4 as compensation for the muddle, despite Judy's surreptitiously pressing a £5 note on me as I drew a £20 note from my wallet. So, I handed the driver £20 and we set off.

The repercussions were immediate. Judy thought I'd been mean and told me so. I pondered the criticism uncomfortably for a few minutes and decided I had to agree with her, so the entire walk was blighted by self-reproach, which ended only with our arrival back in town, when Judy went straight to the taxi office with that additional £5 note. Was even that enough? I have since reverted to my absolute rule – no use of taxis unless in a stark emergency.

At the metal bridge over Craigaig Water, I recalled a telephone call from a member of the Kintyre Way committee the previous year. The caller took his time coming to the point, clearly uncertain as to what my response would be, but, when he finally did, it transpired that he wanted to propose that the bridge be named after me. I had no objections to the proposal, indeed was rather flattered by it, but he left Kintyre later that year and I heard no more about the idea. Since the bridge is hardly a structure of aesthetic distinction, and is probably incapable of any real improvement, I am content that the honour, well intentioned though it was, should drift in limbo.

As Judy and I crossed the moor, we discussed our return route. I favoured the coast, but, as Judy reasoned, had the wind dropped (it did), we might find ourselves labouring north in the debilitating heat of that rocky terrain. At a certain point on the path, Judy suddenly remarked: 'Why don't we go up there?' I looked, and 'up there' was Creag nan Cuilean, a hill to the south which rises to 1166 feet and is joined to its higher neighbour, the Slate (1263 feet). The name translates as 'Rock of the Pups', a presumed reference to young foxes, and although it now applies to the whole hill, the eponymous crag is high on the north-facing slope.[112]

We had discussed for several years climbing Creag nan Cuilean, but considered it a walk more suited to winter than summer. Judy had never been on the hill and I wasn't certain that I had, but I'll return to that matter. We decided to follow an old turf-dyke which climbs the north-facing slope of the hill, after which a dried-up water-course, filled with rushes and bounded on either side by a heathery bank, appeared in sight, so we followed that until it too petered out, then continued to the top. We sat in full view of the grand north-facing flank of Cnoc Moy, but weren't long settled before the wind dropped and midges appeared in clouds. It was time to move, and we moved quickly, heading north and picking a route down to the enigmatically-named Allt Mhic an Tanner, which runs west through a glen dotted with shieling-huts. Owing to our rapid departure from Creag nan Cuilean, we had no time to look for two features which belong to recent history. To be truthful, I wouldn't have known where to begin looking.

Post Office and Captain's Well

The first, known as the 'Post Office', has doubtless rotted away without trace. It was a box, covered with roofing felt and mounted on a pole, on the Lossit side of the hill, and was in use in the 1920s by the McKendrick brothers, Alexander in Killypole and Dugald in Gleneadardacrock, for the exchange of messages. When a note had been deposited by either brother, a wooden flag, which was visible on the skyline, would be raised, and the note could then be collected. They were neighbours, in a sense, but very remote neighbours – their respective steadings were separated by the combined bulk of the Slate and Creag nan Cuilean – and the climb from either steading to the mail-box would have been no stroll.

38. Captain Hector Macneal of Ugadale, c. 1900. Reproduced from Campbeltown Courier, 28/5/1910.

The nearby Captain's Well was named after Hector Macneal of Ugadale, who died in May 1910. The hill and much of the surrounding land was then on Lossit Estate, which belonged to the Macneal family. Shooters would halt and refresh themselves with bottled beer from the cool water.[113] The bottles were doubtless lugged to the top earlier in the day by a gamekeeper or ghillie to ensure the gentlemen's satisfaction. Hector Macneal was born in Edinburgh and attended Rugby School before commencing his military career, which ended with his being invalided home from the Boer War while Captain and Adjutant of the 92nd Gordon Highlanders. He was just forty-seven years old when he died and left a wife and young family.[114]

Two pints of 'Belhaven'

We reached Machrihanish with an hour to spare before the last bus, and decided to pass the time at the Old Clubhouse. In truth, the decision was made on the moors and a brisk pace was maintained to ensure that the beer we'd promised ourselves would flow. Judy, I suspect, was more anxious than I to reach the bar, and when we stopped above Ballygroggan steadings to look at an event out to sea, I detected a note of impatience in her voice as she urged me onward; but I delivered the incontestable rebuff: 'This is what we're out here for.'

We'd been glancing out to sea from time to time and had remarked on how calm it was except for patches of tidal turbulence around Sgeir Mhòr, the big reef off Uisaed; but there was also a much smaller rough patch still further out and it looked different. We trained our binoculars on it and perceived at once its difference. A flock of birds was circling over it and plunging into the turbulence, and these birds could only be gannets. The conclusion was obvious – a shoal of fish breaking the surface, perhaps forced upwards by predators below. We continued to watch the distant frenzy until the water calmed and the gannets ceased their hunting and settled on the surface, afloat and perhaps also replete.

At the Old Clubhouse I ordered two pints of 'Belhaven'. As the beer was being poured, Harry Grogan, the resident quiz-master, approached me and asked if we'd be participating in the evening's entertainment. I declined, explaining truthfully that we'd be catching the last bus into town and couldn't stay for the end of the quiz. A

World Cup quarter-final tie, Belgium v USA, was filling two screens in the bar, and I was tempted to watch the game, but we'd decided to sit outside, so out I went with the glasses. The first question we overheard, as the quiz commenced, was, '"D" is the international vehicle registration number for which country?', and an hour later, as we hastened away for the bus, I heard Harry's voice fade behind us with: 'The town of Swindon in England is ...'

Clegs and ticks

Horseflies (*Haematopota pluvialis*) were a constant nuisance all that afternoon. The local name, of course, is 'cleg' (from Old Norse *kleggi*), which suggests, I fancy, a rather more nasty encounter. I believe I suffered more bites that day on Creag nan Cuilean than ever before. The cleg alights silently and has already bitten – inflicting a sudden pain like the prick of a sharp needle – before you know it's there. I never try to kill them, but anyone who does is likely to be disappointed. They are equipped with amazing vision, and are up and away before the swatting palm or cap can reach them! They appear in much smaller numbers than midges, two or three at a time perhaps, and often a lone raider. Nature in her mercy has so arranged it.

George Newlands, a Campbeltown fisherman, told me he was bitten in the neck by a cleg at Canna while queuing at a spring for a wash. His neck swelled so much that his concerned shipmates took him immediately to Mallaig. The doctor there considered him too ill to send by train to hospital in Glasgow, and, instead, since there was no local hospital, lodged him with an old woman in the village. George maintained that the old woman's herbal poultices and not the doctor's medicines saved his life.

The stealthier ticks, which lie in wait for mammalian blood, were not as much of a problem to me this year as in some other years. The most I had to deal with in a day was five, during an outing to Ru Stafnish. I saw them crawling on my trousers – all of them following the grooves of the corduroy – and was able to remove them before they could attach themselves. Throughout the summer, merely two managed to commence blood-sucking, and they were removed with tweezers as soon as I felt my skin irritated. (Twist the tweezers clockwise, taking care to remove the mite in its entirety, and treat the wound with antiseptic cream immediately.)

Ticks have a complex life-cycle, and have to work hard to complete it, which is why, I suppose, I kill them only when there's no alternative. A tick begins as an egg on the ground and hatches into a six-legged larva, which, the following spring, climbs on to vegetation and attaches itself to a passing host; when fully fed, it drops back to the ground and metamorphoses into an eight-legged nymph, which has to find another host, drink blood and again drop off; it metamorphoses once more, into an adult which has to find a final host and feed again. Once mated, the male dies and the female drops to the ground for the last time and lays her eggs, as many as 18,000 of them. Ticks are able to detect the animal species which best suits their destiny. The one which generally finds humans desirable is the sheep tick.

In some parts of Kintyre I have walked, I ended up 'crawling' with them, but they seldom reach my skin because for many years I have eschewed shorts in the hills, even on the warmest of days. I'll wear a pair of light trousers and tuck the bottoms into my socks. From time to time during the outing, I'll check my clothing, and, when I'm home, will check my body, usually in a bath. A tick or two will penetrate the barriers, but seldom. Of all the places I habitually frequent, Ben Gullion is probably the least troublesome, and that's because there are no sheep and few deer in the forest, so ticks fail to proliferate. In the past decade or so, shepherds and farmers and hillwalkers in Kintyre have become increasingly aware of the dangers of tick-borne Lyme disease. Judy was treated for it in 2013. This is her account.

Some time during the summer of 2013 I was bitten by a tick, but didn't notice it for a few days. As usually happens with tick bites that aren't dealt with straight away, the site became red and sore, so I applied antiseptic cream and expected it to clear up. I noticed some time later that there was a ring around the site of the tick bite, and that this appeared to be spreading. I can't now remember what prompted me to make an appointment at the Health Centre to have it looked at – perhaps an internet news article. I gave a blood sample and was put on a course of antibiotic and told that I should mention the bite should I ever suffer from any of the symptoms of the next stage of Lyme Disease, since a negative result from the blood test in the early stage of the disease did not necessarily mean that I had not picked up the infection, which can, much later, progress to cause joint pain and flu-like symptoms, and can, in rare cases, prove fatal if left untreated. After the antibiotic, the rash disappeared.

6 June 1984

I couldn't remember having been on Creag nan Cuilean before, but had a vague recollection of crossing either it or the Slate. In fact, I was on both thirty years before, as I discovered, to my delight, in an overlooked notebook. The entry opened at the Inneans, but I'd done a lot before then, and still had a lot to do.

I set off by bicycle at mid-day. At Kilwhipnach road-end, I met Isobel McInnes, who had driven her husband Robert to his peat-bank at Lochorodale and was returning to Stewarton. I found him there, a solitary stooping figure on the moor. He was 'fitting up' peats – standing blocks together in little clumps to dry them – and I offered my assistance if he felt like cutting more peats. He welcomed the offer and we worked for a couple of hours, Robert cutting and I spreading. Afterwards, while sitting with him, drinking tea and smoking, the notion of 'cutting away for Creag nan Cuilean' came to me. I left Robert at 3.50, cycled on a bit, concealed the bike beside a burn, and headed into the hills.

I hadn't reckoned on encountering so much ploughed forestry ground, and 'the going was tough', but by following burns for much of the way I got on to the Slate without undue exertion. At the top, I followed a forestry ride which took me to a boundary fence, on the other side of which the ground was unscarred. I crossed that fence and followed it on to Creag nan Cuilean until I was looking down into the Inneans Glen and 'away across Ballygroggan ground to Islay, Jura, Gigha and the Knapdale hills'.

I reached the Inneans Bay just after 6 o' clock, lit a fire for tea and began filling in my journal: 'The hottest day of the year, legs and arms – and head and neck, I dare say, though I can't see them! – are reddened.' Later: 'The sun is clouded over and the air is cooler. Time is now 6.50. I'll have to set off in about 10 minutes, because I shan't be going back by the same way, but going through the glen, which will involve a lengthy walk by road to reach my bike – an unplanned stage of the journey, but then so much of this day has been unexpected. The only expected part of it is being here!'

I left at 7, and fifty minutes later was sitting at Gleneadardacrock ruin, pleased with my progress. By then, the sun was out again, and the heat, for the time of day, so 'extraordinary' that I pulled off my tee-shirt and sat bare to the waist. There the account ends, and there I leave myself, in solitude and silence.

6 July: Arinascavach

In *A Summer in Kintyre* (p 173) I described a walk with John MacDonald in 1982 which should have taken us from the Black Loch to Feochaig, but, when we lost our way in mist, took us instead to Arinascavach. If I ever returned to Arinascavach, I have no memory of it, but the name, which may represent 'Shieling of the Hawthorn',[115] has for long intrigued me.

The forest around 'Scavach' has been felled and replanted, and the steading is difficult to reach, even by the shortest routes. Judy and I went there on 6 July with Margaret McKiernan and Davie Robertson. I'd known for years that Margaret had ancestral connections there through her late mother, Georgina, whose father was Neil Galbraith Campbell, born in 1887 at Dalbuie, near Scavach. Neil's father Malcolm was born in 1857 at Scavach and died in 1891 at Dalbuie. His parents were Archibald Campbell and Janet MacLaren, to whom I shall return.

That Campbell family descends from Stronchormaig/Glenfeochan Campbells in the Oban area, some of whom were still farming at Glenfeochan right up to the beginning of the twentieth century. The line has evidently been traced back to a Dugald Campbell who was born about 1510 in Glenfeochan. Georgina Campbell's line thus extended back through Neil, Malcolm, Archibald, Colin, John, John, Patrick, Duncan, Dugald Og and Duncan to the first Dugald in the early sixteenth century.[116]

Margaret's grandfather, Neil Campbell, was a house painter to trade, but painted in oils as a hobby, and I have several of his landscapes, one of which – of the Maidens' Planting with cattle on the beach and a rowing-boat offshore – hangs in my living-room. Neil's work found a receptive market in Kintyre, but he was prolific, and Margaret has a large collection of his unsold paintings at home, the earliest of which is dated 1925 and the latest 1963, twelve years before his death. Most of the work in Margaret's possession was painted on hardboard, since, as she observed, 'he had no money for proper materials'.

Margaret had only ever been to Scavach in winter, and after our visit there I had to concede that had the vegetation been down we would have come away with a fuller awareness of the place. That said, Sitka spruce were planted so close to the steading that the character of the settlement was destroyed, and felling operations have left the ground littered with brashings even up to the very front of the building. The route we chose from the forest road down to the steading – over a wasteland of tree-stumps, discarded trunks and strewn brashings – was hard-going. There may be a better route, but if so we couldn't identify it.

When Margaret and Davie were last there, on 4 January 2013, they had followed a burn downhill towards the steading, but the crossing of the burn at the bottom of the glen proved to be a trial, so that route was rejected. Margaret's daughter, Katrina Macfarlane, and Katrina's boyfriend, Jimmy MacDonald – since 9 August, her husband – were there that day. Ten years earlier, Margaret and Davie were there with Katrina, her brother Neil, and two Campbeltown Hospital colleagues of Margaret's, Elizabeth Marrison and Denise Fawcett. About twenty-five years before that visit, Margaret's mother had pointed out the steading from a distance away, Margaret's first view of Arinascavach.

We explored the interior right away. It was interesting, but messy. Margaret had glimpsed a 'big white bird' fly off as we approached the steading, and splashes of white excrement and a scatter of large pellets in one of the rooms suggested a barn owl. There was neither sight nor sound of owlets, but I later met Neil Brown, who monitors the barn owl population in Kintyre, and he said he'd ringed six chicks there in what was a remarkable breeding year.

Scavach, like Bordadubh, was an outdoor centre, but its status was unofficial. Peter Morrison informs me that it was adopted as such and occasionally used by Scouts, Sea Cadets and unaffiliated others, and that it may earlier have been a shooters' bothy. The remains of furnishings and bedding still litter the rooms, most noticeably two mouldering armchairs. Margaret mentioned that in 2003 one of the rooms contained benches and a table, around which the party sat for lunch, but they are gone. Judy admired an old 'Rayburn' stove with a boiler and tap at one side of it. But the ceilings are collapsing and some floorboards are stove in, and once the roof begins to go – which may be just years away – the building will be dangerous.

The graffiti had me reaching for my pocket notebook, and I offer the names which most interested me. Jan McInnes wrote her name on 2/4/2002; Katrina Macfarlane recorded her visit, on 4/1/2013, with the note, 'Great 3 Gran died in a well near this house'; James McGown, July 1997; Jamie Girvan, Shawn McDaniel, and Scott Campbell, all 15/4/95; Robert, Kerry, Imogen and Sola comprise the Houston family, who were there on 9/9/2001; the '16th Argyll' was there collectively on several dates in 1992, including, it would appear, '3 Agu' (*sic*); but I reserve to the last the most poignant message: 'Alastair McKinven/26/11/05/lived here from 1939 to 1943.'

When Judy and I emerged from the back of the house, we found Margaret and Davie about to break into cartons of fruit juice. Margaret confessed sheepishly that she had forgotten the flask of tea, which was in Davie's car, parked on the forestry road. Elizabeth Marrison had e-mailed to Margaret's phone a portion of an early Ordnance Survey map which showed Scavach and – the main point of interest – the location of a well there. Margaret and Judy went looking for it, while Davie and I sat smoking on a wall near the adjacent sheep-fank.

Bogie Roll and Rock 'n' Roll

Davie was watching me slice and rub pipe tobacco. He asked was it 'Bogie Roll' and I replied that it was 'Thick Black', a bulkier variant. He then produced an anecdote which was news to me, though I was in it. He and Rosemary Gilchrist – then his girlfriend, later his wife – had joined Joe McGill and me at a table in the Argyll Arms, Campbeltown, one night in the late 1970s. Rosemary had toothache, and I cut a tiny piece off my Bogie Roll and told her to press it into the cavity and she'd find it would dull the pain. It did exactly that, Davie remembered.

I had a raging toothache one week in July 1972 when beyond the help of dentistry. I was in the crew of the Kyle ring-netter, the *Kathryn*, herring-fishing over on the west side of the Minch with the neighbour-boat, the *Mary Ann*. Seeing the agony I was in, one of the old Gillies brothers aboard the boat suggested 'Bogie Roll' for stop-gap relief, and when we put into Scalpay-Harris the next morning, I went ashore, found a shop – perhaps *the* shop – and bought a packet of Mitchell's finest

Archie Docherty, father of Malcolm (p 132), had a small holding at Killeonan, but also did contract work as a drainer. When he was working close to home, young Malcolm would be sent out with his 'piece' and a can of tea, and could usually locate his father on a still day by the reek from his pipe. He smoked an ounce of tobacco a day, Malcolm remembered, a quantity which frightens me even thinking about it. Malcolm's brother Duncan told me in 1997 that his father once found a big salmon astray in a drain near Scavach.

Davie's reference to Joe McGill brought him back in memory along with the Bogie Roll. Genial Joe certainly knew his music back in the 1960s, and doubtless still does. I last spoke to him many years ago when I met him by chance in the Barras, Glasgow. He has lived in the city for most of his life and is still there, according to Davie, who was in a bar in Glasgow in 2013 when Joe materialised from the throng and tapped him on the back. In August 1964, when Manfred Mann came to town to perform in the Victoria Hall, the band's single 'Doo Wah Diddy Diddy' had just topped the popular music chart, and the popular press had also come to town. Joe and I were at the head of the Old Quay mingling with band members while photographs were taken. Joe appeared in a picture published next day in a national newspaper, but I had the consolation – a thrill remembered to this day – of having touched Paul Jones's leather jacket.

Two drownings

Early in 2014, while browsing in old newspapers, I chanced on a report from 1889, headed 'A Woman Drowned in a Well'. The wife of the shepherd in 'Arinskavack', Archibald Campbell, left the house 'ostensibly to fetch water from a well near at hand'. When she failed to return, Campbell went to the well and found her 'lying in the water with her head downwards, and quite dead'. The supposition was that she had fallen and was 'so stunned ... as not to be able to take herself out of the fatal position'. Since the well was 'a small one' and 'not more than three feet' deep,[17] her drowning is curious. Mrs Campbell's own name was Janet MacLaren and she was born in Balquhidder, Perthshire. Her age on the death certificate is seventy. These Campbells were already at Arinascavach by the 1851 census, so most of her life was spent in that remote spot.

Less than three years later, a second mysterious death by drowning occurred in that family. Angus Campbell, forty-five-year-old son of Archibald in 'Scabach', and a shepherd at Feochaig, went into Campbeltown for the Candlemas Fair in February 1892, and never returned. Six days later, his body was discovered on the shore near the New Quay by a police constable. 'On his watch being taken off him, it was found that it had stopped at eight minutes to twelve.'[118]

In the poor rolls for Campbeltown Parish, I noticed a daughter of Archibald and Janet. She was Jessie Campbell and the man she married was John Campbell, so she appeared on the roll as 'Jessie Campbell Campbell'. John Campbell died on 10 November 1895, aged forty-three. In the register of poor he was a 'carter', but in the *Campbeltown Courier* he was described more impressively as an 'entire horse owner and contractor'. He left Jessie with four children, Agnes, Archibald, Janet and John, for whose support she was awarded 4s 6d a week. Both her parents by then were dead. The most poignant part of the poor roll entry, for me, was the note that she married at 'Scavach' on 19 August 1884.[119] I can visualise the celebrations out there, the house full of merry guests, most of them probably Campbells.

39. L-R: Judy Martin, Margaret McKiernan and Davie Robertson at Arinascavach, 6 July 2014. Photograph by the author.

We looked for the well at the north-west end of the steading, but there was no trace of it. Judy fancied that a clump of wild irises might mark the spot, since these flowers flourish on damp ground, but there was no way of knowing. After a couple of group photographs had been taken, with the steading in the background, we set off back to the car. We hadn't had much of a walk, but had enjoyed an afternoon in sunshine. In view to the south-west, as we picked our way across the ravaged landscape, was the little ruin of Knocknagrain, which is Gaelic *Cnoc na Gréine*, 'The Sunny Hill', a beautiful name. It was hard to believe that Duncan MacEachern kept three work-horses there in 1797,[120] before the sheep and before the forest.

Peter Morrison

Peter Morrison's name wasn't inside the ruin, but I knew he'd been there. His first visit, he told me, was in autumn or winter of 1987, with Ross MacGregor and Duncan Westerman. All three were instructors in the Campbeltown Sea Cadets and were keen to find suitable places for adventure training. They knew about Scavach and its use by Scouts, and decided to see it for themselves. They set off from Crosshill Loch one dry but bitterly cold Saturday morning, followed Tomaig Glen to the Black Loch, and entered the forest from there. Having followed a forestry road for a time, they cut off into dense conifers and proceeded along a fire-break towards the burn where they reckoned the building would be. They came to a well-worn path, which they decided to follow, and further on noticed a series of marker-posts which led them to their destination. Having explored the ruin, they left as darkness was falling. This time they kept east of the Black Loch and aimed for the head of Glenramskill. Peter remembers that, during their descent of the glen, 'night vision was blighted by the lights of the NATO jetty which had an oil-tanker visiting'.

Peter's next visit to Scavach was in the spring of the following year, a week-end of brilliant weather. He was accompanied this time by four Sea Cadets, Robert Harvey, Michael Rutherford, Craig Bedson and Ian Smith. They intended to stay overnight, so were laden with sleeping-bags and provisions. They occupied the living-room/kitchen and spent most of the time yarning around the Rayburn, which they had managed to light. Peter hardly slept that night, hearing what at first he imagined to be a 'constant repetitive engine in the distance'. When he finally decided to investigate the noise, he discovered it was coming from the attic, and found 'an owl making a kind of purring noise'. The next day, the party set off back the way they had come, but instead of continuing to the Black Loch, they headed west to Pennygown and from there to Lochorodale and over the Slate to Machrihanish.

I'd heard rumours of uncanny happenings at Scavach and asked Peter if he had experienced anything unusual there. The issue had clearly never bothered him, but he did mention that, on his first visit, the party had found a crude Ouija-board, which one of them threw into the trees. And there was a strange occurrence during his overnight stay. While he and his companions were seated around the stove, a battery-operated radio was on in the background. The reception was perfect, but at about midnight the music inexplicably stopped, and there was silence for about twenty seconds before it resumed. When Jimmy MacDonald visited Scavach in 2013, his antennae detected a sinister presence, and his apprehension was intensified when his mobile phone somehow produced a photograph of the place without his assistance.

Alastair McKinven

Two days after my visit to Arinascavach, I was walking along Burnbank Street and saw someone I wanted to speak to, but I didn't know him to speak to and was reluctant to approach him in the street. He, however, knew who I was, had a question for me, arising from a book of mine he was reading, and decided to approach me. 'He' was Alastair McKinven, whose name and the note '... lived here from 1939 to 1943' (or 1942), I had seen in Scavach ruin. I answered his query as well as I could, then told him I'd seen his name at Scavach and asked him if he remembered anything about his life there. I realised that he must have been a child then and might remember little or nothing, but from the anecdote he produced straight away, I decided his knowledge would be worth exploring. I gave him my telephone number and suggested he call me with a date and a time that would suit for a visit.

An arrangement was made and I visited him on the evening of 14 July. I asked him to repeat the story he had told me in the street (though I had committed it to memory at the time) and here it is; but, first, the terrain has to be cleared of coniferous forest, the ruin at Scavach reconstructed, and a meadow restored to the landscape south of the steading.

There were two men in the meadow, scything hay. One was Alastair's father, Alex McKinven, and the other was the shepherd at Kerran, the McKinvens' nearest neighbour. Scything is warm work and the men were thirsty and in need of a smoke as well, so Alastair's father sent him to the house for two cigarettes and a can of meal and water. While Alastair was extracting the cigarettes from the packet, he decided, on an impulse, to take one for himself. He halved it and put it in a pocket along with a couple of matches. He was about four years old and ready to try smoking. When he returned to the hay-field with the necessities, his father noticed he was behaving oddly and focused on the hand in the pocket. He asked Alastair what was in his pocket and the boy replied, 'Naethin'. His father pulled out the hand and found the hidden tobacco. Alastair bolted at once.

40. Alex McKinven at Dalbuie in May 1955, with his favourite collie, Drift. Alex kept Drift for three years without his showing any inclination to work, then suddenly 'away he went as if he'd been doing it all his life'. Courtesy of Alastair McKinven.

On the day the Scavach pig was to be slaughtered, Alastair was warned not to mention the event to anyone. (The warning was never explained to him, but he has since deduced that the keeping of pigs was probably forbidden in the lease.) However, when the postman from Southend, Jimmy Greenlees, appeared at the door, Alastair opened it and blurted out: 'We skeoched the pig the day!' He did not recall having any sentimental attachment to the doomed animal, but he remembered a pig at Dalbuie, where the family later moved. While it was being fattened, the pig became a pet, and when the day of its death arrived the pig sensed what was coming and refused to leave its house. By then, Duncan McMillan had arrived from Kerran to 'do the business', and Alastair was sent into the shed to drag out the frightened beast, an experience which upset him.

Alastair has a fragmented memory of three soldiers appearing at Scavach in the early part of the Second World War. What circumstances brought them there he never learned, but he guesses that they might have lost their way during a military exercise. Doubtless they would have been taken into the house and given hospitality. He also recalls that his father had been issued with a rifle and gas-mask, which suggests his enlistment in the local 'Home Guard'.

He remembered a pony at Scavach. It was mostly used for carrying 'messages', or provisions, out to the farm from Hugh Smith's grocery van, one of the various travelling shops which served rural Kintyre. Hughie would park and await his customers at a certain time on a Tuesday on the Southend road below Dalbuie. Once, Alastair and his mother saw the van already there as they came over the hill above Dalbuie – Hughie was early, but he waited for them. The hill track which ran from Scavach down past the fanks at Dalbuie was later obliterated by afforestation.

From Alastair's memory of the steading, a clearer idea of the function of the compartments emerged. At the north-west end was the living-room and kitchen. The 'Rayburn' stove, which is still there, replaced an old-fashioned range after the McKinvens left in 1942 and Neil MacMaster moved in. Next were set-in beds and a small 'milk-house', in which butter was churned. There followed stable, byre, and, at the far end, a hen-house and a shed for storing the peats cut each spring on the Sliabh. At the back of the steading, facing on to the sheep-fank, was the built-on corrugated-iron scullery, which is still in place, and, close to that, two small outhouses, since collapsed. One was the 'washing house', containing an iron cauldron in which water for cleaning the family clothing and bedding was heated, and the other was the 'cludgie', or lavatory, containing only a bucket, the contents of which would be dumped 'down the glen'.

There was a well at the foot of an embankment below the front of the steading, but it was little used after the excavation of a water-hole north-west of the steading. The domestic water supply was piped from there to the scullery. The hole was fenced off, but, even so, a sheep fell into it and drowned during Alastair's time there. The mishap went unnoticed until the water began to 'taste funny'.

The McKinvens' tenancy of Arinascavach was preceded by a period at Ballygroggan – Alastair spent the first three years of his life there – and followed by a period at Dalbuie, which ended in 1959. Latterly, when Alastair was grown up, his father herded Dalbuie, 'Eldrick' (Eleric) and 'Crock' (Knocknagrain), while his beat encompassed the further hirsels of Scavach, 'Sleeoff' (Sliabh) and Arinarach.

At 'handlings', i.e. clipping, dipping and marking, neighbours would help one another reciprocally. At Scavach fanks, there would be assistance from the shepherd at Kerran, Duncan McMillan, the shepherd at Glenamucklach, Alex Paterson, and sometimes Archibald Campbell (Dalbuie), Donald McCallum (Achnaglach) and Jim McPhee (Pennygown). The Duke's carter, Willie McMurchy, would come for the wool by a track which ran from Uigle across the Sliabh and down into Scavach. As well as carting away the wool-bags, Willie also packed them. A bag would be suspended from the trams of an up-ended cart, and, after a few rolled-up fleeces had been thrown in, Willie would disappear inside to tramp down the wool. When he was ready for another fleece, 'his hand would appear out of the top of the bag'. Alastair's job, with Alex Paterson, was to 'draw' the sheep out of the fanks to the clippers on their stools, and also to have a mixture of tar and butter to hand for treating any sheep which suffered a nick from the shears, an accident which 'sometimes happened when the sheep struggled to get away'.

Two one-year contracts for Dalbuie survived in Alex McKinven's papers. They are headed 'Argyll Estate Office, Campbeltown', and were signed by William Muir, estate manager (and Alastair Thompson's maternal grandfather). The first ran from 28 May 1948 to the same date in 1949. Alex's wages were 99s per week (total £257 8s), with a weekly allowance for two dogs of 2s 3d each (total £11 14s). From that total of £269 2s was deducted £32 13s: £7 3d for 'house', three cows at £6 10s each per annum, three 'followers' (calves) at £1 10s each, and potatoes valued at £1 10s.

In 1923, Arinascavach had been advertised for let in a package which also included 'Upper Gartloskan', 'Dalbuy', 'Ellerick', 'Arinarach', and 'Knocknagrein', with shepherds' accommodation at Dalbuie and Arinascavach. The stock of black-faced sheep numbered about 1700 and there was 'good Grazing' for about 50 cattle.[121]

When Jimmy Allan finished work at Lussa in 1953 (p 148), he took a job as a driver with Argyll Estate, based at the yard in Argyll Street (now the site of Ciaran Court). His new job took him to parts of Kintyre he'd never seen before. One memorably fine day in the late 1950s, he drove to Auchenhoan farm, and from there, on foot, accompanied the shepherd, Sandy Helm, and Sandy's nephew Davie Helm, out into the hills to gather sheep and bring them back to Auchenhoan. The hills then were free of afforestation, and he was shown, in the distance, Arinascavach, which Sandy told him was uninhabited.

Sliabh

I'll end with a place-name missing from the 1923 list, 'Sleeoff', which is Alastair McKinven's pronunciation of Gaelic *sliabh*, and one I was pleased to hear. Until then, the only time I'd heard the name was in 1983, and I'd jotted it into a notebook in the Gaelic form, and then forgotten how my informant, John McMillan, a retired shepherd, had pronounced it. I could have heard the name, too, from Mrs Hector Galbraith, Polliwilline, whose earliest years, as Mary Balloch, were spent at Scavach, but she died before I became aware of her Scavach connection. (I published, in *Kintyre Magazine* 45, under the title 'A Hill-Farm Girlhood', Mary's interesting memoir of her early life, in which she records that her father was shepherd at Scavach for eleven-and-a-half years, until November 1933, when he took the tenancy of Achnaglach so that Mary, who was seven years old then, could attend school without having to be 'boarded out'. Her spelling, in that article, was 'Sleof'.)

There are many interpretations of *sliabh*, but the most apt for Kintyre is 'moor-slope'. A lease granted to John Turner in 1793 described 'Sleave' as a 'common moor' between his farm, Elerick, and the farms of Knocknagrain and Arinascavach. There are several other *sliabh* place-names in Kintyre, two of them mapped by the Ordnance Survey and all the others, except this one, in locations which cannot be identified; but I have already covered that ground. [122]

I shan't be covering the physical ground encompassed by 'Sleeoff' – from the back of Scavach out towards Uigle, according to Alastair – because a forest was planted over it, the same forest which also erased the old farms of Eleric, Knocknagrain and Arinarach. I hadn't truly realised the scale of the destruction wrought by state and (later) private afforestation in Kintyre until, obligated by research needs, I began to visit places I'd never seen before. It now seems to me that blanket afforestation is not only an environmental tragedy, but a cultural tragedy as well.

41. *In this pre-afforestation photograph, taken from Dalbuie Hill by Alastair McKinven, Sliabh is the distant hill and ridge.*

9 July: The Inneans

In early July, John MacDonald was 'between berths' at the fishing and was keen to introduce his friend, Nicola Coffield, to the Inneans. We had planned to go on the 8th, but heavy rain during the night persuaded John that we should postpone the hike until the following day, when the ground would be dry underfoot and, according to weather forecasts, the sun would be shining. The forecasts were correct, and we set off in Nicola's car in late morning and headed on to the Kintyre Way from the car-park at Ballygroggan.

We had a wander around the bay, noticing that the wooden cross on the Sailor's Grave had broken and that the cross-piece was lashed back in place. It looked weathered and sad. That cross was made and carried round by Neil Brown in Campbeltown (the second one he made for the grave) and is at least the sixth in a succession of memorials which have stood over the remains of the unknown fatality of the First World War. I fear it may be the last, since the dedicated custodians of the grave have either died out or are unfit to reach the Inneans. Perhaps the responsibility should devolve on my own or on a younger generation? Is it sufficient, I ask myself, to merely document a problem? Teddy Lafferty foresees a time when there will be no marker on the grave, only the ring of stones which will finally disappear under turf.

Footnote. John MacDonald, quite independently of the above ruminations, telephoned me early in November to suggest the erection of a more permanent memorial on the grave. He pledged a sizeable sum of money, which I am prepared to match. Should any reader be interested in helping us, financially or otherwise, get in touch with me. The hundredth anniversary of the body's discovery will fall in May 2017, and it would be fitting if a memorial could be in place by then, or even erected then.

10 July: Inneans remembered and Ben Gullion

42. John Watson in Inneans Bay, 2 October 1982. Photograph by the author.

In town the day after that walk to the Inneans, I saw a death notice in a shop window and was shocked to read the name on the card. John Watson had died, aged fifty-five, five days earlier in London (of a cerebral haemorrhage, I later heard). John worked for several years as a postman in Campbeltown before moving away, but I wasn't remembering him as a colleague; I was remembering a day I took him to the Inneans. It was a case of 'third time lucky' – the first hike we planned didn't happen because John 'slept in', and the second one was cancelled owing to poor weather.

The date was 2 October 1982, and we set off after work in John's car, which he left at Glenahanty. When we reached the bay, we lit a fire and brewed a kettle of tea, but not at the customary camp site, which had been wrecked and burnt by vandals two months earlier; we used instead a little fire-place which Teddy Lafferty had constructed nearby. Annoyingly, I was denied my customary fireside smoke, my pouch, knife and tobacco having fallen out of my rucksack en route to the Inneans. That was the second identical loss that year, to which add a beret and a door key.

The tide was higher up the shore than I had ever before seen it, and the sea was roaring in. I photographed John standing on the beach with his back to the west, a stick in his right hand and Knock Layd mountain in Antrim reaching out to 'touch' his upper arm. He himself is lost in silhouette, but I reproduce the photograph, anyway, for the dark-clouded sky and the heaving ocean with its track of sunlight. The sun was well down when we started back, and for most of the walk we were in the gloaming and then the night: 'Coming through Gleann Eadar da Chnoc, there was, for perhaps fifteen minutes, the magnificent and slightly eerie spectacle of long and sharp flashes of horizontal lightning away in the darkness to the east. The stillness out there was intense.'

That evening I headed on to Ben Gullion to gather the early and abundant blaeberries, and for almost two hours my focus was on the ground, my concentration interrupted only by an ant-bite. When I descended to the top of the trail, I saw a man, in vest and shorts, perched on the back of the bench, facing north. Hearing me approach, he turned his head, and I greeted him. He spoke with a thick Ulster accent, well-seasoned with expletives, and asked if there was a way to the top. I pointed out the route I favoured, through a spruce plantation, adding, however, that with increasing age I tended to seek out easy routes, and that, since he was clearly in the prime of life, he might prefer the simplest one, which was straight up the face of the hill. From the ensuing conversation, which lasted mere minutes, I learned that he belonged to North Belfast, had been working in Kintyre and had taken up running. Apart from an enigmatic reference to his trousers being 'ripped to bits', I learned nothing more about him and said goodbye.

On my way down, picking berries as I went, I could hear him talking into a mobile 'phone. At the bend in the track where a picnic table used to be, I stopped to secure the lid on my tub of berries, having finished gathering. I identified the picnic site, which was bare when the table was in use, but is now so overgrown that only those who know that little detail of Ben Gullion history would recognise it. In or around 2006, vandals wrenched out the table and threw it down the slope of the hill. In 2001, my sister Barbara, daughter Bella and I had sat there on the evening of '9/11', and on 19/2 of the same year, as I sat with Bella and Amelia, I carved their names into the wood. When the table disappeared, I wanted the names back and took a saw with me to the hill. I found the table upside-down at the edge of the forest and removed the square of plank I wanted.

I stood for a while watching the *Isle of Arran* manoeuvring into her berth at the New Quay, propellers thrashing and rumbling. My wife Judy and George and Margaret McSporran would be boarding her at 7 the following morning, while I was still in bed. The last of the sunlight was laying patches of gold on fields across the loch, and along the tops of hills in the north streamers of mist hung.

As I continued down the trail, I heard a voice at my back. I assumed it must be the runner's, but I kept going, thinking he was still on his 'phone. Again I heard him, and this time turned and saw him hurrying after me. He wanted to know if the track we were on would lead him back to his van at Narrowfield. I suggested he accompany me, and, further down the trail, cut off on to the loop of a cycle track, which soon took us to the Crosshill farm water-tank, which he recognised from his uphill slog. We had chatted along the way and I found him more personable than before. As we parted, he extended a hand, which I willingly shook. I can be as crafty as an Ulsterman in Ulster, and asked him his name, but in my case the question was genealogical rather than tribal. He gave me only his forename, and when I asked for his surname, he gave me that too, and spelled it.

13 July: Largiebaan Caves

I was at Largiebaan Caves for the first time since my fright with Jimmy MacDonald in 2012.[123] My companion this time was John McCallum, a talented footballer and promising young writer from Campbeltown. Despite the age difference – I am nearly old enough to be his grandfather – we share many interests, one of which is football, and, since the televised World Cup final was to kick off at 8 o' clock that evening, we wanted to be home in time for it.

John collected me from my house at 11.30 in a borrowed car, which he left at the turn-off to Glenahanty, and we walked out to the cliffs from there. Conditions were perfect, sunny with a cool breeze. John had been to the Inneans with his father, Peter, but had yet to visit Largiebaan, and, since Largiebaan is a place I believe should be seen at least once in a lifetime by anyone with an interest in exploring Kintyre, we'd been discussing a trip for months. In recent years, I have been content to sit on the cliff top and look on to the shore, but the caves are central to the appeal of Largiebaan and John was naturally keen to visit them.

We left the Kintyre Way where it turns uphill towards the Aignish and headed down along the cliff edge towards the glen. Past the waterfall – a powerful presence after the previous day's rain – I glanced at my customary route to the shore, a narrow goat-track which threads north across a steep rock face, and decided I'd prefer a different approach, so we scrambled straight on to the shore and made our way across the rocks to the caves. We were now out of the wind and in the pure heat of the sun, which was intensified by the heated rocks. I pulled off my jersey after we had sat in front of the southernmost cave for a late and keenly anticipated lunch. The noise of the surf was echoing behind us on the rock as a continuous restful soughing.

We'd have sat at the mouth of the northernmost and largest of the caves – the main object of our visit – but there was a troop of eighteen goats between us and that cave and we decided to allow them time to decide their next move. I expected them to vanish over the rock face on the seaward side of the big cave (which was ultimately what they did) but allowed that, with the human intruders out of sight, they might choose to trickle back south. Instead, they stood patiently until we were ready to make our way to the cave. They were reluctant to move and allowed us to approach quite close to them before they took off, and I remarked to John on how fearless the goats had become; thirty years before, they'd have been off at once if they saw humans approaching a mile away.

One of the caves – the biggest, I believe – was known in Gaelic as Beul Dearg, 'Red Mouth'; indeed, I've seen them referred to collectively as the 'Red Coves'. As an adjective in Kintyre place-names, *dearg* is rare compared with *ruadh*, also 'red', so it is worth noting another example nearby, Bruach Dearg, the brae at Glenahanty.

We explored the cave with a candle and a small torch, which, despite my having renewed the batteries that very morning, emitted a very feeble glow. Had I been properly prepared, I'd have had a more powerful torch with me. In 1993 I'd taken time to transcribe some of the names and initials on the walls of the cave, 'a marvellous social record', as I enthused at the time. The oldest I found that day – 'J McA' – was dated 1893 and had been carved in the rock, but the vast majority was pencilled on to the sheets of lime which have formed on the walls, and while many of these remain legible over a century later, others – my own included, it would seem – have been lost. Back then, I resolved to return and record all the names and dates I could decipher[124] – the total, by now, is probably in three figures – but I haven't got around to it yet, and may never. That day, I contented myself with two exotics from 1996, 'Diego/Alesandro'.

Some of the names which have appeared in the cave since 1993 surprised me. Largiebaan is a place of immense grandeur, but that grandeur comes from the cliffs and rocks which turn Largiebaan into a risky place as soon visitors begin their descent to the shore. As I read some of the names by candlelight, I thought: how the hell did *you* get down here? John wasn't able to leave his name in the cave because neither of us had a pencil; there were several in my rucksack, but to have fetched one would have taken more time than we thought we had.

Looking at the cliff above the cave, I noticed that since I was last there a huge chunk of it had broken off from about a hundred feet up. I looked on the shore at the mouth of the cave, and there it was, in bits, its relationship with the cliff still evident in its tawny colouration amid the black shore rocks.

There was one dead goat in the cave, a pathetic bundle of wool and bones, and as I passed it I switched on a little film in my head and saw the goat doing goat things on that coast. At the very last it was perched on the top of a skyline rock as though it owned the whole world, and then it stepped into nothingness. In the middle cave there was another dead billy, decomposing blackly near the back, and an old skull with horns intact; in the third – southernmost – cave, a further skeleton.

In that middle cave, several visitors have left their mark in white, red and yellow paint, daubed on in big lettering. The worst offender plastered his whole name over a rock face. From the quantity of paint used and the variety of colours, I assume that pots of the stuff were carried to Largiebaan. Whatever the explanation, it's all in bad taste, and contrasts unfavourably with the discreet graffiti in the big cave. At the very back of the southernmost cave were several hefty branches and lumps of tree-trunk which could only have been deposited there by wave action. I paced the distance from the back to the mouth of the cave and estimated it at 120 feet, so these log-tossing storms would have made spectacular viewing – from well above the shoreline!

43. *John McCallum resting during the climb out from Largiebaan shore, 13 July 2014. Photograph by the author.*

Since Largiebaan is unlikely to receive many visitors interested in butterflies, I was being especially observant that day. The tally from below the cliffs was twenty meadow browns, three common blues, one relative rarity, a grayling, which I noticed basking on a warm rock, and one other – probably a fritillary – which, frustratingly, I couldn't get close enough to identify.

Our route out was to have been straight up the slope from the caves to the cliff top, and we started off on a goat-track, resting frequently on the way. At a certain point, when we should have turned off the track and gone for the top, I decided, lazily I suppose, that we should continue our gradual progress. I had no idea where the track would lead us, never before having followed it further, so I was inviting risk. As it transpired, however, a little climbing over grass and rock took us off the slope and on to the spur we had followed on our way down. Secure now, we were able to rest and relax for a while. I took a couple of photographs of John with the cliffs behind him, and then switched positions with him so that he could photograph me. 'Mind and no' step back when ye're composin' the photo,' I advised him, only half-joking.

There followed a steep uphill slog, broken by several rests, before we arrived back at the Kintyre Way. The entire climb had lasted about an hour, probably a little longer than the direct route would have taken. We reached the car at 6.45, and were home for 7. I was able to cook and eat a meal before setting out for George McSporran's house, where I watched the World Cup won by a single goal in extra time. These two hours would have been better devoted to Largiebaan, but John and I weren't to know that.

15 July: McCambridge's wholewheat bread

On 17 June, I met Les Oman in G10 Bistro – since, regrettably, closed – for our weekly coffee and chat. He had just returned from a Felice Brothers concert in Dublin, where his daughter Tina then lived. He mentioned a loaf he had sampled in Dublin, John McCambridge's stone-ground wholewheat bread, assuming, correctly, that the surname's Kintyre/Glens of Antrim associations would interest me. I asked him why he hadn't brought a loaf back for me, since I could have converted the bread into an item for my work-in-progress (this book). Tina, he replied, would be coming to Campbeltown in a fortnight's time and would bring one. On 14 July, Les duly delivered the (frozen) bread to my door. The following day, I was gathering blaeberries and sat near Fin Rock to eat four slices with cheese-spread.

I have a personal interest in the name MacCambridge, because an ancestor of mine – and of George McSporran, who is a sixth cousin of my own – was Flora McCambridge, whom tradition in Kintyre credits with having spirited the young MacDonald of Sanda heir, Ranald, away from Dunaverty Castle before the infamous massacre of the garrison in 1647. Ranald's grandfather, Archibald Mòr, was executed on the spot, and his father, Archibald Og, was slain later in the year on the battlefield of Knocknanuss in Ireland.

Flora would marry a weaver named MacCaig from Articlave in County Antrim, and it is from him that I, on a maternal line, and George, on a paternal line, descend. Sanda Estate was restored to the MacDonalds in 1660, after ten years' confiscation, and the MacCaig family, by virtue of its link with Flora McCambridge, was subsequently favoured with tenancies of MacDonald-owned farms. Towards the end of the eighteenth century, there were MacCaigs in Coledrain, Penlachtan, Kilmashenachan and Pennyseorach.[125]

'McCambridge' is a peculiar Anglicisation of Gaelic *MacAmbrois*, 'Son of Ambrose', though I suppose it's no more peculiar than the disguises many other Gaelic names in Kintyre assumed. The name, in any form, has long gone from Kintyre, but was taken to the Glens of Antrim from Kintyre and survives there. Alasdair Roberts, in 1990, suggested that the earliest forms of the surname 'Montgomery' in Kintyre – 'McComra', 'McGomirie', etc. – derive from *MacAmbrois*.[126]

If his deduction is correct, and McCambridge and Montgomery are both products of the same Anglicisation trend, then to Flora McCambridge may be added a more illustrious *MacAmbrois*. The Canadian novelist, Lucy Maud Montgomery (1874-1942), whose *Anne of Green Gables* was published in 1908, descended from a Southend couple, Hugh Montgomery and Mary McShannon, who sailed in 1771 in the *Edinburgh* from Campbeltown to Prince Edward Island.[127] And there is yet another famous woman, the American actress Mercedes McCambridge, whose father the late A. I. B. Stewart contacted in the hope of establishing the family's origins; but Mr McCambridge was unable to help.

The words of the well-known Irish song, *Àird a' Chuain*, have been attributed to Eoin Mac Ambróis, otherwise John McCambridge (*c*.

1793-1873), who was born in Glendun, County Antrim. The Gaelic scholar, historian and politician, Eoin MacNeill, who was born in Glenarm, County Antrim, in 1867, and was also likely a descendant of Kintyre immigrants, described McCambridge as the last Gaelic poet in Country Antrim, and – unusual in the Glens – a Protestant to boot. MacNeill's mother knew him well and testified to his passion for the language. MacNeill rescued the song from oral tradition and published it in 1895, but the circumstances of its composition have been disputed. By one version, McCambridge and his wife left the Glens and settled in Ayrshire, from which coast the sight of his beloved Antrim hills inspired the tribute; by another version, he wrote *Àird a' Chuain* before his intended departure and was so moved by his own words that he decided not to go.

An Irish genealogical researcher, Brian S. Turner, recalled that in 1971, in Glendun graveyard in the Glens of Antrim, 'an old lady of the O Haras of that district pointed out to me the very field which she believed to be the site of the McCambridges' first home in Antrim, pronouncing their name in Gaelic as she did so'. Four men of the name were on the 1669 Antrim Roll, living between Glenaan and Glendun, and in nearby Layd churchyard – facing across the North Channel to Kintyre – stands a gravestone cut in 1832. A Gaelic inscription at the head of the stone has eroded to virtual illegibility, but the genealogical information reads as follows:

> Malcolm McCambridge who came from Cantire in Scotland
> A.D. 1625, located in Carnasheerin and died there.
> Daniel his son died in May 1690 aged 94 years.
> Archibald son of Daniel, Nov. 1795, AE 98.
> John son of Archibald 1797 AE 92.
> Francis son of John Sept. 1817 AE 65.
> Daniel brother of Francis April 1832, AE 76.
> Francis son of Daniel April 1832, AE 35 years ...[128]

Notice the name of the progenitor of that McCambridge family in County Antrim. 'Malcolm' is a characteristically Scottish forename, being the Anglicised form of Gaelic *Mael Coluim*, 'Devotee of Saint Columba', and commonly used as a substitute for Gaelic *Calum*. The firm of Irish bakers was founded by one Malcolm McCambridge, who moved from Galway in the west of Ireland and opened a shop in

Raneclagh, Dublin, in 1945. His son John joined the business at the age of fourteen and oversaw its expansion. According to the John McCambridge website, its bakery products now claim a 'one-third share of the Irish market'. Oh, and the bread was very tasty!

20 July: The dog Chomsky

'Chomsky' is a golden retriever who was acquired as a pup from a farm near Matlock in Derbyshire in October 2012 by my daughter Sarah and her partner, Neil. He'd stayed a few nights with us in his first winter and was crazy and destructive, as most pups, I suppose, are. I say 'suppose', because I only ever had one pup, Benjie, and he was crazy and destructive. We again welcomed Chomsky into the house on the day after he arrived on the ferry from Ardrossan with Sarah and Neil and their month-old son, Lachlan, for an eight-day holiday. They stayed with Neil's father Donnie, his wife Heather, and their son Jamie, at Machrihanish, and Judy and I felt we ought to have Chomsky since the Gillieses themselves have a placid collie bitch, Jess.

44. *Chomsky and Judy Martin at Fin Rock, 20 July 2014. Photograph by the author.*

I should explain the name 'Chomsky'. When Sarah was a toddler, Judy's parents were living in Carradale, and the conservatory at 'Kantara' was home to a plastic garden gnome which Alex's brother, Jim Honeyman, had given them as a joke. The gnome, however, was no joke to Sarah, and she quickly formed an attachment to him, necessitating that we find him an identity. I punningly conceived of 'Chomsky', after the American linguist and political activist, Noam Chomsky. Poor Chomsky – the gnome, that is – appears to have disappeared during a subsequent flitting, but Sarah didn't forget him, and when a name was wanted for the pup, 'Chomsky' was her choice. I rather naively imagined he must be the only canine Chomsky in the world, but Neil discovered many others on the internet website 'Instagram'.

Judy and I found ourselves custodians of a much calmer Chomsky than before, but we reckoned he was due a long walk, and took him on to Ben Gullion on the 20th. We chose a side-route I call the 'Peat Road', in the belief that it formed the lower part of a track which led to peat-cutting banks on the top of the hill. It is no longer the rather private route it used to be, because mountain bikers converted it into an unofficial cycle track, but that suits, too, because the track is now maintained, yet remains relatively quiet. As soon as we crossed from Knockbay on to Forestry Commission ground, we let Chomsky off the lead and away he went, but minutes later he found a pile of excrement in the middle of the track and rolled on it. I dragged him off and discovered to my disgust that the deposit was of unmistakably human origin. An excellent start to Chomsky's day on Ben Gullion!

Fortunately, the ordure smear was soon removed as he charged through muddy ditches, plunged into peaty pools, and rolled around with abandon on grassy clearings. He was no trouble on the blaeberry ground at Fin Rock, and stayed with us most of the time, occasionally romping off for a little exploration, but just as content chewing on a heather stalk. We filled two one litre ice cream tubs with berries and then headed home by another route, avoiding the deviant turd.

22 July: The Stinky Hole

Wife Judy, daughter Sarah, grandson Lachlan, and Chomsky had gone to the caravan at Polliwilline early that afternoon, and I said I would follow and spend the night with them. I was late setting off, but the departure time worked in my favour because the journey was eventful.

As I was cycling past Glenramskill, I noticed a huge bank of mist out in Kilbrannan Sound. As mist goes, it was spectacular enough, but I quickly noticed something more remarkable – it had formed into a 'mirror image' of Davaar Island, but higher and reversed in shape. I decided I should photograph the phenomenon, but by the time I chose a stopping place, the formation had flattened out somewhat, and the resemblance had diminished. I stopped again at the Stinky Hole – that aptly-named tidal lagoon just past the Doirlinn – and from there the formation again resembled the island, whose pointed end was 'touched' by the pointed end of the mist-bank, thus enhancing the effect. But I decided I didn't want a photograph, which would probably fail to capture the vision I was actually seeing and describing in my notebook.

45. John Brodie with bicycle at entrance to the Sheep Fanks, looking towards Davaar Island and the mist bank, 22 July 2014. Photograph by the author.

I still had notebook in hand when another cyclist, John Brodie, a former Royal Mail colleague and hiking companion, appeared. I explained the nature of my observations, and he remarked that he had been seeing unusual mist formations for the past few days. He'd been coming regularly to the Stinky Hole to monitor the breeding success of a pair of shelducks which had produced thirteen ducklings and preserved them all. Most years, he observed, only two or three ducklings would survive the depredations of black-backed gulls and other predators, but these parents were stern custodians, and he'd watched them driving off intruders by 'skiting', or skimming, over the surface of the lagoon, making a terrific splashing noise. We had two adult shelducks in view, but no young that day, though I counted ten wonderfully camouflaged mallard ducklings crossing the rotted seaweed at the head of the lagoon.

The Sheep Fanks and Bobby Martin

John accompanied me as far as the Sheep Fanks and we talked for a while there, studying the mist-bank out to sea. From the upthrust formation I'd perceived as Davaar Island, it extended south, low and level, for mile after mile until it disappeared behind Auchenhoan Head. While we were chatting, a red car pulled in at the entrance to the Fanks, and I recognised the driver as Bobby Martin, whom I meet frequently, winter and summer, on that road. I had business with him, and parted from John, who was ready, in any case, to leave.

I'd spoken to Bobby at Kildalloig on 8 June, when he told me he'd been born and brought up at Killocraw, near Bellochantuy. I'd always assumed him to be a thoroughbred 'Toonie', so was interested in his store of rural memories. A couple of days later, I wrote to him suggesting we meet for a chat. I was prepared to visit him at his home, but in the end we agreed that we'd leave the meeting to chance. That chance had arrived.

He moved his car into the Fanks and we sat together on the bonnet for the 'interview'. He was born in 1931 at Killocraw Cottage, the house, he told me, with the date '1906' above the door. Provost Archibald McCallum was also born there, a fact Bobby didn't discover until the day 'Baldy' was buried. Bobby's father, Peter Martin, who suffered shrapnel wounds in the First World War, worked at nearby Putechan in the Cefoil factory which manufactured a seaweed-based wrapping paper, soon to be superseded by cellophane.

Bobby's mother, Mary Borthwick, belonged to a Borders shepherding family which came to Kintyre in the mid-nineteenth century. Mary was dairymaid on the farm, and Bobby, from a young age, helped out by shawing turnips and taking them to the farm by horse and cart, and by leading the horse, Flora, down to the roadside with cans of milk for collection. He remembers drinking oatmeal and water at sheep-clippings.

He and his brother Neil would go into the hills every September to gather white heather. They'd pass the cottage where the shepherd Johnny Mitchell lived with his daughter, Nellie, and continue to the hill where they knew they would find the special heather. From there they could look east, and Bobby remembers seeing the shepherd's cottage at Collusca in the distance.

He recalled the first Luftwaffe air-raid of the Second World War (6 November 1940). When the raider flew in towards Campbeltown over Killocraw, Bobby was carting milk-cans down to the road, and remembers thinking that it might be a German plane. On its way back, the aircraft strafed cars along the West Road as far as Glenbarr before turning away in the direction of Gigha. Bobby remembers hiding fearfully 'ahint the daik'.

The family moved to Campbeltown when Bobby was about eleven years old. He lived first in Saddell Street before moving to one of the new miners' houses in Crosshill Avenue around 1948. Aged about twelve, he started work with West Coast Motors, taking parcels to and from buses, and at the age of fourteen, having left school, began his training with the company as a motor mechanic, an apprenticeship which was interrupted by two years' National Service. When West Coast Motors sold its fleet of lorries to British Road Services, Bobby moved with the lorries. In 1973, he established his own commercial garage, Martin Maintenance, which he ran until his retirement in 2007.

To my knowledge, Bobby and I are not related. DNA analysis would resolve the uncertainty, but I appear to be the only Martin in Campbeltown who has had a test done, and that test established that my DNA group is L193 and that I have more MacLean than Martin relatives on the database. There are four Martin families in Campbeltown whose lines are distinct as far back as documentary records go, and I have already published a brief account of them.[129]

46. Bobby Martin at the Sheep Fanks, Kildalloig, 22 July 2014, with his car in the foreground and wild teasel in the background. Photograph by the author.

Before I left Bobby to resume my journey, I photographed him standing in front of a line of huge teasel (*Dipsacus fullonum*) which had sprouted along the seaward side of the car-park. They had been sown by a local ornithologist, Tony Lambert, and I knew the reason – the seed-heads feed small birds. I'd never noticed teasel growing anywhere else in Kintyre and asked Agnes Stewart if she was familiar with it in the wild. She replied that she had seen the odd one 'at different times, in different places', and attributed these random plants to the droppings of birds which had fed on mixed seed at bird-tables.

23 July: Home by the Learside

I enjoyed my time at the caravan with Sarah, Lachlan and Judy, and members of the Docherty family who were staying with my sister Barbara in her van. But I slept badly that night, as I often do at the caravan, being out of my domestic routine, and as the morning promised another warm day – we were in a mini heat-wave, reminiscent of the previous year's glorious summer – I didn't relish the prospect of my journey back up the Learside.

As I neared the top of the track from the shore to Polliwilline farmhouse, I noticed two other cyclists parallel with me on the main road from Macharioch. It appeared that we would meet at the foot of the Learside road if they too were taking that route rather than the loop to Machrimore Mill. They were ahead of me by mere minutes, a man and a woman in early middle-age. Both were pedalling, but I dismounted for the initial steep part of the brae. He was in front and she was labouring after him, and I noticed that the gap between us remained constant, confirming my long-held conviction that pushing a bike uphill is the more sensible option unless one is young and fit – energy is conserved and the top is gained in much the same time.

Time appeared to be a pressing factor in the couple's outing, but for some reason they stopped together near the top of the hill, perhaps to fix one of the bicycles, and I realised that the unexpected was about to happen: I'd catch up with them and have a chance to quiz them about their journey. But the conversation didn't happen. As soon as they noticed my approach, she mounted her bike and was off again, and he, momentarily delayed, delivered one line by way of engagement – 'A good day, better than being rained on' – and was off after her. So, I didn't discover who they were, and they didn't discover the location of the roadside springs, at which they might have refreshed themselves, or any other particles of local knowledge which might have rendered their journey a little more rewarding.

I stopped at the first of these springs, at the Winny Corner near the seventh milestone, and drank three cups of water, which was flowing vigorously and noisily and was 'bitsy' with vegetal matter. There had been a proper scooped well maintained at the roadside, but it was obliterated several years ago, presumably during ditching operations.

My next brief stop was just minutes away, at the blocked-off track which leads past a quarry and into coniferous forest, since felled. In the previous summer, Judy and I had stopped there to count common blue butterflies (*Polyomattus icarus*, a total of twelve). I couldn't remember the date, but when I got home and checked, it was 7 July, over a fortnight earlier. We walked from town to the caravan that day, and stopped for a while at that overgrown road-end to finish our flasks. There was plenty of common bird's-foot-trefoil (*Lotus corniculatus*) – the food plant of common blue caterpillars – at that spot. I wandered around in the hope of seeing a blue, but there was none. My total for the entire day was four.

From the top of the hill, a few minutes' free-wheeling took me to the Second Water and my customary refreshment halt at the bridge. There was a car parked there and I noticed someone prowling at the north end of the bay. I was nodding off in the heat of the sun when a second car appeared. A young woman, whom I recognised as local, emerged, walked in my direction and then began peering over the landward parapet of the bridge. 'Are you looking for a way down?' I asked. No, she was concerned about adders and wondered if the overgrown banks of the burn would be safe for her sons to play on. Minutes later, a third vehicle sped down the brae and screeched to a halt in the lay-by. It was time for me to go.

As I approached the hairpin bend, wheeling the bike, I heard a car approaching downhill and drew the bike, and myself, closer to the verge. The car stopped on the bend, and the driver, Willie Durance, greeted me. He asked if I recognised his passenger, and I peered in through the window. When Willie told me the man's name, I knew who he was, but no longer recognised him as the man I remembered. During our brief conversation, Willie recalled that he had once seen a fellow on a mountain bike cycle up the brae we were stopped on without 'getting off his seat'. Many years ago, while I was standing at the bridge, a young man on a racing bicycle sped down Corphin brae at about fifty miles an hour and shot straight up the opposite brae without pause. The incident has stuck in my memory because he appeared and disappeared without warning, all in the space of a minute, and had I happened to step into the road he would certainly have struck me.

Willie was himself once a keen cyclist and belonged to a cycling club in Bishopton, Renfrewshire. He'd cycle all the way to Campbeltown for a week-end's camping, a journey of eleven to sixteen hours, depending on wind strength. He and his companions would set off after work on the Friday and travel through the night, stopping at Loch Lomond for a brew-up. This was just after the Second World War when roads were relatively traffic-free,[130] but I wouldn't fancy the journey myself, traffic or no traffic! Our conversation was interrupted by the appearance of another car on the brae. I reckon that was about the busiest I'd ever seen the Learside road, thanks to blue skies and a sweltering sun. I next met Willie in Amelia's Café Bistro in town on a stormy day in December, when I reminded him of that lovely day in summer.

28 July: Five cyclists on Ben Gullion

I was on Ben Gullion gathering blaeberries, but didn't go as far as I'd expected to; I didn't have to, because there was good picking along the middle bicycle trail. Two young boys cycled past without noticing me, one of them calling to the other, 'It's rough here'. I didn't manage to fill my tub from the bike trail and decided to finish at the top of the walking trail, where berries are always abundant. While I was there, mist closed in and the landscape vanished – all that remained was a line of spruce in the east, which could have been anywhere.

On my way downhill, picking as I went, I heard a slight clicking sound and guessed that someone was approaching. A man in his thirties appeared, pushing a mountain bike. 'You're at the blaeberries, then?' he remarked. After he'd passed, I thought – not many folk would know what I was picking, and, even if they did, probably wouldn't have used the Scottish form of 'blueberry'. Having run out of fruit bushes, I jumped on to the track to pack the tub in my rucksack. I also took the opportunity to update my notebook, and while I was scribbling, the thought came to me that the cyclist might soon be heading downhill at speed and that I'd better remove myself from the track. Simultaneously with that thought, a wood pigeon shot noisily over my head and startled me.

The cyclist didn't reappear on that track, but emerged on to the lowest bicycle trail by some irregular side-route. I heard a shouted conversation, and two other cyclists – a man and a girl – appeared briefly and turned east in the direction I was heading. I didn't recognise them at the time, but the lone cyclist, who was stopped further along the trail, told me they were a father and daughter.

This time I got talking to him and asked if he was a visitor. He told me he had come to Kintyre to work and was indulging his passion for cycling. He enthused about Ben Gullion's merits for mountain biking and mentioned that he and a local cyclist had been creating side-routes – in fact, he was poised at the upper end of one, and would soon shoot down it. He also enjoyed cycling on roads, he said, and mentioned the Learside. I asked if he was capable of going the whole distance without dismounting on the hills, and he looked at me as though I had said something stupid, so I changed the subject. He asked me how I had done at the blaeberries and I told him the weight I'd picked. His mother, he said, made blaeberry jelly in the part of Scotland where he was brought up, which explained his familiarity with the fruit.

I would encounter him for a third time at the end of the trail near Kilkerran graveyard, and the two other cyclists were with him, chatting. 'You'd better go home and wash these hands,' he remarked to me as I passed. I held out my red-stained palms to the father and daughter and told them, 'I've just committed a murder – my best friend is lying up the hill'. I hope the joke was explained to them after I'd gone!

31 July: Knockbay

Going on 8 p.m., at home, I happened to glance at a window and saw sunshine. That week's weather had been mixed and I hadn't been out at all that day, so I grabbed binoculars and camera, pulled on a jacket and set off. I'd intended going up the Knockbay road at the graveyard, but met Judy's daughter Doreen, and, since she was walking home to Ardnacraig Avenue, I decided to turn up that way and head on to Crosshill from the Grammar School.

I crossed the fence at the school playing-field and, looking around, noticed that the ridge opposite the wood at Limecraigs, with its rope-swing, had been part-cleared of bushes. There had been a diagonal track through the bushes from the field on to the ridge which rises to Crosshill itself, and I'd often used it in the past. Now, I saw, I could walk straight on to the ridge in a minute, and that's what I did. Still, I preferred the old path and the intimate contact with trees and bushes which following it entailed. There was a gnarled hawthorn one had to practically crawl under to pass, and I dare say it was there when I played on that hill as a boy.

The fence which ran from east to west along the grassy ridge had been removed and only a few bits of barbed wire and rotten stobs remained. I remembered writing a poem, 'Across the Sagging Fence', on the ridge one evening. It took only a few minutes to scribble into a pocket notebook and required little revision. It had emerged from an emotional response which demanded expression, and I can't say that of many poems I've written in the past several years. The date of its composition was 26 March 2010, and I'd gone out impulsively on an evening stroll and just kept going.

It appeared in *Paper Archipelagos* in 2011, and the poem I paired it with, 'Crossing a Field, Knockbay', had a similar emotional origin which brought with it a charge of creative energy. My dog Benjie was with me that evening, 1 July 2007, and, as we passed the ruin in the field at the back of Limecraigs Cottage, which has a big dead tree standing next to it, ruin and tree conjoined in my imagination. Lines were going through my head, and, when we reached Crosshill Loch, I sat in the middle of the dam and wrote them down. Judy admired the poem when I showed it to her, and it still pleases me as the finished statement of a momentary vision. Here are the two poems.

CROSSING A FIELD, KNOCKBAY

Dead tree and ruined house together
leafless, roofless in a world
from which a shining feather
to an outer abyss hurled

would merely falter to the ground
the fillet of some gentle dream
a crown of buds worn all around
children splashing in the avid stream

but light there's more of light
bare branches hold no shade
rooms darken only in the night
where even time has languished and decayed.

ACROSS THE SAGGING FENCE

I look across the sagging fence
into a space already darkening
beneath its canopy of trees and bushes
and see a path I used to follow
except the path is in my mind
for grass has repossessed its own.

I halt the shuddering reel of memory
before it casts me forms and faces
out from the archive of my losses
and turn to face the hill again
from which I'll bid the sun farewell
with all the birds who sing it down.

I carried on to the top of the ridge and stopped at a rock outcrop which George McSporran and I know as 'Sandy's Wee Shop'. When George took his son walking on the hill as a child, Sandy adopted the rock as an imaginary shop. I usually insert a coin into a crevice in the rock, an illogical custom – I dare say I've been buying 'good luck' all those years – which I forgot to observe that evening. At the top of the Ben Gullion trail, and visible from the rock, there is 'Shop Ridge', where my daughters Sarah and Amelia would play in the early 1990s, while Judy and I gathered blaeberries. They, too, had an imaginary shop. I wondered what the modern equivalents would be – 'Sandy's Wee Supermarket', 'Supermarket Ridge'? Somehow, these names don't sound as much fun.

Seeing the *Isle of Arran* coming up Campbeltown Loch, I decided to hurry to the New Quay to watch her berth and disgorge her vehicles and passengers, a spectacle which, as the summer progressed, increasingly diverted me. Caledonian MacBrayne is contracted to run the service for only one more year, but I earnestly hope it will be extended. The arrivals of the majestic *Isle of Arran* bring to Campbeltown harbour a stir which has been missing since the *Claymore* was withdrawn from the Irish run in 1999 and the *Duchess of Hamilton* sailed out of Campbeltown for the last time in 1970.

5 August: Dreams

I headed on to Ben Gullion in mid-afternoon to gather blaeberries, but I was heading into rain. It wasn't alarmingly heavy, but by the time I returned home I was soaked. On my way up, I decided to shelter in trees at a spot beside the east trail where the spruce plantation ends. My daughter Bella and I sometimes sat there and drank a cup of cocoa during night walks with Benjie. While in there, a fantasy emerged and I indulged it, fast-forwarding to the very end. Everyone who had ever walked that trail was coming uphill, and I watched a procession of thousands pass. Every face was looking straight ahead as though in a state of enchantment, and no one knew I was there. I counted those faces I recognised, and after the last person had passed I had a total of 385.

In a disturbing dream on 21 October, I saw runners on Ben Gullion. I woke from it at 4.25 a.m., with the wind howling outside, and wrote it down. My daughters were with me as children. We were at the top of the trail in the night and I was hearing cattle and worrying about a bull being among them. While I was fumbling in my rucksack for a torch, a group of runners appeared silently out of the darkness, 'without even one of them turning a head'. We all simultaneously exclaimed: 'The fright I got!'

Daughter Amelia later had a dream so terrifying she hadn't put it behind her weeks afterwards. It was of the type which is difficult to escape from, each perceived exit leading to an impasse, until finally one breaks free, grateful but shaken. I remember, from her narrative of the nightmare, only one detail: I myself was somewhere in the dream, muttering lugubriously, 'I'm not going to be around forever, but that's all right'. Strangely, on 29 November, round about the time of her dream, I was on Ben Gullion with Chomsky and heard Amelia's voice saying 'Dad?' It was an urgent appeal, as though I had disappeared and she was wondering where I'd gone. The voice was so clear that I listened and looked around, supposing there might be other people on the hill, but I failed to detect any human presence.

On 5 August, when I reached the top of the trail, Chris was on his mobile phone and acknowledged me when he ended the call. He had walked up the opposite trail and would follow it back down. His wife is from Campbeltown and they had travelled from East Anglia to visit her family, completing the journey by the Ardrossan ferry.

Higher on the hill, Kenny appeared by a route on which I seldom see anyone. I suspended the berry-gathering to chat, and discovered that his fiancée is from Campbeltown and that they were visiting her parents. I'd worked briefly with her father back in 1978, and allowed genealogy to sneak into the conversation. Kenny admitted that her parents' penchant for the subject passes him by, and I sympathised. My daughters, I confessed, become frustrated when I start making connections – this one's daughter married that one's son by his first marriage, and his second wife was a cousin of his brother's girlfriend – which are of no interest when the parties are unknown or dead. He shook my hand and carried on downhill. A couple of hours later, in misty and midgy conditions, I followed him.

7 August: Feochaig to Glenahervie

George McSporran and I had last been on the Learside together on 26 May, when we'd reached Feochaig at the end of our second futile search for the Pirate's Grave. I could hardly believe it was so long ago, and now summer was almost gone. We wanted to do the final bit, Feochaig Bay to Glenahervie Bay, which would take us to the familiar coastline north of Polliwilline, where George too has a caravan. We were fortunate with the weather – just a shower at the start – and the tide was still ebbing, allowing us to step on rocks for most of the way, avoiding the overgrown foreshore.

We hadn't gone far south of Feochaig when I let out a cry of delight which had George momentarily puzzled. I had recognised a sandstone rock, hollowed out on its seaward side so that it resembles the gaping mouth of an immense clam. Looking through slides several days before, I had noticed one of my niece Barbara Docherty huddled inside that same rock maw, and George now suggested that he photograph me inside it. I clambered stiffly into position and smiled for the camera. When I returned home, I looked again at the slide, which was captioned 'Young Barbara enveloped in rock, South Learside'. The date was 11 September 1984, so I had been back at the rock almost thirty years later. That photograph, regrettably, has too much shade in the wrong parts to be worth reproducing here.

47. *The author in the maw of a rock, Feochaig shore, 7 August 2014. Photograph by George McSporran.*

George also photographed the Giant's Chair, a feature named for the Ordnance Survey in 1866 by Allan MacLean, farmer in Feochaig, and described in the Southend Parish Name-Book as a rock about 30 feet high which 'somewhat resembles the form of a Chair hence its name'. Duncan McLachlan and companions used to shelter at it, and Duncan slept below it one night.[131] The next feature on the map which George photographed, 'Natural Arch', is a description rather than a place-name, but neither of us could see an 'arch', only a narrow sea cave.

We sat for lunch on a flat rock near 'Wood Bay', which Teddy Lafferty named from the piles of driftwood cast ashore there by tide and storm. When he and Billy Russell camped there for a week one summer in the late 1950s, the farmer, Iain MacIntyre, would visit them in the morning while going round his sheep, and towards the end of the week he remarked on the difference their fires had made to the driftwood. From the top of the hill he could see the shore getting barer and barer further and further away from the camp, as the nearest of the wood was burned.

Another friend of Teddy's, Tommy Thompson, was a farm-hand at Glenahervie at that time, and would visit them in the evenings after work. They gave him half-a-crown to buy milk from the farm and biscuits from one of the grocery vans that travelled the countryside, but Mrs MacIntyre in the farm – Iain's mother – wouldn't accept payment for the milk or the biscuits. Mostly Teddy and Billy were eating tinned food, but they had half-a-dozen square sausages with them, which they boiled, two at a time in a National Health Service dried milk tin with a wire handle, and ate between sliced bread. At the foot of the little stream in the bay, Teddy formed a shallow basin in the shingle and, using a cup, scooped out water for tea and cooking.

He returned to Wood Bay once, alone and without a tent, for a night. He lay on the shingle beach wrapped in a heavy blanket, but, as he admitted, he didn't sleep much. When young, he occasionally liked to 'push' himself, but the motivation wasn't 'macho' – those little endurance tests were for his own satisfaction. I told him, after my trip there with George, that his name for the bay was no longer apposite. There is very little wood there now; in fact, I carried the best of it home in my rucksack. Later that month, I visited him to look through his collection of photographs. I had seen them all before and there were two in particular I wanted for this book. One of them was of Wood Bay looking north, taken in the early 1980s, and I noticed at once that amid all the driftwood there was scarcely a branch. Most of it consisted of planks and boards, so, even into the plastic age, the remains of wooden fish-boxes and other containers lingered on the beaches. The ratio is now reversed.

48. 'Wood Bay', looking north, c. 1982. Photograph by Teddy Lafferty.

On the day Teddy took that photograph, he found a wooden crate smashed on the rocks. Lemons had spilled out, and some of these, he noticed to his amusement, had beak holes in them where birds had tested their edibility and doubtless been repelled. Teddy selected half-a-dozen of the best lemons, carried them home, sliced them into a big bowl, added sugar and hot water, and drank the concoction a couple of days later, enjoying it as much for the memories it stirred as for its refreshment.

Adders again

One morning in the 1950s, when Iain MacIntyre visited the camp, he and Teddy were standing chatting. Iain was asking him what gave them the notion to camp in that remote, rocky spot when there were nicer bays – Feochaig and Glenahervie – they could have picked. Billy Russell, who was lying on the tent's flysheet, spread on the ground to dry, suddenly sprang to his feet, and Iain and Teddy exclaimed at once: 'An adder!'

George had a couple of adder stories related to that very spot, but the whole Learside coast is snaky, and I'm loath to walk it during the greater part of the year. On that warm day, I was particularly nervous and seldom ventured from the tidal zone on to the foreshore, and, when I did, my eyes were searching keenly ahead. George's stories served only to intensify my anxiety.

During a holiday one August around 1970, George decided to follow a track down from the main road on the north side of the Bastard, but before he reached the shore he saw that 'all the rocks seemed to have adders lying on top of them, so I just about-turned'. Thirty-odd years later, he and his son Sandy took the same route down to examine the 'Natural Arch' to the north. While seated on a foreshore rock, they noticed several adders basking round about. 'We certainly had to watch our step coming off,' he concluded.

George and Sandy had a rare winter encounter with an adder on 9 December 2013 while walking from High Glenadale to Largiebaan. George told me he 'got a shock' when he noticed the snake coiled on the track. Sandy touched it with a stalk of dried-out bracken to establish that it was actually alive – it was.

While dining with Alex Kempshall and Yvonne Wilkin in June (p 111), Yvonne mentioned an encounter with adders around 2003 during a hike from Ballygroggan to the Inneans to see the Sailor's Grave. The trouble started on Beinn na Faire, when Yvonne, who was behind Alex, saw one and then another adder. She called out, but he had already ascended the slope and was oblivious to her predicament. As Yvonne nervously followed, she saw a third adder, lying where she was about to place her hand, and she froze. Alex, finally realising something was wrong, turned back, and he too began seeing snakes. They continued cautiously, and finally reached a point on the hill from which they could see into the Inneans Glen and identify a route down to the bay, but they also saw 'an ominous swathe of mist creeping up the glen from the sea', and decided not to risk a descent. They have still to visit the grave.

49. *Teddy Lafferty with tent at the north end of Glenahervie Bay, c. 1982. Photograph taken by himself using timer, which allowed him eight seconds to press the shutter and position himself on the fish-box. The mug is empty and is merely for effect!*

In 1981, when I tape-recorded Teddy Lafferty about his coasting experiences, the subject of adders came up. He told me he'd capture them – only possible on open ground – and take them home in a lemonade bottle, but they wouldn't eat in captivity and he would always release them, near the English Graveyard at Tomaig, before they starved to death. He remembered them as 'vicious' when caught, and striking at him through the glass. On occasion, he killed and skinned adders for belt-coverings; the skins would be stretched over a leather belt and sewn in place. At his first attempt he committed the error of making the incision along the snake's back, thus spoiling the pattern. The dark underbelly was where the cut should have been made, and the edges sewn together; but he was never able to secure enough skins to make a belt, anyway. There seems to have been a craze for snake-belts in the 1960s. A primary school classmate of mine was rumoured to have made one from skins got on Ben Gullion, but I've never seen even one adder on Ben Gullion and never saw the fancy belt, if it even existed.

McEachrans and McKerrals, Glenahervie

In Glenahervie Bay, George and I crossed the burn and sat at a 'port', a cleared tidal passageway for boats. This, I am certain, was the 'harbour' which Colin McEachran constructed in the early nineteenth century and asked Argyll Estate for financial help in extending. He received a grant of £100, no small sum considering the annual rent of his farm at Glenahervie was £35. Local farmers were using the harbour for importing Irish limestone for fertiliser, and this boon to the Estate's agricultural improvement schemes doubtless recommended McEachran's initiatives to the Duke of Argyll. Two of McEachran's sons were operating a 24-ton smack from the harbour, and, like the harbour itself, McEachran had built the vessel, in 1807.[132]

When Colin applied for Estate assistance in October 1817, he was tenant of the 'South Shore Division' of 'Glennahervy'. The farm by then had been divided, the other portions being: 'West' (Donald Oloynachan), 'High' (John McEachran) and 'North West' (Robert Hall). In 1777, Glenahervie was still a single unit, with Neil Brolochan, John McIlreavy, John McEachran and Donald Oloynachan in joint-tenancy, paying a combined rent of £48, but, in accordance with the old system, obliged to top it up with produce and labour. The name McEachran in Glenahervie goes back at least to 1709 and the first extant Argyll Estate lease, and in 1711 three men of the name were granted the lease of the farm by 'Our high and potent Princess Elisabeth, Dowager Duchess of Argyll': Angus Bain ('Fair'), John, merchant in Campbeltown, and Eacharn in 'Sockoch' (Socach, a nearby farm), who signed himself 'Acharn McAcharn'.[133]

These Glenahervie McEachrans contributed to my own genetic make-up through my mother's line, but the connection is remote. John

McEachran (above) and his wife Christian McIlreavie were my great-great-great-great-great-grandparents, but I have sixty-four pairs of them – we all have! Their daughter, Barbara McEachran, married Neil McKerral, who was tenant in High Glenahervie in 1830 along with his father-in-law. McKerral, incidentally, when presented with the lease, 'declared he could not write, never having been taught'. On 21 February 1833, his son, John McKerral, who was born at Kilmashenachan in 1810, married Amelia McKay, born in 1806 at Erradil.

Amelia McKay, Erradil

I have already looked at Erradil and its clever and interesting McKay family,[134] so brevity must prevail here. It was one of several farms near Glenahervie which were emptied in the mid-nineteenth century to accommodate a sheep stock. Just before the sturdy little bridge at the bottom of the hill down from Glenahervie, a track leads left past a disused silage-pit. That track leads to Erradil, and, beyond, to the ruins of Socach and Cantaig, before it re-joins the main road near the top of the brae opposite the Bastard. Only heaps of stones remain at Erradil to mark the site of the settlement, and in 1995 the glen, with its fine old arable fields, was ploughed for afforestation.

I familiarised myself with Erradil in 1988, after we got our caravan at Polliwilline, and after one visit wrote a three-part poem titled 'Erradil', which was published in *The Larch Plantation* and dedicated to my baby daughter, Amelia, since the poems were inspired by her great-great-great-great-grandmother, Amelia McKay. On the evening of that visit, there was snow drifting over Erradil as I left the glen for a night's stay alone at the caravan, and my pockets were 'heavy with shards/of china, each glaze-veined/with the dark earth's ageing'. I'd lifted them from the old midden site there, and imagined Amelia clasping, and dropping, one of the bowls of which I now held a fragment.

> Here is a curved, blue-patterned
> rim fragment of a drinking bowl;
> perhaps your young girl's lips were on that bowl
> when someone called you from the fire
> and startled you,
> 'Amelia! Amelia!'

Amelia McKay became for me a romantic spirit from the past, as the poems reveal, and the name 'Amelia' was itself part of that allure. My mother was Amelia McKenzie, she had an aunt Amelia Boyle, my middle daughter is called Amelia Martin, and the name goes right back to that Amelia McKay at Erradil. Many years after the poem was written, I was going through the files of the *Campbeltown Journal*, and in the issue of 26 September 1851 I chanced on a report of the Inveraray autumn court: 'Amelia McKay or McKerral, charged with theft at Campbeltown, pleaded guilty, and was sentenced to 15 months' imprisonment at Inveraray.' There could have been no other Amelia McKay who married a McKerral, and I was momentarily shocked. Amelia's disgrace was 'news' to me, but it affected me as though it had happened just the week before.

I later found a fuller record of her misdemeanours on the Inveraray Jail website. She was employed to clean a house in Kirk Street, Campbeltown. The family there consisted of Rose MacQuistan, a bedridden 'imbecile', and her two blind sons, Finlay and Neil, a 'situation ripe for an unscrupulous person to exploit', as the website scribe sagely observed. Between 1 April and 15 August 1851, Amelia removed from the house twenty-one items of clothing, three 'half-blankets', two bed-covers, two baskets, two metal pots, a mahogany tea-tray and a candlestick. When arrested, she had thirteen pawn tickets on her. Perhaps, I tell myself, she intended all along to recover the goods from pawn and restore them to the MacQuistan household when money came her way, but – surprise! – there never was money, except what she was receiving from Archibald Hamilton, pawnbroker, in the downward spiral of her pilfering. Though described as 'single' on the website, she appears to have been widowed by then and was doubtless in poor circumstances.

Her romantic allure has been swept away, but I regard her now as a victim herself, and theft has always been punished heavily in law. By contrast, in the following year, Archibald McCoig, labourer at Dunglas farm, Southend, beat a fellow-servant on the farm, Michael Flynn, so brutally that he died of his injuries a month later. His sentence after trial? Twenty shillings or twenty days in jail if he couldn't raise the fine.[135]

Two cliff fatalities

North of Glenahervie, in April 1878, a shepherd, James Lees, fell almost hundred feet to his death from 'a precipice called the Dune'. The more usual spelling is 'Doune', which is Gaelic *dùn*, a fort or rounded hillock. In this case, there was a fort, on the summit of a low hill, but only an 'irregular band of wall debris' remains, the rest of the structure having been removed for building nearby enclosures.[136] When Lees, who was the Glenahervie shepherd, failed to return home, the shore was searched and he was found at the foot of the cliff.[137] He left a wife – Marion McConnachy, born in Killean Parish – and two children, who found themselves on Campbeltown poor roll, in receipt of two shillings a week. James and Marion had a total of eight children by previous marriages. Four of his were already working, another, Archibald (8), was with his paternal grandfather, and Mary (6) was with Marion, as was his son by Marion, Alexander (1). Her daughters from her former marriage, Catherine and Margaret MacNab, were of working age.[138]

Twenty-one years earlier, in August 1857, a little herd-girl, Catherine Norris, also fell to her death on that coast. She was a servant with Alexander McFarlane, farmer in Polliwilline, and while herding cattle along the shore she saw a lamb stuck on a cliff. While trying to rescue it, she lost her balance and fell.[139] Her death registration gave her age as eleven, date of death 17 August, and cause: 'Killed by falling over a precipice. Death immediate.'[140] She was a daughter of David Norris, Balquidder-born shepherd at Glenahervie, and in the 1851 census living, with his wife Margaret McKie and three children, Catherine among them, at 'Erridale'. Three years after Catherine's death, Norris took the lease of Laggan farm in Glenlussa, and remained there for the standard term of nineteen years, after which his stock was sold at public auction.[141]

14 August: Butterflies and blaeberries

I aimed to supply a friend in Southend with blaeberries for jam-making before the gathering season ended, so in the early afternoon I headed for Ben Gullion. It was a sunny day – one of the dependable few we had at the tail-end of that summer – but breezy, too, and I knew that as long as these conditions lasted I wouldn't be bothered by midges. As I have already observed, one's vision of the world when picking berries narrows to the ground at one's feet, so whatever might be happening in the surrounding landscape or sky generally goes unnoticed, unless one is alerted by sounds. The mind is soothed, but the notebook tends to remain empty.

On my way up the hill and before I began picking, I noted four butterflies. The first was a small copper (*Lycaena phlaeas*), which alighted at my feet as I crossed Crosshill Reservoir dam. It was a little beauty and I looked closely at it for a while, which is what one must do to familiarise oneself with the different species. Until a few years ago, I didn't seriously observe butterflies and didn't realise just how aesthetically pleasing they can be, some more than others, naturally. Now I view them as airborne art galleries.

One of the most exotic-looking of the local butterflies, and also one of the biggest, is the peacock (*Inachis io*), and I later saw three of them. It is unmistakable, with its brightly coloured eye-like markings, resembling the spots on a peacock's tail. The three I saw on the uphill trail were in pristine condition, and all the more attractive for that. The peacock is an overwintering species, and when it wakes from its long sleep may look a bit tatty, but its offspring, which emerge from the pupal stage in late summer, are perfect. The first one I noticed was on the path in front of me and I decided to photograph its vivid beauty, but by the time I found my camera, the peacock's outstretched wings were folded in, and it now resembled an age-blackened leaf. What a transformation! – almost like 'good' and 'evil' rapidly demonstrated in the one organism. I waited for several minutes, hoping it would spread it wings again, but it didn't; nor did it move when I walked by it.

I saw two peacocks during a walk with my daughter Amelia to Kilchousland on 22 August. We were by-passing Macringan's Point along a path trampled by cattle when I noticed the second one at my feet. Assuming it was dead, I lifted it to show Amelia the 'eyes', but as I began to prise the wings apart I realised that the butterfly was now standing on my finger, so I placed it on a wild iris leaf at the side of the track and left it to its fate. Since its lower wings were missing and it was generally in bad shape, I concluded that it was not a candidate for successful hibernation.

The earliest sighting of a peacock in Kintyre that I know of is 28 January. On that day in 2006, while walking from Feochaig to Dalbuie, Agnes Stewart and Ian Teesdale saw the butterfly about a mile south-east of Arinarach Hill and a mile east-north-east of Arinascavach, 'pretty far from human habitation and the chance of a nice sheltered barn in which to over-winter', as Agnes observed. Jimmy MacDonald saw one in fine condition at Innean Beithe sheep-fank on 5 November 2014. I wouldn't have known about it had I not met him the day after and remarked that I'd been at Largiebaan, further north, and missed the summer colours of butterflies and flowers.

Another insect species caught my attention that day on Ben Gullion, and it was one I hadn't expected to see (though I later found a record from Ben Gullion dated 25 August 2004). It was the St Mark's fly (*Bibio marci*), so named because it appears around St Mark's day, 25 April. I have always associated the fly with spring visits to the caravan at Polliwilline, but here it was, numerous in late summer. It is the largest of the *Bibio* genus and is conspicuous by its long dangling legs, resembling the undercarriage of an aircraft about to land.

19 August: Knock Scalbert and the Queen's Silver Jubilee

I was writing up my account for 21 May, 'Painted Ladies on Knock Scalbert', on 19 August, which was sunny with a fresh westerly breeze, and took a notion to head for Knock Scalbert in the afternoon to check for mushrooms. I found one just below the summit, dislodged from the ground, presumably by a sheep. It was tiny and desiccated, but I considered it a promising sign.

While looking through Teddy Lafferty's photograph albums two days earlier, I noticed a black and white print of a gathering of people around a bonfire. Teddy couldn't remember the occasion, but recalled that he had met his old headmaster, Hector MacNeill, there, and enjoyed a bit of banter with him. Through force of habit, Teddy had been addressing him as 'Sir', and Hector laughed and told him he could call him 'Hector' now. I wasn't interested in the photograph at the time, but noticed that it was taken at or very close to a spot on Knock Scalbert which often produced a 'fairy ring' of horse mushrooms (see photograph in *By Hill and Shore in South Kintyre*, p 18, dated 5 August 1998). I decided to visit the spot on the chance that mushrooms might have appeared there. There was none, but as I headed back to my bike at Auchalochy I decided to investigate what was going on in the photograph.

The Queen's Golden Jubilee in June 2002 seemed the likeliest explanation, so I went that evening to the Library and consulted the *Campbeltown Courier*. In the issue of 7 June, there was a report of the celebrations on Monday 3 June, which included 'a beacon lit on Knock Scalbert'. I was mistaken, though. When I next visited Teddy and examined the photograph in detail, I realised, as Teddy already knew, that it was much older. The fish sheds at the end of the Old Quay, the R.N.L.I. buildings on the New Quay, and the Rex Cinema were all in place; and, in any case, Hector MacNeill had died in 1998. We finally concluded that the photograph had been taken at the time of the Queen's Silver Jubilee, 3 June 1977, when celebratory bonfires blazed all around Britain.

The bonfire torch was lit on Kinloch Park by ex-Provost A. P. MacGrory, assisted by 'Miss Kintyre', Lorna McCallum, and passed to Campbell McMurchy, the first of a relay of fifteen Boy Scout runners who were to carry the flame to Summerhill. The torch was received on the hill by Rear-Admiral Robin Mayo and put to the wood-pile as a maroon was fired from the life-boat station.[142]

The Scottish Independence Referendum

The following month, on 9 September, I noticed a large 'YES' spread out on Knock Scalbert. It was the most audacious local propaganda statement I'd seen ahead of the Scottish Independence Referendum on the 18th of that month, and that it was also close to where the Queen's Silver Jubilee bonfire had been lit was doubtless a coincidental irony. I decided I'd like a closer look and went on to Knock Scalbert the following afternoon. I left my bicycle, as usual, at the anglers' car-park at Auchalochy, and climbed on to the summit and sat there for an hour. Bird sightings included a hen harrier and a kestrel, the latter my first of the year (I read later that numbers of the latter species have been in serious decline nationally). I then descended the hill in search of the 'YES', but failed to find it. I hadn't gone far enough, as I discovered when I looked more carefully at the hill from town.

Three days later, on Ben Gullion with Chomsky, I noticed the sign from where I sat, but half-an-hour later, at the back of five o' clock, when scanning the hill again, I failed to see it. Assuming that a trick of the fading light had obscured it, I trained my binoculars on the spot and saw, instead, three figures – two of them draped in blue – making their way downhill. The message had been removed, and I speculated, from my parochial perspective, that I might be the only witness to the 'climb down'. I heard later that its propaganda value had been compromised when some hostile party rearranged 'YES' into 'SEX'.

I was disappointed, but not surprised, by the result of the Referendum. On the morning after, unable to sleep, I rose at 5 a.m., fetched a radio into the bedroom and switched it on. At first the trend of the voting was unclear from the interviews, but after about five minutes' listening, the outcome was unmistakable. If the opportunity was missed to replace corrupt government in London with a model designed on sounder ethical principles, the Referendum debate at least politicised the Scottish public, its youth in particular, and that legacy should energise politics in Scotland for years to come.

26 August: Killypole

On 12 September 1988, when walking across Kinloch Green with daughter Sarah, I met Mr and Mrs Dugald McKendrick, who lived nearby in Queen Street. He told me he had recently seen my name written in Killypole ruin. He had been with his sister, Mrs Jeannie Johnston, their first time together there in sixty-odd years. She was born in Killypole, but Dugald was born in Ballochnafraesan, three conjoined farmworkers' houses on Lossit Estate.

Dugald spent twenty years of his life in Killypole, and his mother, Catherine Jackson, died there on 13 March 1924 at the age of forty-six, when Dugald was in his early teens. She belonged to a shepherding family which came to Kintyre from Eskdale in the Borders in 1855. The mother of renowned engineer, Thomas Telford, born in 1757 in Westerkirk, was Janet Jackson, a member of that family. Her husband John Telfer died four months after Thomas's birth, and the child was raised with the help of Janet's brother, Thomas Jackson.[143] The closest Telford got to Kintyre was Tarbert, whose harbour improvements he directed in the second decade of the nineteenth century.[144]

I seem to remember Hugh MacFarlane (p 157) telling me that Telford's initials, 'TT', were carved in one of the coping-stones on 'The Bielding', the man-made island from which sailing ships were warped into the inner basin when winds were contrary. I have an even vaguer memory of having gone out to the building at low tide to look for the initials; but, I ask myself, did I? And if I did, did I find them? I have no written record, and can't be certain. Are the initials even there? I asked Ian Macintyre in Tarbert if he had heard the tradition. He had, but had yet to see the evidence for himself.

Dugald himself would marry into another Borders shepherding family in Kintyre. His wife was Mary Helm, a sister of Sandy's (p 98), and Sandy's wife was Margaret McAllister, one of the 'Moss McAllisters', so-called, to which Archie, the fiddler, belongs (p 23). Intermarriage between Highland and Lowland shepherding families was nothing unusual by then.

On 26 August, I walked to Killypole from the top of Lossit brae in sunshine and an easterly breeze. On arrival, I went straight to a corner of the old garden to check the rhubarb patch – it survives, though it cannot be said to be flourishing. Still, I was glad to see several leaves showing above dense nettles. In 1986, when the patch was more robust, Judy cut sufficient stalks to make a batch of memorable chutney. Dugald told me that his mother had planted that rhubarb, so it must be around a century old, and he mentioned that a 'mavis', or thrush, nested in the patch one spring. Catherine McKendrick also planted lilies there. Sixty-odd 'rucks' of hay were cut in the meadow below the steading, he said.

He mentioned, also, several place-names in the area, including Dougie's Glen, on the march between Lochorodale and Lossit Estate, named after a Dugald MacPherson in Lochorodale who herded there, and Jean's Glen, past Killypole, going towards the Inneans, after a girl who courted there, but I never got precise locations from him. Later that year, he wrote out for me a list of thirty minor place-names in South Kintyre, some of them familiar to me, but most not. He died in 1997 at the age of eighty-seven, and I now wish I'd questioned him more about his years in Killypole.

I sat out of the wind on the south side of the steading and, having eaten, decided to examine the names inside. As I made my way to the front door, I disturbed a lovely small copper, which flew briefly and then alighted at my feet. I reached for my camera, but, by the time I had it ready, the butterfly had folded its wings and resembled a fawn-coloured leaf.

From that very spot, on 25 May 2013, I'd noticed a hooded crow perched watchfully on the chimney-head of the ruin. It reluctantly flew off at the sight of me, and then I noticed, a short way off, a small fox with a bird in its mouth. It watched me watching it for longer than I thought was reasonable, ran off, then inexplicably reappeared directly in front of me and stopped again, watching me. I noticed then that the bird in its mouth was a young crow, which I suppose explained the living crow's vigil. The fox finally collected its wits and ran off south towards the forest. I probably missed the killing by mere minutes.

The first name I looked for inside the ruin was my daughter Amelia's, scratched in a cement surface on 8 August 2013, but it had already disappeared. As I remarked in *A Summer in Kintyre* (p 109), 'I photographed the inscription and told her that I'd think of her whenever I returned'. In an early draft of the book, I'd written, and decided to delete, 'I photographed the inscription for no particular reason ...' Now I understood the reason. I thought of her, anyway; she'd returned to Glasgow by bus that morning. That disappointment decided me to transcribe all the legible names remaining on the walls, and here is a selection:

Annie & David McKillop, 9/3/2000
Owen + Rhuairidh 6/2/05
Tommy + Jessie 11/4/03
Angus Martin June 1991
Alex Docherty 1990
Mary Armour
Nicola M
Mary Butler   Robert Pollock 19/1/1992
Ryan Ferguson 1994
Dougie Ferguson 17/10/1993
Katie McLean
Lauren + Daniel Oct 89
Calum + Val Buchanan 14-III-89
Peter Morrison 18/6/93
Martin Brown wiz ere 3/9/88
Mags + Sleepy

I noticed several splashes of white excrement inside the ruin, but, since it is entirely roofless, I gave no thought to the possibility that a barn owl might be responsible. Two days later, however, Elizabeth

McTaggart, Drumlemble, was there with her friend, Catherine Dobbie, and Catherine's friend, Anne Kerr, and they disturbed a roosting barn owl. Elizabeth always stops for a cup of tea at Killypole, as I myself do. It's that sort of place – restful and beautiful. On 31 August, three days after my visit, Davie Adam, my postman, and his partner Jean were also there. Her father is a Drumlemble Thomson, as was Catherine's mother.

27 August: The Maidens' Planting and bramble-gathering

I had taken a couple of tubs with me to Killypole in the hope of filling them with brambles, but though the bushes along the track down to High Tirfergus were well-berried, only a small proportion was ripe. On a walk to Kilchousland five days earlier with Amelia, however, we were picking ripe berries all the way, so I decided to head for the Maidens' Planting, and bought a big plastic bucket. The purchase was an act of faith, but was justified, because I returned home after four hours' picking with eighteen pounds of ripe berries, which a friend in Southend collected the following morning for jam-making. By then rain had arrived, but my afternoon was spent in breezy sunshine, hearing the restful lapping of waves on the shore.

While eating lunch in the Planting, I heard a voice from the other side of the wall and guessed that a dog-walker was passing. Later, when back on the track, gathering, he and dog appeared. 'He' was David McIntyre, the piper, and we chatted for a while. He mentioned that his mother had preferred jelly to jam, and after he'd gone I remembered my own mother and her jelly-making: the 'jeely-bag' suspended over a pot on broom handles between two chairs, and the slow drip of the juice from the mash in the bag; her testing for consistency by dropping a spoonful of the boiling mixture of juice and sugar into a saucerful of water; the ladling of the jelly into jars, which were sealed with a circular waxed paper cover over the jelly and a larger circular transparent film over the jar, held on by a tiny rubber-band; and, finally, the attachment, to the outside of the jars, of a little gummed paper strip with contents and date written on it.

When I meet Mrs Mary Lavery, a neighbour from the Crosshill years, she sometimes reminds me of my mother's setting off for the 'Wuds' (Woods) to gather berries, with a following of children, her eager, chattering helpers. The Wuds, being handy, was the usual gathering place, and I don't recall having gone anywhere else as a child and teen-ager. There had been a dense plantation there, but when I remember the place – which was a natural playground for children – the trees were sparse and in decay. A gull's ghost was rumoured to haunt the Wuds, but I never saw it, nor, I dare say, did anyone else. The Wuds and all its bramble thickets disappeared under the Kintyre Gardens housing development in 1979, and the only 'ghosts' there are the children who run through my memory, their voices resonant in vanished summers.

Keil Cave and Travellers

Beside the burn, where I sat for lunch, generations of Travellers had camped, and I recalled the canvas tents and the scent of wood-smoke. It was certainly a hard life, but has the 'civilised' alternative turned out any better for their descendants? The family I remember there was named Townsley, which is still the commonest Traveller name in Kintyre, except that Travellers here don't travel any more. 'Townsley' is an English name and must mask a Gaelic original, presumably Irish *Duinnsliabh*, 'Brown Mountain'. The family itself believed it came to Kintyre from Ireland about 250 years ago and occupied Keil Cave as blacksmiths and tinsmiths, a tradition aired in a thirty-minute BBC documentary about Kintyre Travellers broadcast in 1960.

The story seemed familiar, and I found something similar in the transcript of a tape-recording I made in 1977 with Archibald Cameron, a retired Southend farmer, who told me that 'the tinkers used to cast iron down in Keil Cove'. He'd been told that as a boy by Ned McCallum, blacksmith in Machrimore, who was then about eighty, and Ned had been told by his father, which dated the tradition, Archie reckoned, to from 150 to 200 years back. Ned's father, himself a smith, judged the tinkers' iron work to be 'very rough'.

The Big Cave at Keil was excavated a decade after Saint Kieran's Cave and revealed intermittent occupation since about the 3rd century AD. The excavation appears to have been more efficiently conducted, yet there was something of the pantomime about it, too. When Ludovic Mann and J. Harrison Maxwell arrived in Southend on 19 July 1933, they found the 51st Renfrewshire Boy Scouts camped at Keil and immediately enlisted the whole camp as labourers!

Large quantities of charcoal fragments and lumps of iron slag were uncovered, and these, combined with fire-blackened stones and other material, suggested the site of a small iron foundry. Maxwell noted in his first report a local tradition that 'the Big Cave was used by gipsies [sic] for forging iron, and that they made excellent coulters and ploughshares for the local farmers'. In the following year, 1934, he received the tradition first-hand and seemed genuinely interested in it. 'From a gipsy camped on the shore at Keil Lodge, Mr Maxwell learned that the gipsy's great-grandfather, Alexander Townsley, had smelted iron in Keil Cave and fashioned smoothing-irons and coulters, "then he left Keil and went to Ireland, but came back and worked iron at Tayinloan". (Will local antiquarians follow this clue in caves in that neighbourhood?)'[145]

In the 1881 census there were six Travellers in Keil Cave: John McFee, tinsmith, his wife and son, and a cousin, Alex McCallum, basket-maker, with his wife and daughter. All six had different birthplaces: Inverness, Paisley, Roseneath, Ross-shire, Argyll and Stirlingshire. The entry was later annotated: 'not a house.'

I recently noticed a reference to that BBC documentary, *It Happened to Me*, in the *Campbeltown Courier* of 25 February 1960, but few families had television sets then and I didn't get to see it until a friend loaned me a copy on video tape in 2014. Most of the filming was done at Lintmill, a ruined wool-manufacturing hamlet near Stewarton, and a favoured Traveller camp site. The film is in black and white and was shot in bleak winter conditions. Had the camp been filmed in summer, the atmosphere would have been altogether lighter; but there was a clear propagandist message throughout the documentary – the beleaguered Travellers' unanimous desire for council housing. There were four families – 26 people in all, including 17 children – living there in tents. The presentation is sympathetic but narrow, and the huge cultural storehouse of the Travellers – the music and stories – was unvisited.

'Bill' Townsley was an eloquent spokesman and described his experience of the 'tinker brand', the stigma attaching to his outcast people. As a child in school, he said, other children wouldn't sit beside him, yet he had been in the army during the Second World War and served in the North African campaigns. The name 'Townsley' meant nothing in the army, he said, but when he returned to Kintyre from the war, he was just a 'tinker' again. In 1958, he took his wife and children on the road, and in Carlisle he found work on a building site, earning £20 a week, good money then. He and his family lived in a caravan in a farmer's field, but were removed and couldn't find a house. He returned to Kintyre, 'and now I am a tinker in a tent once again'.

50. *A Travellers' camp in Kintyre, c. 1935. The man on the left is weaving a basket.* Photograph by Dugald Semple, from his Looking at Nature *(1946).*

Traveller families throughout Scotland sometimes chose to spend their winters in houses, but at the first signs of spring they'd go back on the road. In the winter of 1965, six of the twelve Kintyre Traveller families – all Townsleys – were camped in Kintyre, one was in Arran and the other five were housed in Glasgow and Kilmacolm. Argyll County Council was then considering providing permanent housing on sites selected by the Travellers themselves, but, of the six families in Kintyre interviewed, none was prepared to commit to all-year settlement. Two sentiments, however, were unanimously expressed: the 'miseries of camping in winter' and the 'great ordeal' consequently suffered by the children. The total number of Kintyre Travellers – including those wintering elsewhere – was estimated at eighty-nine.[146]

The last Travellers at Lintmill were Anthony Stewart, his wife Jean Townsley, and their family, who were living in caravans rather than tents. During a sudden afternoon gale on 11 January 1984, Mrs Stewart, who was thirty-two years old, was killed when a caravan she was trying to secure blew over on her. I remember meeting Mr Stewart at the Second Water one summer before his tragedy; we talked for a while and he played me a tune on his bagpipes.

Those Lintmill Travellers captured on film alluded to their use of 'Romany-cant' when wishing to exclude outsiders from their conversation, and gave the interviewer a few simple examples, but there is little Romany in the Highland Travellers' *beurlacheard*, or 'lingo of the cairds', according to the pioneer in the field of Traveller culture, the late Hamish Henderson: 'That this is a very ancient cover-tongue is shown by the fact that some of the vocabulary which it reflects and deforms is archaic Gaelic.'[147] That the Kintyre Travellers' original tongue was Gaelic is clear from censuses, but, along with the settled population, they entirely lost the language.

Allister Stewart has a story which illustrates the Travellers' canny philosophy of acquisition. His father, Peter, was employed on Kildalloig Estate at the time and was on his way to work one wet morning when he met 'Bonny' Duncan Townsley. Duncan asked him for some tobacco and Peter loosened off his oilskins and searched his pockets. 'Gosh, Duncan, A'm afraid ye're oot o' luck. A'm away withoot my tobacco.' With that, Duncan produced a chunk of Bogie Roll, cut off a bit and handed it to Peter. 'Here, wait a minute, Duncan, I thought *you* asked *me* for tobacco?' – 'Och aye, Peter, but ye don't ask when ye're oot o' it.'

I won't get away with romanticising the Traveller culture – some readers will recall, for example, the drunken battles between rival families in the streets of Campbeltown – but, historically anyway, the Travellers' attitude to personal property, to say nothing of the paucity of their worldly goods, ought to shame the gross materialism of settled society. The very idea of a family's quarrelling over a dead relative's belongings was incomprehensible to Travellers, whose own few possessions were generally burnt when they themselves were gone.

A farmer's wife near Campbeltown told me she once admired a gold ring worn by a Traveller woman who called at her door. A few days later, the woman returned and gave her the ring, saying it would be burnt when she died, anyway; but the truth was that since the farmer's wife, in all innocence, had 'eyed' the ring, there could be no luck in keeping it.

Small Tortoiseshells

On my way to the Maidens' Planting, I'd noticed two butterflies on a sheltered buddleia bush on Low Askomill, one a peacock and one a small tortoiseshell. In *A Summer in Kintyre* (p 63), I reported a cluster of ten small tortoiseshells overwintering on the stairwell ceiling of 13 Saddell Street. They began dispersing in mid-April 2014, and by the 27th only one remained. On 27 August, I noticed that two had come in and attached themselves to the ceiling. Exactly four months had passed, and another generation had arrived with an intimation of winter. I looked at them with some sadness.

A colony of around fifty tortoiseshells ultimately assembled in the stairwell, in a new location, above the doorway, apart from three which chose the plaster ceiling over the window. Towards the end of November, I noticed that these three had gone, but I gave their departure little thought. Early next month, however, I discovered to my astonishment that all the others had also disappeared without trace. Had the unseasonable warmth of November triggered awakening and flight? I have no idea, but that midwinter mass dispersal was unprecedented in my experience.

The longer I live, the more I realise that thousands of talented writers, artists and musicians practise in relative obscurity, and whether one ever gets to know of them depends to an extent on chance. I had never heard of Anna Adams until sent a copy of *Open Doors*, a selection of her poems edited by John Killick and published in 2014. I was vexed to discover she was three years dead, because her poems express a perception of the world which I believe I share, and I would have told her so. Readers who are familiar with the subject of the following poem should 'get it' all the way; for others, I trust that Anna Adams will be an illuminating guide.

TORTOISESHELLS OVERWINTERING

In my bedroom ceiling's shadiest corner
   a dark encampment of inverted tents
is sitting out the tyranny of Winter.

Like Israelites that keep God's covenants
    in sober arks, or nomad Bedouins
who hide rich mats in fustian tenements,

they fold the magic carpets of their wings,
    concealing hieroglyphics of the meadow
clapped between tatter-bordered coverings.

As dingy as the withered nettlebed,
    as drab as marbled bibles, charred by fire,
or chips of bark or stone, they could be dead

but hang by wiry legs, as fine as hair,
    close-clustered near the plaster desert's edge
like a proscribed religious sect at prayer.

This bivouac preserves the Summer's page
    during eclipse of dandelions and daisies;
it bears pressed sparks of sun through this dark age:

one night between oasis and oasis.

17 September: Auchenhoan

September was a dry month, with many sunny days. There were still a few butterflies – mostly peacocks – to be seen, and I logged two at Auchenhoan, the second of them at the boulder on top of the hill overlooking the Second Water, described in *A Summer in Kintyre* (pp. 120-24). It was an idyllic afternoon – sunny and windless – and I sat on the boulder for an hour, reminiscing contentedly. I'd been hoping to find horse mushrooms, but found none. From Ballinatunie I cut on to the main road and from there down to the Blin' Man and along the top of the little cliff until I came to the route to the shore which I'd first used on 5 April, at the beginning of this book. To get there, I was wading chest-high in bracken, and wrecking, with unvoiced apologies, innumerable spider webs. When got there, the descent was so overgrown I hardly recognised it. I was stung by nettles and scratched by briers, but reached the shore. A couple of branches had been washed in since I was last there more than five months earlier and I lifted them and carried them up the Second Water brae to my bike at the top and sawed them there by the gate.

20 September: Small Coppers

I left my bike again at the top of the Second Water brae and walked south along the shore. Nothing much had changed since my springtime walks. The flowers were different and fewer; there was still some wood to be gathered, mostly branches I'd propped against rocks to dry (they did); there were still seals – eight of them – crooning on the reef north of the Dummy's; and the birds were much the same (only eiders were noticeably absent).

When I emerged from the shade of the cliffs into the little bay at the Dummy's, its beach white with multitudinous washed-in limpet shells, the grassy foreshore was still in sunlight. I saw first a peacock butterfly in that bright corner and then, darting about together, two small butterflies which I guessed must be small coppers. I waited and watched, and when they flew back in my direction, one of them helpfully alighted on the edge of a fish-box a few feet from me. It was indeed a small copper, and I was delighted to see it so late in the year. Had I arrived ten minutes later, it is unlikely I would have seen any butterflies, because the bay by then was in shade. By a neat coincidence, my first small copper of the year, on 16 May, had also been at the Dummy's.

This book, which began at 7.15 p.m. on 4 April, ends at 4 p.m. on 20 September.

Sources

1. D. Colville and A. Martin, *The Place-Names of the Parish of Campbeltown*, 2009 edition, pp. 37, 51, and 57.
2. A. Martin, *Kintyre: The Hidden Past*, pp. 181 and 180.
3. The Merchant Shipping Act 1894, Report of Court No. 8044, m.v. 'Quesada (O.N. 300586), held in Campbeltown from 7 to 10 November, 1966, before Sheriff Donald John MacDiarmid. HMSO 1967.
4. T. Pennant, *A Tour in Scotland and Voyage to the Hebrides*, pp. 195-96.
5. *Campbeltown Journal*, 12/8/1852, 'Southend'.
6. *Campbeltown Courier*, 9/9/1894.
7. *Ib.*, 10/4/1926.
8. N. Morrison, *My Story*, pp. 254-58.
9. A. Martin, *Kintyre Places and Place-Names*, pp. 3-4.
10. R. Black, e-mail 27/8/2014.
11. *Argyllshire Herald*, 16/3/1889.
12. D. Colville and A. Martin, *op. cit.*, p 24.
13. *Campbeltown Courier*, 7/5/1964.
14. D. Colville and A. Martin, *op. cit.*, p 12.
15. *Kintyre Magazine* 45, 'By Hill and Shore', p 20.
16. A. Martin, *Kintyre Places and Place-Names*, p 173.
17. *Campbeltown Courier*, 13/8/1993.
18. *Ib.*, 7/5/1898.
19. www.richieunterberger.com/whales.html
20. Duncan Docherty, 15/3/1999.
21. *Campbeltown Courier*, 6/1/1894.
22. A. Martin, *Kintyre Country Life*, p 11.
23. A. Martin, *Kintyre Places and Place-Names*, p 152, and A. Martin, *Kintyre: The Hidden Past*, p 178.
24. D. C. MacTavish, *The Commons of Argyll*, p 2.
25. A.I.B. Stewart, 'Presbyterian Rebels in Kintyre', *Kintyre Magazine* 33, pp. 3-5.

26. Register of Poor, Campbeltown Parish, No. 20, Argyll and Bute Council Archive, CO 6.
27. *Campbeltown Courier*, 24/2/1923.
28. *Ib.*, 17/5/1924.
29. A. Martin, *A Summer in Kintyre*, p 236.
30. 2002, pp. 88-89.
31. *Justices of the Peace in Argyll*, ed. Frank Bigwood, 2001, p 10.
32. *Ib.*, pp. 61-62.
33. *Kintyre Instructions*, E. R. Cregeen and A. Martin, 2011, pp. 147-48.
34. *Justices of the Peace in Argyll, op. cit.*, p 101.
35. Murdo MacDonald, letter, 22/11/2014.
36. *Campbeltown Courier*, 24/5/1879, 'Melancholy Drowning Accidents'.
37. *Ib.*, 18/8/1923, 'Kintyre Sheep Dog Trials'.
38. *Argyllshire Herald*, 15/2/1902, 'Largieside Agricultural Society Annual Ploughing Match'.
39. *Campbeltown Courier* and *Argyllshire Herald*, 15/2/1902, 'Death from Exposure at Carradale'.
40. *Argyllshire Herald*, 1/2/1902.
41. *Ib.*, 8/2/1902, 'Boy Perishes on High Knockrioch Farm'.
42. A. Martin, *Kintyre Places and Place-Names*, pp. 56 and 257.
43. *Argyllshire Herald*, 28/12/1912.
44. *Ib.*, 17/1/1874, 'Presentation to the Oldest Shepherd in Kintyre'.
45. D. C. MacTavish, *The Commons of Argyll*, p 3.
46. *Campbeltown Courier*, 13/2/1875, 'Melancholy Case of Drowning'.
47. A. Martin, *An Historical and Genealogical Tour of Kilkerran Graveyard*, p 60.
48. Precognition, Scottish Record Office, AD14 21/170.
49. A. Martin, *Kintyre Country Life*, p 134, and D. Colville and A. Martin, *op. cit.*, p 37.
50. Marjorie Heggen, 'The Holmes Family of Campbeltown', *Kintyre Magazine* 59, pp. 3-4, and James L. Caw, *William McTaggart ... A Biography and an Appreciation*, 1917, p 32.
51. N. Morrison, *My Story*, p 237.
52. *Campbeltown Journal*, 6/11/1851.
53. J. M. Scott, *Gino Watkins*, 1937 edition, p 45.
54. *Campbeltown Courier*, 23/5/2014.
55. A. Martin, *The Ring-Net Fishermen*, pp. 168-69.
56. *Argyllshire Herald*, 1/12/1866, two reports.

57. *Ib.*, 8/12/1866.

58. *Ib.*, 14 and 21/11/1874.

59. A. Martin, *By Hill and Shore in South Kintyre*, pp. 240-42.

60. *Campbeltown Courier*, 19/1/1935.

61. A. Martin, *Kintyre: The Hidden Past*, pp. 112 and 144.

62. *Argyllshire Herald*, 11/1/1913.

63. *Campbeltown Courier*, 29/3/1924, 'The Wreck of the "Charlemagne"'.

64. *Ib.*

65. Precognition, Scottish Record Office, AD14 35/158.

66. Register of Poor, Campbeltown Parish, No. 2577, Argyll and Bute Council Archive, CO 6, and *Campbeltown Courier*, 15/6/1929.

67. *Campbeltown Courier*, 9/11/1935, 'How History Repeated Itself last Week-end at Feochaig'.

68. C. Mactaggart, *A Ramble Through the Old Kilkerran Graveyard*, p 27.

69. *Campbeltown Journal*, 9/5, 4/7, 29/9 and 3/10/1851.

70. *Argyllshire Herald*, 25/9/1863.

71. Register of Births, Campbeltown Parish.

72. *Campbeltown Courier*, 30/11/1935, also 9/11 and 23/11, and Rae MacGregor, 'Aground at Feochaig – the S.S. *Elisabeth*', *Kintyre Magazine* 50, pp. 9-10.

73. *Campbeltown Courier*, 18/5/1912.

74. A. Martin, *An Historical and Genealogical Tour of Kilkerran Graveyard*, p 53.

75. *Campbeltown Courier*, 18/2/1983.

76. *Kintyre Places and Place-Names*, p 154, and *A Summer in Kintyre*, p 44.

77. A. Martin, *Kilkerran Graveyard Revisited*, p 70.

78. J. Halsby and P. Harris, *The Dictionary of Scottish Painters: 1600 to the Present*, 2010 edition, p 106.

79. M. MacDonald, *Kintyre Magazine* 71, p 12.

80. A. Martin, *By Hill and Shore in South Kintyre*, p 157.

81. *Campbeltown Courier*, 21/12/1967.

82. *Justices of the Peace in Argyll*, op. cit., p 100.

83. *Campbeltown Courier*, 30/4/1938.

84. *Ib.*, 11/2/1948.

85. *Kintyre Magazine* 33, pp. 25-26, 'Three Lochs in North Kintyre'.

86. *Ib.* 75, p 27.

87. *Ib.* 70, pp. 29-31.

88. A. Martin, *Kintyre Places and Place-Names*, p 104.

89. *Campbeltown Courier*, 3/8 and 24/8/1940 and 6/11/1943.

90. *Ib.*, 17/3/1945.

91. A. Stewart, e-mail 10/5/2014.

92. *Campbeltown Courier*, 27/7/1950.

93. N. Morrison, *My Story*, p 159; his police record, Argyll and Bute Council archive, Lochgilphead, CA/1/8/19.

94. A. Martin, *Kintyre Places and Place-Names*, pp. 218-19.

95. A. Martin, *Sixteen Walks in South Kintyre*, pp. 20-21.

96. A Martin, *The Silent Hollow*, p 21.

97. *Kintyre Magazine* 49, pp. 4-6, A. Martin, 'A Poet at Park', from the memories of Mary McCallum, Campbeltown, a daughter of Donald and Annie MacDougall, and *Laggan Days*, A. Martin, 2008, p 8.

98. *Campbeltown Courier*, 27/6/1974.

99. *Ib.*, 27/8/1932.

100. A. Martin, *Kilkerran Graveyard Revisited*, p 32.

101. *Campbeltown Courier*, 12/3/1949.

102. Killean and Kilchenzie Old Parish Register.

103. *Campbeltown Courier*, 1/11/1956.

104. *Ib.*, 23/2/1958.

105. Killean and Kilchenzie Old Parish Register.

106. *Campbeltown Courier*, 27/3/1915, 3/2/1917, and 9/2/1901.

107. A. Martin, *Kintyre: The Hidden Past*, p 208.

108. *Argyllshire Herald*, 16/8/1861.

109. A. Martin, *Kintyre Places and Place-Names*, pp. 283 and 227.

110. *Argyllshire Herald*, 4/1/1908.

111. *Campbeltown Courier*, 25/2/1922.

112. A. Martin, *Kintyre Places and Place-Names*, p 88.

113. D. Colville and A. Martin, *op. cit.*, pp. 56 and 49.

114. *Argyllshire Herald*, 25/3/1910.

115. A Martin, *Kintyre Places and Place-Names*, p 7.

116. Stewart Campbell, e-mail to Margaret McKiernan, 27/1/2004.

117. *Argyllshire Herald*, 5/10/1889.

118. *Ib.*, 13/2/1892.

119. Register of Poor, Campbeltown Parish, 1593, Argyll and Bute Council Archive, CO 6, and *Campbeltown Courier*, 16/11/1895.

120. A. Martin, *Kintyre Places and Place-Names*, p 171.

121. *Campbeltown Courier*, 4/8/1923.

122. *Kintyre Place and Place-Names*, pp. 279-82.

123. *A Summer in Kintyre*, p 39.

124. A. Martin, *By Hill and Shore in South Kintyre*, p 49.

125. A. Martin, *Kintyre Places and Place-Names*, p 182.

126. 'Retreat from Kintyre to the Glens: The Evidence of Family Names', *The Glynns*, Vol. 18.

127. A. Martin, *Kintyre Families*, p 61.

128. B. S. Turner, 'Distributional aspects of family name study illustrated in the Glens of Antrim', unpublished doctoral thesis, pp. 205-7, 1974.

129. A. Martin, *Kilkerran Graveyard Revisited*, p 74.

130. A. Martin, *By Hill and Shore in South Kintyre*, p 124.

131. D. McLachlan, tape-recorded by A. Martin, 6/2/1981.

132. A. Martin, *Kintyre: The Hidden Past*, p 99.

133. Kintyre leases, extracted by Duncan Colville from originals loaned to him by the Duke of Argyll in 1958.

134. A. Martin, *By Hill and Shore in South Kintyre*, pp. 60-62 and 72-76.

135. *Campbeltown Journal*, 19/2/1852.

136. *Argyll: An Inventory of the Ancient Monuments. Volume I, Kintyre*, 1971, p 86.

137. *Argyllshire Herald*, 27/4/1857.

138. Register of Poor, Campbeltown Parish, No. 867, Argyll and Bute Council Archive, CO 6.

139. *Argyllshire Herald*, 28/8/1857.

140. Register of Death, Southend Parish.

141. *Campbeltown Courier*, 15/11/1879.

142. *Ib.*, 7/6/1977.

143. A. Martin, *Kintyre Families*, p 22, from the late Nancie Smith, 17/1/2010.

144. *Argyll: An Inventory of the Ancient Monuments, op. cit.*, p 191.

145. *Campbeltown Courier*, 14/1 and 1/9/1934, 'Archaeology in Kintyre'.

146. Argyll County Council report, 'Housing of Tinker Families', 19 January 1965.

147. *A Companion to Scottish Culture*, ed. David Daiches, 1981, p 378.

Index

Owing to the frequency of references, 'Campbeltown' 'Kintyre' and 'Learside' have not been indexed.

Accord, MFV, wreck of, 27-28

Achnafad (725 513), 106

Achnaslishaig (645 135), 93, 119

'Across the Sagging Fence', poem, 195, 196

Adams, Anna, poet, 219

adders, 8 (ill.), 18, 61, 127, 128, 154-55, 193, 202-4

Aignish (596 152), 95

alcohol, 20, 29, 60, 81, 82, 83, 100, 106, 128, 161, 218

Allan, Jimmy, Campbeltown, 145, 148, 175

Allt Mhic an Tanner (624 170), 160

alpacas, 129

Amelia's Cafe Bistro, 193

Amod, Barr Glen (707 381), 48

Anderson, Robert, Campbeltown, 11

Andrew, Stuart, photographer, 63

archaeology, 16-18, 64, 106, 207, 215-16

Ardshiel Hotel, Campbeltown, 20

Argyll Arms Hotel, Campbeltown, 29, 73, 111, 167

Argyll Estate, 73, 151, 155, 174, 175, 204

Argyll's Rebellion, 36, 59

Argyllshire Herald, 56, 73

Arinanuan (733 390), 48, 51-52, 53, 55

Arinarach (724 150), 174, 176, 209

Arinascavach (721 138), 165-75, 209

Armour, John, Ballybrennan, 155

Armour, Robert 'Robina', Campbeltown, 78

Arnicle (710 381), 47, 48, 53, 145

Arran, 22, 52, 72, 77, 111, 133, 217

Auchadaduie (690 368), 52, 56

Auchalochy (726 226), 74, 209, 210

Auchenbreck (783 440), 53

Auchenhoan farm (760 168), 3, 10, 22, 23, 26, 35, 52, 87, 88, 89, 90, 99, 101, 103, 122, 124, 175

Auchenhoan Head (764 170), 9, 14, 20, 21-22 (with derivation of name), 62, 64, 67

Australia, 79, 80, 81, 90, 189

Ballimenach (755 183), 90

Ballimenach brae, 37, 67, 90, 102, 110, 127, 152

Ballinatunie (762 160), 22 (derivation of name), 35, 68, 69, 123, 220

Ballochnafraesan (636 195), 211

Ballochroy Glen (745 515), 87, 106, 107

Ballybrennan (682 139), 155

Ballygroggan (622 191), 45, 158, 161, 164, 174, 176

Balnabraid (753 158), 97, 103-5, 154

Balnabraid Glen, 3, 9, 104

Baraskomill (740 210), 129

Barbour, Catherine & Cameron, Keil, 45-46, 92

Barr Glen, 47-55, 58

Bastard (758 123), 78, 89-90, 202

Bedson, Craig, Campbeltown, 170
bees, 103
Beinn an Tuirc (752 361), 138, 150
Bell, Hugh, Low Ugadale, 108
Bellochantuy, 51, 58, 138
Ben Gullion (721 181), 27, 101, 106,
    163, 178-79, 187, 194, 197-98, 207,
    209, 210
Benjie, dog, 74, 101, 106, 195, 197
Beul Dearg (595 149), 181
bicycles, cycling & accidents, 35, 41,
    66-67, 88, 91, 114, 115, 123-28, 132,
    133, 155, 164, 188, 192, 193, 194-95
Black Loch (716 176), 54, 165, 170,
    171
Black Rock of Corphin, 69
Black, Alex, fisherman,
    Campbeltown, 111
Black, Frances McIver, daughter of
    above, 111
Black, Ronald, 22
Black, Sandra (née MacDougall),
    133
blaeberries, 178, 179, 184, 187, 194,
    197, 199, 207
Blin' Man (767 161)/Blindman's
    Rock (768 164), 3, 4, 220
Bloody Bay (766 167), 12, 22, 24,
    26-29, 89
Blue family & name, Collusca,
    148-49
Bonar, Captain C. G., 87
Bond, Margaret, 29
Bordadubh (725 314), 136-44, 151
Boyle, Gary, guitarist, 153
Boy Scouts, 166, 170, 210, 215
bracken, 10, 32, 47, 90, 111, 220
brambles, 214-15
bramble jelly, 215
British Road Services, 125
Brodie, John, Campbeltown, 188-89
Brodie family, Lochgilphead
    district, 131

Brolachan families, 63, 131
Bronze Age sword, 64
Brown, Dr James, 29
Brown, Neil, ornithologist, 166
Brown, Neil (Sailor's Grave), 176
Brown, Robert, 114
Bruach Dearg (629 143), 33, 91, 92,
    93, 115, 119, 181
Brunerican Bay (695 075), 45
Buchanan family, East Skeroblin,
    134
Bullinger, salvage tug, 87
buses, 34, 45, 47, 53, 61-62, 68, 111,
    161
butterflies: common blue, 155, 183,
    192; grayling, 183; orange-tip, 115;
    painted lady, 74; peacock, 33,
    208, 209, 220, 221; small copper,
    208, 212, 221; small tortoiseshell,
    74, 219-20
By Hill and Shore in South Kintyre,
    209

Caledonian MacBrayne (Calmac),
    50, 197
Cameron, Archibald D., Southend,
    215
Campbell, Archibald, 9th Earl of
    Argyll, 36
Campbell, Lord Archibald, 15
Campbell family, Arinascavach, 165
Campbell, Colonel Charles of
    Barbreck, 49
Campbell, Colin of Skipness,
    executed rebel, 36
Campbell, Ewan & family, Minen,
    108
Campbell, George Douglas, 8th
    Duke of Argyll, 83, 129
Campbell, Iain, Campbeltown, 20,
    67, 88, 89, 126, 128
Campbell, Janey Sevilla (née
    Callander), 15

Campbell, Major John, Cleongart, executed rebel, 36

Campbell, John, Marquess of Lorne, 129

Campbell, John, schoolmaster, Ballochroy Glen, 87

Campbell, Mary, daughter of above, 87

Campbeltown Courier, 81, 87, 92, 121, 128, 137, 140, 144, 151, 169, 216

Campbeltown Grammar School, 6-7, 10, 11, 85, 206

Campbeltown Journal, 79, 84, 206

Campbeltown Library, 90, 94, 121, 210

Campbeltown Museum, 18, 64

camping, 87-88, 99, 193

Canada, 87, 125, 131, 184

Canna, 162

Cantaig (751 132), 205

caravans, 9, 44, 128, 191, 217, 218

Carradale, 52, 58, 73, 143, 187

cars & accidents on Learside, 122-23

cats, 128

Cats' Cove (743 101), 32, 128

cattle, 36, 88, 108, 111, 139, 141, 149, 174

caves, 14, 15, 31-32, 64-66, 128-29, 180-82, 215-16

Cave Picture (759 198), Davaar Island, 15, 16

Cefoil factory, Putechan, 189

Charlemagne, wreck of the, 73, 79-83

children's graves, Bordadubh, 138

Chomsky, dog, 186-87, 198, 210

Chomsky, Noam, 187

Clachan (764 561), 62, 94, 109

Clark, Archie, South Beachmore, 114

Claymore, Irish ferry, 197

clegs, 162

Cleongart (670 342), 36, 106

Cnoc Moy (611 152), 34, 115, 160

coasters, 9

Coastguard, H.M. Auxiliary, 26, 27, 53, 86

Coffield, Nicola, Campbeltown, 135 (ill.), 136, 176

Collins, Judy, 31

Collusca (714 328), 145, 148-49, 190

Colville, Duncan, 16, 75

Cook, Hugh, Campbeltown, 54

Cook, Malcolm, Campbeltown, 67

Cooper, Dr Doug, Canada, 59

Corphin (769 146), 35, 37, 40, 71, 72, 74, 94, 155-57

Corrylach (705 303), 143, 145

cotoneaster, 102-3

County Antrim, 149, 178, 183-85

Courshelloch (751 513), 108

crabs, 30, 31, 45

Craigaig (610 184), 155, 159

crannog, 109

Creag nan Cuilean (619 167), 158-61, 164

crooks, shepherds', 33, 99

Crosshill, 54, 195

Crosshill Avenue, Campbeltown, 7, 88, 127, 190, 214

Crosshill Loch/Reservoir, 101, 170, 196, 208

'Crossing a Field, Knockbay', poem, 195-96

crows, 6, 213-14

cuckoo superstitions, 37-38, 42

Dalbuie (691 139), 155, 165, 173, 174

Dalintober, 41, 60

Dali, Salvador, 95

Dalsmirren (643 132), 97

Darroch, Donald. ploughman, 54

Davaar Island, 11, 15, 188

Davison, Rab, 7, 8, 9, 10, 88, 89, 123, 125

Deuchran (766 433, Mòr), 54

Dhurrie (686 224), 54
DNA, 190
Dobbie, Catherine, Campbeltown, 214
Docherty, Archie, Killeonan, 168
Docherty, Barbara, Drumlemble, 121, 123, 128, 132, 179, 191
Docherty, Barbara (daughter of above), 21-22, 75, 78, 199
Docherty, Christine, 75
Docherty, Donald, 92
Docherty, Duncan, Campbeltown, 168
Docherty, Malcolm Snr., Drumlemble, 132, 168
Docherty, Malcolm Jnr., 128, 131, 155
Docherty, Peter, Campbeltown, 123
dog-rose, 157
Doirlinn (745 200), 188
Dotteril, wreck of the, 38-41
Dougie's Glen, 212
Doune, The (754 115), Glenahervie, 207
Drain, John, Glenahervie, 82
dreams, 197-98
driftwood, 5, 9, 18, 20, 21, 38, 41, 42, 45, 68, 71, 200, 221
Duchess of Hamilton, 197
Duke's Seat, The (745 100), 129
Dummy's Port, The (771 143), 25, 30, 32, 35, 43, 44, 68, 69, 71, 75, 157, 221
Dun, The, Machihanish (754 115), 5
Dunaverty, massacre at, 184
Duncan, Gordon & Helen, Campbeltown, 65
Duncan, Christine, East Skeroblin, 133, 139
Dunglas (703 091), 35
Dunn, Douglas, poet, 104
Dunsmuir or Dunsmore, Thomas, cave-dweller, 32
Durance, Willie, 193

eagles, 48, 114
earradhris, 157
East Skeroblin Cottage (707 269), 134
Easter eggs, 42-43
Eastin, Charlotte Brodie, 129-31
eider ducks, 43-44, 221
Elerick/Eldrig (712 145), 174, 175, 176
Elisabeth, grounding of at Feochaig, 85-87
erosion, coastal, 45-47
Erradil (745 124), 205
Esther's Bay (752 107), 128
Evans, Terence, Campbeltown, 25-26

Faber Book of Twentieth Century Poetry, The, 104
'Farewell to Tarwathie', 31
Fawcett, Denise, 166
Feochaig (763 133), 75, 77, 78-79, 80, 83, 84, 85, 86, 87, 88, 89, 94, 97, 98, 165, 169, 199
Ferguson, Duncan, Torrisdale, 60-61
Fiddler's Rock (765 169), 22-25
First Water, 3-4, 5, 6-11, 12, 19 (ill.), 20, 22, 25, 111
Fisherman's Cottage (757 181), New Orleans, 65
fishing, 28-29, 35, 44, 45, 50, 68, 72, 78, 89, 136, 162, 167
Flora of Kintyre, The, 102
Flynn, Michael, Dunglas, assault victim, 206
Foresty Commission, 37, 47, 137, 138, 150, 187
foxes, 159, 213
Fraser, Robert, Drumore Inn, 58
fulmars, 95

G10 Bistro, Campbeltown, 153, 183
Gaelic language, 37, 48, 55-56, 69, 87, 89, 108, 117, 133, 157

Galbraith, Mary (née Balloch), Polliwilline, 175
Galloway, Mr and Mrs T. Lindsay, Kilchrist, 16
gannets, 68, 131, 161
Gartgreillan, 119, 146 (ill.), 148
Gartnacopaig (627 145), 91-92, 94
Garvalt (719 389), Barr Glen, 47, 48, 53, 58
geese, 141
Giant's Chair (765 125), 200
Gilchrist families, 94, 109
Gilchrist, Catherine, Leslie Hunter's grandmother, 94
Gilchrist, Duncan, Bath, 27
Gilchrist, Isabella, widow of John MacMillan, 140
Gilchrist, John, 22
Gilchrist, Rosemary, Campbeltown, 167
Gillies, Donnie, Machrihanish, 151, 186
Gillies, Lachlan, Glasgow, 97, 133, 151, 152 (ill.), 186, 187, 191
Gillies, Neil, Glasgow, 151, 152 (ill.), 186, 187
Girl Guides, 118
Girvan, Roddy, Campbeltown, 97-99
Glasgow, 72, 73, 101, 127, 131, 153, 162, 168, 213, 217
Glemanuill (641 071), 121
Glenadale, High (627 115), 114-121, 202
Glenahanty (630 143), 33, 114, 178
Glenahervie (747 107), 82, 87, 199, 200, 204-5, 207
Glenbarr, 23, 47, 56, 61, 145
Glen Breackerie & School (659 106), 117, 118
Gleneadardacrock (621 156), 165, 178
Glenramskill (735 179), 110, 155, 170, 188

goats, 34, 49, 180, 181, 182
Gobagrennan (706 285), 150
Goings, The (601 069), 102
Gortan (702 214), 52
Gray, Marion, 29
Greenlees, James, postman, 173
Grianan Dheardruin (593 147), 95
grocery vans, 173, 200
Grogan, Harry, Machrihanish, 161
grouse, red, 34
gulls, 6, 30, 31, 43-44, 189
Gulls' Den (594 155), 95

Hall, Robert, Glenahervie, 204
Hamilton, Archibald, pawnbroker, 206
Harvey, John, Gartnacopaig, 91-93, 132
Harvey, Peggy (née Ramsay), mother of above, 92
Harvey, Robert, Campbeltown, 170
Hay, George Campbell, poet, 133-34
Hay, John Macdougall, novelist, 134
hazel, 108
heather, white, 190
Heatherhouse, 82
hedgehog, 22
Helm shepherding family, 8, 175, 212
Helm, Sandy, 98-99, 175, 212
Henderson, Rev C. M., Campbeltown, 92
Henderson, Hamish, 218
hens, 108
hen harrier, 210
High Park (694 257), 133
Honeyman, Alex, 93, 187
Honeyman, Dr T. J., 93-95
Hood, Iain, Peninver, 64
Hood, John, *Charlemagne* survivor, 80-81
horses, 80, 81, 108, 147 (ill.), 170, 173, 190

horseflies – see clegs
Houston, Esther, cave-dweller, 128-29
Houston, Robert & family, Campbeltown, 167
Huie, Alexander, drowned fisherman, 28-29
Hunt, Donald, 118
Hunter, George Leslie, artist, 93-94
hut at First Water, 8-11
Huy, Samuel, banished rebel, 36
hydro-electricity – see Lussa
Hynd, Iona, 119-20
Hynd, Jan, Glasgow, 118, 119-20

innean place-name, 26
Innean Beithe (594 127), 209
Inneans, The (598 165), 77, 118, 164, 176-78, 203
Inveraray Jail, 206
Isle of Arran/Ardrossan ferry, 50, 72, 85, 110, 179, 186, 197, 198
Isotope, 153
ivy growth on Fiddler's Rock, 25
'Ivy Cave' (760 175), 64

Jackson shepherding family, 211
Jean's Glen, 212
Johnston, Charlie, Campbeltown, 77, 78
Johnston's Bay (768 158), 43, 111
Johnston's Point (769 129), 30, 39, 74, 75, 77, 89, 102, 103
Jones, Paul, singer, 168
juniper, 102

Keil Cave (671 077), 215-16
Kempshall, Alex, 111, 202-3
Kerran (715 124), 172
Kerry, Angus, *Charlemagne* survivor, 81-82
Kerry/McKerry/McKarry, James, father of above, 82

kestrel, 210
Kilchousland, 7
Kildalloig, 29, 110, 189, 218
Kilkerran Graveyard, 96, 195
Killeonan (687 181), 168
Killick, John, poetry editor, 219
Killocraw (660 306), 58, 189-90
Killypole (640 178), 53, 211-14
Kintyre Antiquarian & Natural History Society, 16, 47, 75, 107
Kintyre Country Life, 55, 120
Kintyre Magazine, 106, 175
Kintyre Photography, 63
Kintyre Places and Place-Names, 49, 54, 55, 87, 95, 117, 118
Kintyre Rotary Club, 137, 138
Kintyre Scientific Association, 15
Kintyre: The Hidden Past, 56, 57, 68, 129
Kintyre Way, 33, 98, 119, 138, 150, 159, 180, 183
Kirnashie (794 412), 60
Knockbay (724 192), 54, 154, 187, 195-97
Knock Kilmichael (786 405), 58
Knock Layd, 178
Knocknagrain (716 136), 170, 175
Knock Scalbert (730 222), 73-74, 209-11

Lafferty, Teddy, Campbeltown, 8 (ill.), 9, 14, 19 (ill.), 20, 24, 25, 27, 64, 66, 77, 98, 99, 110, 177, 178, 200-4, 209-10
Lagloskin (726 468), 108
Lake, The (618 196), 45
Lambert, Tony, Campbeltown, 191
Lang, Angus, 82
Lang, Archie, shepherd, 25, 26
Lang, Catherine, wife of James Kerry, 82
Langlands map, 49, 143
Larch Plantation, The, 103, 104, 205

Largiebaan (614 143), 33, 34, 83, 95-96, 118, 119, 121, 180-83, 202, 209
Lavery, Mary (née McPhee), Campbeltown, 214-15
Lees, James, cliff fatality, 207
Lees, Marion (née McConnachy), wife of above, 207
Leitch, Archie & Mary, Minen and Auchavraid, 109
lemons, 202
Lena, loss of the skiff, 28-29
Leys, Donald, Campbeltown, 137
life-boats, 12, 27, 39, 86, 210
lilies, 120, 212
Limecraigs Cottage, Campbeltown, 196
limestone, 204
limpets, blue-rayed, 6
Lintmill (688 199), 216, 218
Lismore, 133
litter, 71
Littleson families & name, 55
Livingstone, Neil, Campbeltown, 101
Loch an Fhraoich (747 471), 50
Loch Beag (734 401), 50
Loch Garasdale (765 510), 109
Lochgilphead, 62, 144
Loch Mòr (730 404), 50
Lochorodale (659 160), 164
Lochsanish (664 205), 59
Louise, Princess, 129
Loynachan, Catherine, Ballinatunie, 68
Loynachan, Lachlan, Ballinatunie, 69
Loynachan, Neil, Feochaig, 84
Lussa hydro-electric scheme and Reservoir (709 301), 132, 135, 142, 144-48
Lyme disease, 163-64

MacAlister, Alexander, Torrisdale Glen, 61
McAllister, Archie, Campbeltown, 151
McAllister, Archie, fiddler, nephew of above, 23
McAllister, Duncan, father of above, 23
Macalister, John, gamekeeper, 155
Macalister, Keith, Glenbarr, 56
McAllister, Margaret (née Mitchell), 151, 152 (ill.)
MacAmbróis, Eoin, poet, 184-85
MacArthur, Archibald, Auchenrioch, 54
Macarthur, Campbell, 75
MacArthur, Donald, Auchenrioch, 53-54
McArthur, Mary, farm servant, 54
MacArthur, Neil, builder, 16
McAulay, Donald, Feochaig, 84-85
McAulay, John, father of above, 85
McAulay, James, alleged poacher, 77
Macaulay, Margaret, Penicuik, 104
MacCaig families, Southend, 184
McCaig, James, Campbeltown, 40
McCallum, Alex, Traveller, 216
McCallum, Provost Archibald, 189
McCallum, Donald Snr., 121
McCallum, Donald Jnr., 121, 154
McCallum, Donald, Achnaglach, 174
McCallum, Gilbert, Collusca, 148
McCallum, Gilbert, Campbeltown, 121
McCallum, Jessie (née McInnes), 118, 121
McCallum, John 'Jock', Campbeltown, 118,121
MacCallum, John, Bordadubh, in 1810, 139
McCallum, John, Bordadubh, in 1926, 143
MacCallum, John, Narachan, 54

McCallum, John, Campbeltown, 180-83

McCallum, Lorna, 210

MacCallum or MacLean, Mirren, 36

McCallum, Ned, blacksmith, Machrimore, 215

McCallum, Thomas, Feochaig, 84

MacCambridge name & families, 184-85

McCambridge's wholewheat bread, 183, 184, 185, 186

McCambridge, Flora, 184

McCambridge, John, Gaelic poet – see Mac Ambrói s, Eoin

McCambridge, Mercedes, actress, 184

McCartney, Paul, 133

McCavish, Donald, Corphin, 36

McCoig (McCaig), Archibald, Dunglas, 206

McConnachie, A. & P., bus company, 145

McConnachie, Archibald, Strathmollach, 151

McConnachie, Gilbert, Strathmollach, 151

McConnachie, Jeanie McDonald, 151

MacCorkindale family, Port a' Bhorrain, 56-57

McDiarmid, Archibald, Auchenhoan, 52

MacDonalds of Sanda, 184

Macdonald Publishers, 104

Macdonald, Angus, flesher, 80

MacDonald, Duncan, shepherd, 121

MacDonald, Ian, 62, 109

MacDonald, Jimmy, Campbeltown, 5, 12, 13 (ill.), 14, 19 (ill.), 20, 24, 25, 43, 105, 111, 115, 118, 136, 166, 171, 180, 209

MacDonald, John, Campbeltown, 69, 75, 78, 126, 127, 135, 136, 165, 176, 177

Macdonald, John, Auchenbreck, 53, 54

MacDonald, Murdo, Lochgilphead, 92, 94, 107, 109

MacDougall family, Park & West Skeroblin, 133-34

Macdougall, Duncan, Glenbarr, 47, 48, 50, 51

MacDougall, Duncan, Tonaduppin, 61

McEachrans in Glenahervie, 204-5

McEachran, Alistair, shopkeeper, 88

MacEachern, Colin of Killellan, 49

McEachran, Colin, Glenahervie, 204

McEachran, Donald, Feochaig, 84

MacEachern, Duncan, Knocknagrain, 170

McEachran, Euphemia, wife of John McAulay, 85

McEachran, George, life-boat coxswain, 86

MacEachran, Janet, Corphin, 36

McEachran, John, Glenahervie, 204

McFarlane, Alexander, Polliwilline, 207

MacFarlane, Dugald, Tarbert, 57

MacFarlane, Hugh, Tarbert, 57, 157, 211

MacFarlane, Jenny, Campbeltown, 35

MacFarlane, John, Tarbert, 57

Macfarlane, Katrina, Campbeltown, 5, 111, 166, 167

MacFarlane, Mary, Tarbert, 57

Macfarlane, Neil, 166

McFee, John, Traveller, 216

McGeachy, William, alleged poacher, 77

McGill, Joe, 167, 168

MacGougan, John, Arinanuan, 54, 55

234

MacGougan, Willie, Largie, 55
MacGregor, Rae, Inveraray, 87
MacGregor, Ross, Campbeltown, 170
MacGrory, Provost A. P., 210
McHaffie, Heather, botanist, 103
McInnes, Duncan, Campbeltown, 64
McInnes, Isobel (née McCallum, wife of Robert), 119, 164
McInnes, Robert, Stewarton, 117, 118, 119, 164
MacIntyre family, Auchenhoan, Feochaig & Glenahervie, 85-87, 200, 201
McIntyre, David, Campbeltown, 214
Macintyre, Ian Y, Tarbert, 212
McIsaac familes, Learside, 35-36, 68, 84, 94
McIsaac, Donald, 'The Dummy', 35-36, 75
MacKay brothers, Kirnashee, 60
McKay, Amelia, Erradil, 205-6
MacKay, George, butcher, 11, 88
McKendrick, Alexander, Killypole, 160
McKendrick, Dugald, son of above, 211, 212
McKendrick, Dugald, Gleneadardacrock, 160
McKerral, Donald, Campbeltown, 134
McKerral, John, Glenahervie, 103
McKerral, Pctcr, Peninver, 147 (ill.)
McKiernan, Margaret, Campbeltown, 165, 166, 169 (ill.)
McKillop, William, Campbeltown, 23
Mackinnon, Mr and Mrs Alex, Cleongart, 106, 107, 109
MacKinnon, Monsignor Donald, 47
McKinven, Alastair, 155, 167, 171-75

McKinven, Alex, father of above, 172, 174
McKinven, Alex, Campbeltown, 29
McKinven, Andrew, drowned fisherman, 28-29
McKinven, Derek, Campbeltown, 7, 8, 10, 31-32, 123, 124
McKinven, James, Campbeltown, 29
McKinven, Lawrence, Campbeltown, 29
McLachlan, Duncan, Campbeltown, 62, 78, 85, 200
MacLaren, Janet – see Campbell family, Arinascavach
MacLean, Allan, Feochaig, 73, 78, 82-83, 200
MacLean, Annie – see MacDougall family
McLean, Donald, writer, Campbeltown, 56-57, 80
McLean, Donnie, Southend, 44, 45
McLean, James and Euphemia, High Glenadale, 116
McLean, Janet, High Glenadale, 120
MacLean, John, Glenahervie, 82
MacLean, John, Stockadale, 49
MacLean, Neil, shepherd, Deuchran, 54
Maclean, Will, artist, 68
McLellan, Willie, Campbeltown, 32
Macleod, Murdo, Southend, 7, 8
MacMaster, Neil, Arinascavach, 173
MacMillan, Angus, Stockadale, 49
McMillan, Betty, Bordadubh, 140-43
McMillan, Charlie, 9
McMillan, Charles, father of Duncan below, 127
McMillan, Duncan, cycling fatality, 127
McMillan, Duncan, Kerran, 173, 174
MacMillan, Duncan, Deucheran, 49
McMillan, Hugh, Bordadubh, 138

McMillan, Isabella 'Sweetie Bella', 32
McMillan, John, shepherd, 175
MacMillan, John, Stockadale, 49
MacMillan, Malcolm, Bordadubh,
  138-40
McMurchy, Campbell,
  Campbeltown, 210
McMurchy, Willie, Duke's carter,
  174
MacNab, John, Minen, 108
McNair, John, Campbeltown, 22
McNaughton, Frank, Glenbarr, 50
McNaughton, Neil, Feochaig, 84
Macneals of Ugadale & Lossit, 52, 160
Macneal, Captain Hector of
  Ugadale, 160 (ill.), 161
McNeil, Christina, Gobagrennan, 150
MacNeill, Eoin, Irish scholar,
  historian and politician, 185
MacNeill, Hector F., Campbeltown,
  209
MacNeill, Iona (née Pursell), wife
  of above, 90
MacNeill, Ina Erskine, Duchess of
  Argyll, 129
MacPhail, Adam, Skernish, 47, 106
MacPhail, Angus, Kilchamaig, 109
MacPhail, Flora, Clachan, 109
McPhee, Jim, Pennygown, 174
McPherson family, Arinanuan,
  51-52
MacQueen, Prof John, 48
McQuilkan, John, Tarbert, 58
MacQuistan, Rose & sons,
  Campbeltown, 206
McRoberts' Shop, Campbeltown,
  128
MacSporran name, the change to
  'Pursell', 90-91
McSporran, George, Campbeltown,
  3, 14, 27, 30, 37, 45, 67, 68, 71, 74-
  75, 77, 89, 101, 105, 122, 133, 179,
  183, 184, 197, 198, 199, 200, 202

McSporran, Sandy, son of above,
  27, 45, 104, 197, 202
Mactaggart, Colonel Charles, 16, 83
McTaggart, Elizabeth,
  Drumlemble, 213-14
McTaggart, William, artist, 63, 71,
  94

Macharioch (733 093), 44, 129, 161,
  192
Machrihanish, 5, 33, 34, 158, 171
Maidens' Planting (738 207), 165,
  214, 219
'Malcolm MacKerral', poem, 103-4
Mallaig, 162
mallard, 189
Man-Faced Rock, 5
Manfred Mann, 168
Mann, Ludovic McLellan, 16, 17, 215
'Marilyn' hills, 115
Marrison, Elizabeth,
  Campbeltown, 107, 166, 167
Martin, Amelia (née McKenzie),
  author's mother, 121, 206, 214
Martin, Amelia, author's daughter,
  50, 53, 72, 85, 118, 179, 197, 198,
  206, 208, 213, 214
Martin, Angus, author's father, 89,
  121
Martin, Bella, author's daughter,
  97, 157, 179, 197
Martin, Bobby, Campbeltown, 189-91
Martin, Judy, author's wife, 14, 44,
  47, 50, 53, 64, 65, 72, 74, 75, 92,
  96, 105, 110, 117, 118, 129, 132, 135,
  158-62, 163-64, 165, 169 (ill.), 179,
  186 (ill.), 187, 191, 196
Martin, Mary (née Borthwick), 189
Martin, Neil, 190
Martin, Peter, 189
Martin, Sarah, author's daughter,
  44, 53, 64, 65, 75, 97, 105, 118,
  186, 187, 191, 197, 211

Martin, Stuart, author's cousin, 126
Maxwell, J. Harrison, archaeologist, 215-16
Mayo, Rear-Admiral Robin, 210
Meenan, James, Campbeltown, 12
Menzies, George, Auchenhoan, 22
Menzies, Gregor, Campbeltown, 154
Menzies, John, Campbeltown, 154
Menzies, Mary (née Macalister), 155
mermaid on Learside, 68-69
midges, 135, 160
milestones, 97-98
Minen (766 515 & 756 521), 106-10
mist, 25, 188-89
Mitchell name & families, 59-60
Mitchell, Archibald, shepherd, 58-59
Mitchell, Dugald, Tarbert author, 5
Mitchell, Isabella (née Martin), Torrisdale, 60, 61
Mitchell, Johnny, shepherd, Killocraw, 190
Mitchell, Willie, Campbeltown, 120, 123-24
Moira, MFV, 12
Montgomery, Lucy Maud, 184
Morran, Jamie 'Loafs', 9
Morrans, Dan, 9
Morrison, Norman, 16-19, 63-64, 127, 128
Morrison, Peter, Campbeltown, 166, 170-71, 213
Muasdale, 56, 57, 112
mucag, 157
Muir, Garry, Campbeltown, 64
Muir, Gilbert, Auchenhoan, 3, 8, 10, 25, 26, 98, 124, 125
Muir, Willie, Ballymenach, 174
mushrooms, 74, 110, 122, 209
music & musicians, 23, 31, 153, 168

Narrowfield (710 195), 101, 159, 179
Natural Arch (764 123), 200, 202
Negro's Head, The (638 207), 5

Nelson, Rev W. C., Southend, 92
Newlands, Duncan, Campbeltown, 39
Newlands, George, Campbeltown, 39, 162
New Orleans (757 179) & Glen, 32, 62-64, 90, 104
Norris, Catherine, cliff fatality, 207
Norris, David, father of above, 207
Norse in Kintyre, 18, 27, 48, 70
Novena prayer, 71

oatmeal & water, 172, 190
O'Hara, Pat, 98
Old Clubhouse, Machrihanish, 161
Old Road (749 182), 20, 22, 64, 110-111
Oloynachan, Donald, Glenahervie, 204
Oman, Les, Campbeltown, 31, 153, 183, 184
Oman, Tina, 183
O'May, Norrie, Campbeltown, 101
Open Doors, 219
oranges, 72
Ordnance Survey, 49, 62, 117, 143, 167, 175
otters, 30, 111
outdoor centres, 118, 137-38, 166
owls, barn, 101, 166, 171, 213
owls, short-eared, 105
oyster-catchers, 19, 46, 131

Paper Archipelagos, 195
Paterson, Alex, 174
peat, 47, 119, 139, 164, 173
pellets, bird-, 6
Peninver, 70, 148
Pennant, Thomas, 15
Pennygown (691 143), 171
pennywort, 156
photography, 12, 14, 67, 96, 105, 111, 118, 148, 171, 188, 199-200

pigs, 139, 172-73

Pirate's Grave (691 132), 14, 30, 74-77, 78

Place-Names in the Rhinns of Galloway and Luce Valley, 48

Place-Names of the Parish of Campbeltown, The, 22

Plancy, John, scrap merchant, 39-41

poetry, 103-4, 129, 195-96, 205, 219-20

police, 26, 39-40, 60, 128, 142

Polliwilline (735 100), 47, 106, 122, 128-32, 187, 191, 205, 209

Pollok, Mrs Gladys, Ronachan, 109

poor rolls and poorhouse, 36, 82, 169

Port a' Bhorrain (660 359), 56-57

Port nam Marbh (655 271), 73

Porter, John, Hove, 53

Post Office, The, 160

potatoes, 98, 139, 174

Pursell family & name, 90

Quaintain, James, Feochaig, 84

Queen Esther's Bay (767 165), 12-14, 20, 21, 30, 64, 66

Queen's Jubilees, 210

Queen's Head, The (638 207), 5

Quesada, loss of the, 10-12

rabbits, 33, 56

rain, 20, 86, 197, 218

Rankin, Billy, 77, 86

ravens, 25

Referendum on Scottish Independence, 210

Regan, Roddy, archaeologist, 64

Reid, John, Brackley, 53, 54

Reid, Captain W., *Charlemagne*, 79, 81

Rennie, Doreen, Campbeltown, 129, 195

rhododendrons, 96

rhubarb, 212

Riddell, Bobby, 98

Robertson, Davie, Campbeltown, 136 (ill.), 137, 138, 165, 166, 167, 168, 169 (ill.)

Robertson, Janet, Blary, 52

rocks, 12, 13 (ill.), 199

Roddick, Campbell, 39-41

Royal Artillery, 121

Royal Commission on the Ancient & Historical Monuments of Scotland, 16, 18, 109

Royal Highland and Agricultural Society, 113, 148

runners, 97, 179, 197

Ru Stafnish (771 139), 9, 35, 38, 39, 44, 45, 67, 68, 70, 101-2

Russell family, Ballimenach, 90

Russell, Billy, Campbeltown, 200, 202

Russell, Edward, Campbeltown, 25-26

Rutherford, Michael, Campbeltown, 170

Saddell Street, Campbeltown, 81, 122, 190, 219

Sailor's Grave (598 166), 77, 176-77, 203

Saint Bridget, 19

Saint Ciaran, 15, 27

Saint Kieran's Cave (765 170), 14-19, 22, 64, 65

St. Kieran's R.C. Church, 20

St Mark's fly, 209

salmon, 168

Saltire Society, The, 104

SAS, 101

saxifrage, opposite cross-leaved golden, 154

Scally, Andrew, 39-41

scarts (cormorants and shags), 95

schools, 51-52, 87, 108, 117, 141, 142, 175

Scott, Peter, Campbeltown, 101
Scott, Tom, customs officer, 77
Sea Cadets, 166, 170
seals, 30-31, 69, 221
Second Water (767 154), 3, 5, 9, 32, 35, 67, 96-101, 106, 154, 190, 193, 218, 220, 221
Second World War, 121, 134, 173, 216
Semple, John, Campbeltown, 50
Semple, Richard, Campbeltown, 33
Shaw, Robert, Carradale, 91 (ill.), 92
sheep & shepherds, 14, 23, 34, 52, 81, 85, 109, 119, 139, 140-43, 148-52, 168, 169, 174, 175, 205, 207
Sheep Fanks (755 184), Kildalloig, 20, 64, 65, 112, 113, 189
shelducks, 189
Shields, Jock, Campbeltown, 126
shinty, 60
shipwrecks, 11-12, 27-29, 38-41, 78
Signore, Danish dog, 86
Sillars, Donald, transported, 84
Sinclair, Ian, Glenbarr, 61, 62
Sinclair, Sileas, musician, 23
Skeroblin, East and West (709 267 & 708 267), 134
Skye, 128, 133
Slate (633 164), 159, 160, 164, 171
sliabh place-name, 175
Sliabh, 173, 174, 175
slow-worm, 61
Smerby Castle (756 224), 47
Smith, Hugh, grocery van driver, 173
Smith, Ian, Campbeltown, 170
Smith, Jock, Campbeltown, 66, 75, 77, 78-79, 85
Smith, Marianne, 78, 79
Smith, Tony, camper, 64
Smith, William Jnr., 5
snow, 38, 54, 119, 139
Socach (744 128), 205
Southend, 33, 45-46, 83, 92, 132

sparrow-hawk, 33
Speed, Malcolm, journalist, 140
Speed, Neil, fishing skipper, 12
Spence, E.T.F., 137
spruce on seashore, 38
Starke, Captain Eric, 87
Stewart, Anthony, 218
Stewart, A.I.B., Campbeltown, 184
Stewart, Agnes, Campbeltown, 25, 33, 37, 38, 41, 50, 51, 102, 115, 120, 123, 132, 137, 138, 156, 191, 208
Stewart, Allister, husband of above, 25, 33, 51, 132, 138, 218
Stewart, John Lorne, 73
Stewart, Peter, father of Allister, 218
Stinky Hole (746 195), 188
Stockadale (731 393), 47-51, 58, 61
Stone, Eddie, 101
Strang, James, Courshellach, 108
Strathmollach (715 304), 139, 140, 148, 150-52
Summer in Kintyre, A, 3, 14, 118, 165, 213, 219, 220
superstitions, 15, 37-38, 218
swallows, 65
Sweetie Bella's Quarry (766 160), 110, 111, 123

Tangy, picnic beach, 67-68
Tarbert, 5, 57, 58, 211
taxis, 101, 158-59
teasel, 191
Teesdale, Ian, Campbeltown, 103, 208
Telfer, James, lawyer, 49
Telford, Thomas, engineer, 211
Thompson, Alastair, 3, 4, 6-11, 88, 89, 98, 99-100, 123-25, 174
Thompson, Tommy, 8 (ill.), 200
Thomson, Cathy, shopkeeper, 128
Thomson, Hector, Glenbarr, 62
ticks, 162-63
tobacco, 167-68, 172, 178, 218

Togneri, Ronald, Campbeltown, 10
Tolmie, Peter, Campbeltown, 88
Tomaig (708 195), 170, 203
toothache relief, 167
Torrisdale Glen, 60-61
Townsley families, 54, 66, 215-18
Travellers – see above
trees, 38, 49, 90, 93, 104, 138, 164,
  166, 170, 176, 197
Turner, John, Eleric, 175
Turner, John, Minen, 109
turnips, 112-14, 190

Uigle (695 168), 119, 174
US Navy SEALs, 79

wagtails, pied, 128
warbler, sedge, 67
Wareham, James, line-fishing,
  28-29
Wareham, James and Jessie,
  Campbeltown, 68
Warren, Carol, author's sister, 44,
  63
Watkins, Gino, explorer, 69
Watson, John, 177 (ill.), 178
Watson, Willie, Campbeltown,
  112-14
Wee Man's Cove (760 176), 32-33,
  64, 65, 66, 104
wells, 47, 78, 90, 161, 167, 168, 170,
  174, 192, 200
West Coast Motors, 190
Westerman, Duncan,
  Campbeltown, 148, 170
Westport (654 264), 73
whales, 31, 72-73
Whistler, James McNeill, 15
Wilkin, Yvonne, 111, 202-3
wilks & wilkers, 32-33, 123-24, 132
Wilson, Hugh, Feochaig, 77
winkles & winkle-pickers – see
  wilks & wilkers

Winny Corner (766 136), 192
Wood Bay (762 121), 200-1
World Cup 2014, 132, 162, 180, 183
Wuds, The (718 197), 214-15
Wylie, Bob, New Orleans, 62, 63

9 781845 301552